A Human Comedy: Physiognomy and Caricature in 19th Century Paris

La cinquième acte à la Gaîté.

1 *Frontispiece* DAUMIER, 'The Fifth Act at the Gaîté Theatre',
Whatever You Like, 1848. D.1674

Judith Wechsler

A HUMAN COMEDY

Physiognomy and Caricature
in 19th Century Paris

Foreword by Richard Sennett

With 161 illustrations

 The University of Chicago Press

The University of Chicago Press, Chicago 60637
Thames and Hudson Ltd, London
© 1982 by Thames and Hudson Ltd, London
All rights reserved. Published 1982
Printed and bound in Great Britain by William Clowes (Beccles) Limited
89 88 87 86 85 84 83 82   54321

Library of Congress Cataloging in Publication Data
Wechsler, Judith, 1940–
    A human comedy.

    Bibliography: p.
    Includes index.
    1. Paris (France)—Social life and customs—
Caricatures and cartoons. 2. Paris (France)—Population—Caricatures and cartoons. 3. Gesture—Caricatures
and cartoons. 4. France—Social life and customs—19th
century—Caricatures and cartoons. 5. French wit and
humor, Pictorial. I. Title.
NC1495.W4   741.5'0944   82-70647
ISBN 0-226-87770-1   AACR2

Contents

To Charles Eames
in memory

Foreword

THE CITIES of the nineteenth century were landscapes of the unknown.
Masses of people were thrown together in the great migrations to cities,
people who often did not speak the same language or who, in Great
Britain, France and Italy, spoke dialects others had difficulty in understanding. The rivers of people flowing into London, Paris and Berlin did
not resemble the streams of urban migration which had occurred in the
eighteenth century. In the *ancien régime*, the voyage to the great city was
characteristically made by a young, single person; land enclosure forced
some families to move, but not many. After the Napoleonic wars, a
century-long agricultural crisis unfolded in Europe, caused by new
commercial and technological conditions. It began in Ireland, north-east
France and the northern reaches of the Austro-Hungarian empire, then
spread into the centre of Europe; its effect was to send whole families, or
fragments of large families, into the cities, generation after generation of
rural refugees flowing into cities where they did not want to live, and
where they did not understand how to live. This new form of migration
was compounded in its effects by a smaller number of persons, but highly
visible, who were political refugees or casualties from the constant
revolutionary tremors which shook all of Europe after Napoleon.

Judith Wechsler's study of gesture in the nineteenth century explores
one of the ways in which this mass of the mutually unknown sought to
communicate with each other. It was at once a highly specialized and,
for several decades, immensely popular means of communication. This
language of gesture has its roots in code books of physiognomy, such as
that written by Le Brun in the seventeenth century, and in the theories of
physiognomy built by Lavater and others in the eighteenth century. The
art of gesture was developed in the mime theatres which became so
popular in the Restoration and the July Monarchy during the nineteenth
century; it was displayed in the caricatures and 'pen portraits' of the mass
newspapers of the time. And this art of gesture was made use of by great
writers such as Balzac and artists of the stature of Daumier.

The physiognomists believed there was a direct correspondence
between people's inner being and their outer physical appearance. The
gesture of a hand, the shape of a skull, a nose, the colour of an eye, all

7

revealed the character of a person. The caricaturists further believed that these revealing appearances could easily be put into categories, and manipulated as codes: thus, to draw the eyebrows of a phlegmatic, the mouth of a sensualist, and to put both into the skull of a criminal, would permit not only the artist exactly to describe a person, but would also make of this person a psychological portrait which other people could immediately recognize, by reading elements of the code. Thus the stranger becomes a figure whose nature can be understood by analysing his or her appearance. The problem of coping with an environment of strangers becomes manageable through the science of physiognomy and the art of stylized caricature. The mimes, caricaturists, writers and painters whom Judith Wechsler describes were the teachers of this code to the Parisians.

To appreciate the work of these artists of gesture, I think we have to make an effort of historical imagination which defies commonsense. For us, the growth of cities during the nineteenth century seems in retrospect the fulfilment of a great historical plan, the plan of industrial capitalism. The Parisians of Balzac's time were ignorant of this destiny. Coupled with the confusion about who was in the city was a confusion about what the city would become. Parisians of the last century perceived urban growth in terms of metaphors of overturning, pulling apart, metaphors which expressed a strongly felt idea of the impermanence of the city and its ways of life. For example, many people in Paris in the 1840s predicted that the tide of population would ebb from the city as rapidly as it had flowed in. Or again, they spoke of industrialism not as of a destiny but as an economic system which had grown to aberrant proportions; thus Balzac could imagine cutting out the 'tumour' of industrial production if it swelled any larger in the body of society.

People faced with what seem irreversible, destined changes in their lives can believe, out of resignation if nothing else, that the meaning will eventually come clear of its own accord. But the citizens of Paris and London in the mid-nineteenth century had no such comfort that society in the fullness of time would reveal its grand design. There thus arose a hunger in the lives of these people to impose order, to fix meaning, to arbitrate in the midst of chaos. Caricature and stylized gesture, of the sorts Judith Wechsler presents, were such codes of arbitration. For the essence of this art of gesture was to present a fixed character, a stable personality, an ideogram. It is no accident that this art drew so heavily on physiognomic theory. The physiognomist attempts to analyse permanent traits of character from mostly fixed forms of appearance: the skull's shape, the width between the eyes, their colour. Even in the most subtle work of physiognomic theory of the nineteenth century, Darwin's *The Expression of the Emotions in Man and Animals*, analysis of bodily movement

8

and momentary expression is constantly brought back to some permanent, fixed type of emotion. The uncertainty and intimate knowledge of disorder in the lives of the Parisians, as in those in Berlin and London who flocked in great numbers to the mime theatres and sought out the caricatures and 'pen portraits' in the popular press, made them willing to believe in a code system which froze personality into fixed and static forms. Sometimes the artists of gesture are called 'illusionists', but I think this demeans them. They were artists of a necessary illusion – a stranger's mask can be a reliable guide to his soul – for people in need of it.

Judith Wechsler comments on a difficulty with this sign language which I think needs to be emphasized. The greater the artist, the more disposed he was to modify the signs he used. We know from contemporary accounts that Deburau was considered a mime of genius because he conveyed to his audiences highly developed and particular characters through his gestures. Daumier is a great caricaturist not because his types are so recognizable but because he could infuse each typical figure with a strong sense of individual life. And, despite his great debts to Lavater and his life-long fascination with 'the characters of Paris', Balzac is Balzac because his descriptions so far transcend the language of classification. The art of gesture in the hands of its leading practitioners was fatally undermined by their art also of particularizing.

Judith Wechsler's study itself avoids easy classification, drawing as it does upon art history, literature, the history of the theatre, as well as upon political and social documents. It takes its coherence as a study instead from its subject: the art of gesture constituted a discipline for its practitioners; they deployed this discipline in various media of expression. Such subject-oriented studies which cut across neat academic lines have in recent years renewed our understanding of urban culture; this book is a companion work to T. J. Clark's *The Absolute Bourgeois*, a study of artists in the Revolution of 1848 in Paris, Carl Schorske's *Fin-de-Siècle Vienna*, and Anthony Vidler's *The Street in History*. During the 1950s and 1960s, studies of urban culture tended to be about material conditions – the buildings, bureaucracies, and street-planning of cities – with relatively little attention paid to what sense people made of these conditions. The neglect of the interpretation people in cities made of their lives is now being remedied by a new generation of scholarship, an effort in which this book occupies a worthy place.

RICHARD SENNETT

9

2 Public reading room. *Le Diable à Paris*, 1845–6

Preface and acknowledgments

Les Enfants du paradis, Marcel Carné's film of 1944, made an irreversible impression on me at the age of fourteen. Its romantic partiality has not weakened its force as an exemplary work of recreation. I have learned since how much of its lyricism came directly from the passionate research of its art director, Alexander Trauner. The delicacy and assurance of Jean-Louis Barrault's portrayal of the mime Jean-Baptiste Gaspard Deburau, and the exuberant force of the world around him, were unforgettable. Some seven years later, when I became a performing mime and a student of Etienne Decroux (who had played the father of Deburau in the film), I came to realize the discipline necessary for articulate expression and the freedom of performance. Again, seven years passed and I had become a student of art history. For my own diversion, while writing my dissertation, I began looking at the work of Honoré Daumier, and was struck by the physiognomy, bearing and gesture of his figures and their resemblance to the forms of movement I had learned as a mime. I began exploring the relationships between caricature and mime – and over the years the subject grew and the present study developed.

Walter Benjamin has been a model throughout. His *Paris: Capital of the 19th Century* and *Charles Baudelaire: A Lyric Poet in the Era of High Capitalism* are the most profound and perceptive studies of the period, and his powerful receptiveness to every kind of evidence is a model to history and to criticism alike. One cannot enter his terrain without paying homage.

I am deeply indebted to certain friends and mentors. The lectures of Professor Meyer Schapiro at Columbia University from 1963 to 1965 sparked my interest in nineteenth-century French art and first alerted me to the motif of the spectator. Our conversations over the years helped me hone the ideas presented in this study. Jean Adhémar, Conservateur-en-Chef emeritus of the Cabinet des Estampes at the Bibliothèque Nationale, confirmed my ideas of the parallelism of Deburau and Daumier and encouraged me in the initial stages of my research, suggesting a number of profitable leads and unveiling the mysteries of the library's great holdings.

Professors Linda Nochlin and Rosalind Krauss read parts of the manuscript and offered helpful suggestions concerning procedure, content and structure. Their insights deepened my thinking on a number of issues. I cannot express my gratitude sufficiently to Jehane Burns who did the translations from the French and saw the manuscript through every stage of its development, offering unstinting aid – she is a true accomplice in this enterprise. Without her the book would not have reached its present form.

Benson Rowell Snyder, my husband, has been a source of support, advice and encouragement: he read draft after draft acutely and untiringly. A. William Menzin has helped spring traps. My father, Nahum N. Glatzer, has been a model of scholarship, and my mother, Anne Glatzer, of lively engagement. Josie, my daughter, strengthened me in countless loving ways.

The photographs for the book were mainly taken by Charles Eames and Bill Tondreau at the time we were making our film, *Daumier, Paris and the Spectator*, 1977. Charles Eames' vision has meant a world to me.

JUDITH WECHSLER

Picture acknowledgments

Bibliothèque de l'Arsenal, Paris 21–3, 26, 29–31, 57; Bibliothèque Nationale, Paris 27, 28, 33, 50, 52, 55, 56, 70–2; Cabinet des Dessins, Musée du Louvre, Paris 134; Armand Hammer Collection as collected by George Longstreet 42, 62, 65, 66, 88, 92, 93, 105, 110, 111, 113–16, 118, 120–1, 123, 126, 130–2, 142, 144, 145, 147, 153; Houghton Library, Harvard University 95; Musée Carnavalet, Paris 17, 18, 40, 89, 90, 97–100, 109; Musée National des Arts et Traditions Populaires, Paris 34–8; Benjamin A. and Julia M. Trustman Collection, Brandeis University, Waltham, Mass. 4, 12, 47, 48, 53, 58–61, 63, 64, 67–9, 91, 107, 112, 117, 119, 122, 124, 125, 127–9, 133, 136–41, 143, 149, 152, 154–8, 161

Key to abbreviations of catalogue acknowledgments in the captions

B Emile Bouvy, *Daumier, l'oeuvre gravé du maitre*, 2 vols, Paris 1933
D Louis Delteil, *Le Peintre-Graveur illustré: Daumier*, 10 vols, Paris 1925–30
Maison K. E. Maison, *Honoré Daumier. Catalogue Raisonné of the Paintings, Watercolours and Drawings*, New York and London 1967
s. Gottfried Sello, (intro.) *Grandville. Das Gesamte Werk*, 2 vols, Munich 1969

Introduction

PARIS in the mid-nineteenth century is a prototype of the modern city. In the course of a century, the city underwent four revolutions (of 1789, 1830, 1848 and 1870), a fourfold increase in population (from half a million to two million), and complete physical redesign, from a medieval city to a modern one. Under these pressures, together with radical technical changes in communication and transportation, cultural emphasis shifted towards those forms which could respond with alacrity to topical urban themes – journalism, popular theatre and caricature. This encounter with the ephemeral data of city life as prime material for art and letters is the beginning of a social self-consciousness which is one of the components of modernity.[1] Honoré de Balzac, Honoré Daumier and Charles Baudelaire – from our perspective, the novelist, the draughtsman, and the critic and poet par excellence of this period – all practised within the framework of journalism. All three, in their portrayal of 'modern life', focused on Parisian 'types'; and Balzac and Baudelaire typically introduced their urban characters by description *from without*, as they would be seen by a stranger (as the caricaturist does, per force) rather than by direct statement of character or origins.[2]

This study, which is restricted to the decades between the July Revolution of 1830 and the founding of the Third Republic in 1870, is about the description of people from without: the Parisian's characteristic preoccupation with visible bodily clues to class, profession, character and circumstances. Through caricature, popular writing and theatre, Parisian types and their distinguishing traits were codified; in the way they made sense of the city to itself, these arts were the antecedents of more formal models of the urban population in sociology, demography and criminology.

People are changed by the city and they are the city and the city changes. As people moved from the provinces to the city, and city neighbourhoods lost their autonomous character, traditional roles were lost, traditional obligations were unenforced, and traditional behaviour seemed inexpedient or naïve. Upward mobility may not have been a reality for much of the bourgeoisie and petite bourgeoisie,[3] but it was a constant preoccupation; there was an eager market for tales of ambition and self-improvement. New informal codes of behaviour emerged, for orientation,

13

for emulation and simulation, to recognize others and to hold one's own. The illustrated newspapers were a vehicle for identifying, deciphering and communicating the signals and norms of urban exchange.

Our cross-section through these cultural shifts is approached primarily by way of caricature in the daily press. When caricature is discussed in the history of art, although its political and social context is acknowledged, formally it is analysed in relationship to prints and drawings. But caricature can also be looked at in relation to the tradition of classification and codification of human types.

The year 1830 marks the founding of the major caricature journals; the 1870s see the introduction of photogravure, which undercuts the informative role of draughtsmanship. The major work of Daumier, Gavarni (Guillaume Chevalier), Grandville and Henry Monnier falls within these four decades. Scores of other caricaturists were at work; illustrated journals and cheap editions proliferated, reaching a very broad audience at a time when half the population of Paris was still illiterate.

Only the most distinguished of this material has entered the history of art; but, considered altogether, it forms a pictorial contribution of extraordinary quality to cultural and social history. Caricature recorded moods and attitudes of city life – boredom, alienation, social displacement, political unrest and self-consciousness.

Three main strands can be distinguished in caricature, and each has its own relation to our theme. One is the *portrait charge*, which depicts an individual, usually a political figure, with more or less exaggeration of his characteristic features of face or body. Often this exaggeration has a satirical message, in the ancient tradition of animal-human analogies used as a code for human character. (A caricaturist stressing the owlish eyes and small beaky nose of Adolphe Thiers, politician and historian, was not merely finding a humorous formula to refer to a public figure, he was commenting on Thiers's political personality, his affectation of sharp-sighted wisdom, the owl's traditional attribute.)

The second strand is the allegorical interpretation of public events. Nations, factions, or abstractions such as Peace or Diplomacy, are represented by single figures with recognizable characteristics, and the action of the caricature is a transposition of, and a comment on, the public situation. Emblematic figures, such as Robert Macaire and Joseph Prudhomme, who represented the characteristics of their period, were a popular device for social and political comment. Here there is an element of riddle-guessing and of punning, involving the audience in the pleasures of deciphering a silent code.

The third strand, which is explored more fully than the others in this study, is social caricature – the satirical presentation of typical characters in everyday situations. This element predominated during the periods of

14

political censorship, from 1835 to 1848 and from 1852 to 1866; Chapters Three and Five discuss some of the political content of this social analysis. Whether it employs the grotesque deformations of Louis-Léopold Boilly or Joseph Traviès, the fantastic transformations of Grandville or the benign stylization of Gavarni, social caricature is thematically affiliated with *genre* painting, which by definition portrays *types* rather than individuals, and modest, often domestic, situations rather than the exalted personages of history painting.

Social caricature in the newspapers went out to find its public in the streets and cafés; it was consumed casually, as Baudelaire pointed out, along with the news and morning coffee. To be successful with its public, it had to develop a pungent and rapid communicative vocabulary, exploiting the graphic limitations of its means of reproduction.

The journalistic draughtsman, often working directly on the lithographic stone, was a performer, in daily dialogue with the public who were also his subject matter. Daumier's drawing has a communicative bravura and economy which is comparable to the discipline of mime, with its succinct evocation of character and situation. Both caricature and mime drew artistic advantage from their marginal status. (Another generation had to pass before studio painting and 'official' theatre could allow themselves to profit from the advances in realism which had been won in these popular arts.) Both caricature and mime use vernacular codes directly reflective of daily life. Both are directed to the eye – they show what the urban spectator *sees*, through highly articulate, and at times subversive, silence.

Caricature draws on and develops a twofold tradition: that of physiognomics, the classification of people into character types according to outward bodily signs, such as the shape of the eyes, forehead, mouth, and so on; and that of pathognomics, the interpretation of changing emotions by facial or bodily expression. In nineteenth-century Paris, in a context of urban pressure, dislocation and mass communication, this visual lore of physiognomy, bearing and gesture gained currency, immediacy and artistic power. The caricaturists drew their silent vocabulary in part from the academic rules for the pictorial 'expression of the passions' and in part from more informal models also familiar to their audience.

The *interpretation* of bodily signs, on the premise that traits of inward character are linked with outward traits of body and feature, goes back to a treatise on *Physiognomics*, attributed in the Middle Ages to Aristotle, and thought to be a prudential guide for his pupil Alexander. (The text makes extensive use of the analogy from the forms and imputed 'character' of animals: 'persons with hooked noses are ferocious; witness hawks'). In Chapter One (and its footnotes) I briefly discuss Johann Caspar Lavater's late eighteenth-century *L'Art de connaître les hommes par la physionomie*, first published in Paris in 1806–9, which established this tradition of physiognomic sign-reading as part of the culture of nineteenth-century France.

Another schema or set of conventional signs which was familiarly present, especially to the caricaturist, was that of the manuals for painters, giving rules for *depicting* emotion and character. This tradition, too, whose principal text in nineteenth-century France was Charles Le Brun's *Conférence sur l'expression générale et particulière* (1698), is closely linked with the treatises on physiognomics: it reads the same code, as it were, in the opposite direction. Where physiognomics, from pseudo-Aristotle through Lavater, starts from the outward sign and teaches how to interpret it in terms of inward character, the treatises for painters start from an emotion or disposition and teach the signs which will express it; and in this they are paralleled by guides to gesture for actors and orators.

Every physiognomic codification is also a classification of human character types: pseudo-Aristotle's *Physiognomics* has its near-contemporary complement in Theophrastus' *Characters*, short vignettes which describe, in terms of social behaviour rather than physiognomy, the 'tedious man', the 'idle man', and so on. Through Jean de La Bruyère's *Les Caractères de Theophraste, traduits du grec, avec les caractères ou moeurs de ce siècle* (1688), these vignettes are the source for a continuing 'literature of *moeurs*' (mores: social behaviour, habits, customs, manners). This essayistic classification of human types interacts with physiognomic analysis, and is widely used in our period; the popular *Physiologies* – paperbound books on Parisian types – are descriptions of *moeurs* rather than of bodily features.

The *Physiologies* also bear witness to the familiarity of another schema of classification of living beings inherited from an earlier century. For comic effect, the *Physiologie de l'étudiant* (1841) describes the varieties and behaviour of the species Student in forms that recall a natural historian's account of a species of butterfly, Georges Louis Leclerc de Buffon's *Histoire naturelle générale et particulière avec la description du cabinet du roi* (1749–1804, 44 volumes) was almost as familiar a text in the mid-nineteenth century as La Bruyère. In Chapter One I touch on Buffon's model of observation and classification as a frame of reference for Balzac, who transposes it, not merely for comic effect, to social description.

One last cross-section through this manifold of sign-giving and sign-reading is provided by the rules for decorum, which also formed part of the popular literature of our period. The *Codes* (see Chapter One), like a certain kind of popular sociology-cum-self-improvement literature in our own time, appealed both as entertaining social comment and as guidelines for the naïve and/or ambitious. We shall see in Chapters Four and Five how Monnier and Daumier make satirical use of the commonplaces of decorum and self-presentation.

The premise explored in this study is that these combined traditions of classification and characterization provided a functional base for a corpus of social description, in which the work of the caricaturists is central. In this enterprise, whose motto was Daumier's – 'One must be of one's time' – writers and graphic artists, Romantics and Realists, were equally engaged.[4]

We shall see how the exemplary spectators of our period, Balzac, Daumier and Baudelaire – as well as Jean-Baptiste Gaspard Deburau, the mime, Charles Philipon, the impresario of caricature publications, and Monnier, the actor-writer-caricaturist – were all praised in their time for having updated the vocabulary of their respective arts, making it complex and subtle enough to represent new urban relationships. Contemporaries recognized an analogy, even a symmetry, between the talents and oeuvres of Balzac, Deburau and Daumier: each was a master of silent expression. Both Deburau and Daumier, of artisan status by birth, and working in strictly popular art forms, were hailed as 'great artists': George Sand challengingly set the populist Deburau alongside the great classical actress and actor of the first half of the nineteenth century, Rachel and Talma; Baudelaire classed Daumier with Ingres and Delacroix. Each was perceived as fulfilling, in his own art, Balzac's programme of *La Comédie humaine*.

Overleaf
3 Bird's-eye view of Paris: view from the clock-tower of Saint-Louis en l'Ile.
Texier, *Tableau de Paris*, 1852–3

Champin

One Parisian panorama: codes and classifications

Interpersonal relationships in big cities are distinguished by a marked preponderance of the activity of the eye over the activity of the ear.
GEORG SIMMEL[1]

THE mid-nineteenth century is the period of the bird's-eye view. The panorama was a comprehensive and distancing conceptual mode – and a device of perspective in literature and the visual arts: Victor Hugo's opening scene in *Notre-Dame de Paris* (1831); Eugène de Rastignac in Balzac's *Père Goriot* (1835), gazing down on Paris from the Père Lachaise cemetery; the frontispieces to three popular compendia on Parisian life, *Le Diable à Paris* (1845–6), Edmond Texier's *Tableau de Paris* (1852–3), and *Paris dans sa splendeur* (1861); the dioramas and panoramas offered as public spectacles of the city, of which Louis-Jacques-Mandré Daguerre's was best known; Daumier's depiction of Nadar photographing from his aerial balloon; the early photographers, Daguerre, Nicéphore Niepce and Henry le Secq's view of Paris from the tops of buildings.

Honoré de Balzac (1799–1850) occupies a key position in this study. As a man of letters he was steeped in Enlightenment and earlier models of characterization and classification: La Bruyère's *Moeurs de ce siècle*, Buffon's *Histoire naturelle*, and Lavater's idiosyncratic *L'Art de connaître les hommes par la physionomie* are the three which most directly concern us.[2] And as a prolific day-to-day writer for the popular press, Balzac combined and exploited these models informally. His preoccupations underlie our whole theme: his insistence on social mobility, his fascination with bodily expression as a manifestation of social conditioning and his interest in manipulation of expression for social ends.

Balzac's master-image of his own enterprise is that of an abstraction of his subject, society, spread out and scanned from above: a bird's-eye view, a panorama, a map or a schematic diagram where types are re-arranged into a matrix or a hierarchy. This is essentially different from the Realist master-image of the novel as 'a mirror which one walks along the street'.[3] The eighty novels and stories that comprise Balzac's *La Comédie humaine*

20

4 DAUMIER, 'Nadar Elevating Photography to the Level of Art', 1862. D.3248

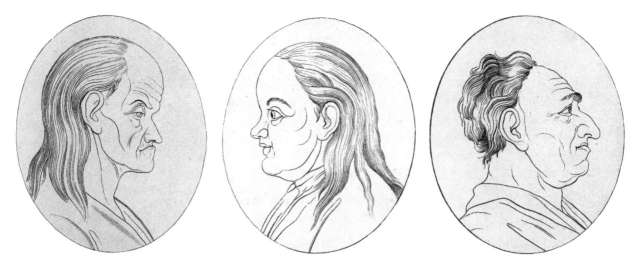

5, 6, 7 LAVATER, melancholic, phlegmatic and choleric types. *Essay on Physiognomy*, 1789.

(the title was first used in 1842 as a partly retrospective characterization of his work) are explorations of a chart which Balzac imagines as complete and simultaneously present.

In *Théorie de la démarche* (A Theory of Bearing)[4] – one of the semi-serious 'analytic studies' attached to *La Comédie humaine* – Balzac presents a full-scale eulogy of the Observer, who must have both a high viewpoint and an eye for detail:

> The observer is incontestably the man of genius. All human inventions come from an analytic observation in which the mind acts with an incredible rapidity of insights. Gall, Lavater, Mesmer, Cuvier . . . Bernard de Palissy, the precursor of Buffon . . . Newton, and also the great painter and the great musician, all are observers . . . those sublime birds of prey who, while rising to high regions, have the gift of seeing clearly in matters here below, who can at the same time abstract and specify, make exact analyses and just syntheses.[5]

Although Balzac's list of great observers rather pointedly refers to Buffon only to omit him in favour of De Palissy, there is a striking parallel between his account and a passage in Buffon's *Histoire naturelle* (1749). After an acknowledgment of the prodigious multiplicity of nature, far beyond any one student's capacity, Buffon gives his requirements for the good investigator:

> There is a kind of mental courage in envisaging . . . nature in the innumerable multitude of her productions, and in believing oneself capable of compre-hending and comparing them. . . . one may say that the love of the study of nature presupposes two qualities of mind which seem conflicting: the large

views of an ardent genius which embraces everything in one *coup d'oeil*, and the small attentions of a diligent instinct which attaches itself to one single point.[6]

Buffon's insistence on the status of *individuals* within a formal system of classification is also pertinent to our theme: 'The more we increase the number of divisions in the productions of nature, the closer we shall approach to the true, since nothing really exists except individuals.'[7] Buffon's ideal calls for a combinatory lexicon of distinguishing characteristics.

In relation to humankind, Johann Caspar Lavater (1741–1801), the Swiss physiognomer, proposed a larger lexicon of distinguishing signs than any previous author; the massive popularity of his treatise all over Europe at the beginning of the nineteenth century indicates a growing market for characterological interpretation. His physiognomic study first appeared in Germany in 1775–8.[8] It was published in France in between 1781 and 1803, under the title *Essai sur la physiognomonie destiné à faire connaître l'homme et à le faire aimer*, and then in a more popular and successful edition, annotated and illustrated in four volumes in 1806–9, edited by Dr Moreau de la Sarthe, under the title *L'Art de connaître les hommes par la physionomie*,

8 Lavater, 'A Group of Mean Faces', *L'Art de connaître les hommes par la physionomie*, Paris 1806–9

23

and reissued in 1820 in ten volumes.[9] Numerous other editions, some abridged, even in pocket size, were issued over the hundred and fifty years after the book's first appearance. Lavater was a basic resource in a gentleman's home, to be consulted when hiring staff, making friends and establishing business relations.[10]

Lavater's premise was the correspondence of physical appearance and moral character: he taught 'the science or knowledge of the correspondence between the external and internal man, the visible superficies and the invisible contents'.[11] He intended his work primarily as a moral and prudential guide and, collaterally, as a source book for painters.

The codification which had begun with pseudo-Aristotle's *Physiognomics* and became a pragmatic system for painters in Le Brun's *Conférence sur l'expression générale et particulière*, first delivered in 1668, was expanded by Lavater into a system of classification and codification of the forms of the parts of the human body and their corresponding moral traits.[12] Lavater maintained the tradition of animal-human parallels as a basis for moral interpretation. Each person is an individual soul and each single feature has 'the nature and character of the whole' and can serve as a key to the person's character.[13] Chapters are devoted to the variety of single features – eyes, noses, mouths, and so on.

Like Aristotle, Descartes, Le Brun and Hogarth,[14] Lavater maintained that often-repeated emotions leave their mark on the permanent expression of a person, so that, for example, an angry man will bear the marks of his disposition in a permanent scowl: 'Our gait and deportment are natural only in part and we generally blend with them something borrowed or imitated. But even these imitations and the habits they make us contract, are still the results of nature and enter into the primitive character.'[15] Education, training, even one's profession, he thought, had an effect on bearing: 'Trifles often decide much concerning the character of man. The manner of talking, holding or returning a teacup is frequently very significant. It may be affirmed that whoever can perform the smallest office with entire circumspection is capable of much greater.'[16]

Lavater conceived his work in the established tradition of physiognomic writing.[17] He cited his authorities – the Bible, Pliny, Cicero, Michel de Montaigne, Gottfried Leibniz, Johann Gottfried von Herder and Immanuel Kant – as testimony to the correspondences between inner and outer states. For method he cited Carolus Linnaeus, Jean-Baptiste Lamarck and Buffon; for his illustrations he drew freely on Le Brun as well as on Raphael, Leonardo da Vinci, Albrecht Dürer and Hogarth.[18]

Although Lavater's work never became a textbook as did Le Brun's guidelines to painters, his encyclopedia of characters prefigured and supported (in part through Balzac's mediation) the panoramic, anecdotal and prudential literature of nineteenth-century Paris. Balzac owned and

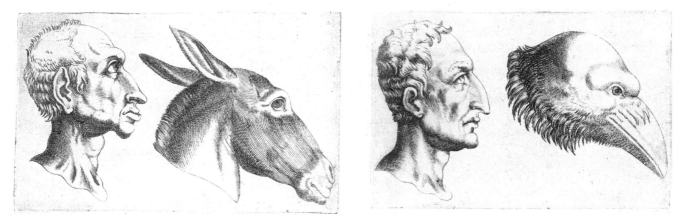

9, 10 LE BRUN, 'De humana physiognomica': comparison of animal and human physiognomy

referred to either the 1806 or 1820 Moreau de la Sarthe edition, with its
augmented and updated notes which reflected the personal interests of its
editor and the presumed interests of its audience.[19] Lavater's work was
presented with emendations and excursions on current research into
phrenology and physiognomy, as well as sections on J. J. Engel's
eighteenth-century observations on the analogies between physiognomy,
acting and painting and Denis Diderot on expression.[20] Especially pertinent and interesting to Balzac was the attention given to professions and
métiers. Although he had cited various occupations and their visible
effects on bearing, Lavater had been more concerned with inborn than
with acquired characteristics.

In his chapter, 'Observations sur les signes physionomiques des
professions', Moreau develops Lavater's notes on this distinction:

> The major varieties of the human species have been well observed and well
> described; it would be no less interesting and useful to study the detailed
> varieties, which are so numerous, and which derive from the diversity of
> conditions of life among civilized peoples. Each métier, each profession, should
> in general be regarded as a particular education, continued through life,
> which develops, exercises, strengthens certain organs, and establishes a specific
> relationship between the individual and his environment.
>
> In general, the different professions announce themselves, either by the
> condition of the forehead and eye, or the state and configuration of the wings
> of the nose and the mouth, according to whether, in the exercise of those
> professions, exalted meditation, observation, profound and lasting feelings
> predominate, or the superficial attention, quick perceptions and small passions
> of worldly people.
>
> Skilful and very experienced surgeons have in their physiognomy a par-
> ticular dominant trait, which comes from an habitual movement of raising the

25

upper lip – which can be attributed to the effort they make to resist the impression caused by the sight of suffering and pain which they have before their eyes during major operations.[21]

Certain professions – business, law, diplomacy, politics and prostitution – give the observer frequent occasion to exercise both physiognomic discrimination and dissimulation: 'It is noticeable especially that people of the world, courtiers, all those who cultivate appearances very much, who make it their business to be agreeable, have a very marked mobility of the nostrils and the upper lip, whose muscles are more developed than in other men.'[22]

In his *Physiologie du mariage*, Balzac made his acknowledgment to Lavater explicit: 'Lavater's Physiognomy has created a real science, which has taken its place at last among human knowledge.'[23] And elsewhere: 'The laws of physiognomy are exact, not only as they apply to character, but also as they apply to the destined course of life.'[24] Balzac used the language of physiognomy as well as phrenology in many of his first introductions of the dramatis personae of *La Comédie humaine*.[25]

Balzac was concerned both with the classification of Parisian types and their immediate and specific social context. It was primarily through him that a new repertory of Parisian types emerged in nineteenth-century narrative: the bureaucrat, the confidence man, the social climber, the banker, the money lender, the stock-market player, the industrialist, the journalist and the commercial writer.[26]

He presented a view of Paris at the time it was beginning to undergo staggering growth and dramatic change from a medieval city to a nineteenth-century urban centre. One's view of Paris at this time is inescapably coloured by that of Balzac. He projected on to his characters his own preoccupation with decoding of visual clues and the capacity to dissimulate. As the demographer Louis Chevalier has pointed out, Balzac did not describe all of Paris: his Paris was essentially bourgeois.[27] The streets he cited were largely those inhabited by small investors and tradesmen – Rue St Honoré, Rue des Bourdonnais and, above all, Rue St Denis. His characters rise through the strata of the bourgeoisie. His descriptions of working-class characteristics are less faithful and complete.[28] His descriptions of métiers are at least partially based on Louis-Sébastien Mercier's picturesque *Tableaux de Paris* (1781) which was reissued several times in the nineteenth century.[29]

Balzac repeatedly used physiological and anatomical metaphors for the whole of the city as an organism which can be analysed and studied: 'Paris is a sentient being, every individual, every bit of a house is a lobe in the cellular tissue of that great harlot whose head, heart and unpredictable behaviour are perfectly familiar to them.'[30] Paris is also like a delightful monster: 'Its head is in the garrets, inhabited by men of science

26

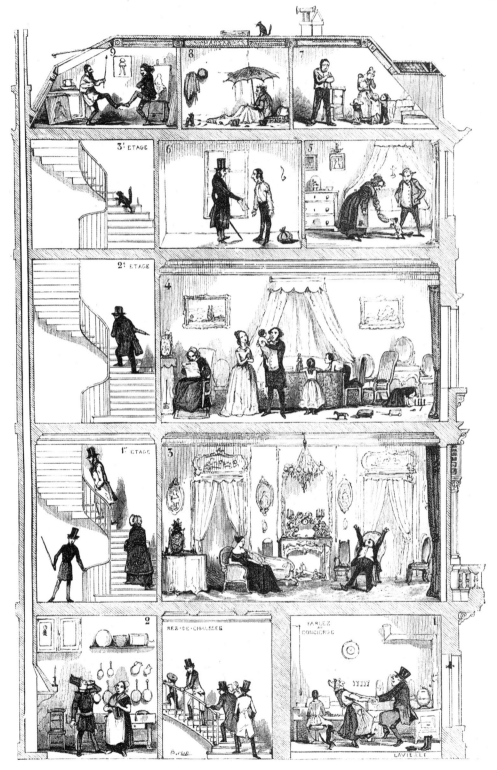

11 'Cross-section of a Parisian House, 1 January 1845: Five Stages of the Parisian World,' *Paris Comique*, 1845

and genius; the first floors house the well-filled stomachs; on the ground floor are the shops, the legs and feet, since the busy trot of trade goes in and out of them.'[31] He repeatedly remarked on the correspondence between the Parisian and his neighbourhoods, echoing the eighteenth-century axiom that the part reflects the whole. For instance, in *La Femme de trente ans* (The Woman of Thirty), he wrote: 'The influence exercised by the locality on the soul is a remarkable thing';[32] and in *Ferragus*:

> In Paris the different types contributing to the physiognomy of any portion of that monstrous city harmonize admirably with the character of the *ensemble*. Thus, the concierge, doorkeeper or hall porter, whatever the name given to this essential nerve-system in the Parisian monster, always conforms to the quarter in which he functions, and often sums it up. The concierge of the Faubourg Saint-Germain, wearing braid on every seam, a man of leisure, speculates in Government stocks; the porter of the Chaussée-d'Antin enjoys his creature comforts; he of the Stock Exchange quarter reads his newspapers; porters in the Faubourg Montmartre work at a trade; in the quarter given over to prostitution the portress herself is a retired prostitute; in the Marais quarter she is respectable, cross-grained, and crotchety.[33]

In *Les Splendeurs et misères des courtisanes* (A Harlot High and Low), another example, one of many: 'Who can fail to observe that [in the crush room of the Bal de l'Opéra] as in every other zone of Paris, there is a mode of being which reveals what you are, what you do, where you come from and what you are after.'[34]

Histoire des treize (History of the Thirteen) begins with an evocation of the physiognomy of the city: 'The streets of Paris have human qualities, and such a physiognomy as leaves us with impressions against which we can put up no resistance.'[35] Those who savour Paris 'are so familiar with its physiognomy that they know its every wart, every spot or blotch on its face'.[36]

Balzac intersected his anatomy and topography of city life with the vertical axis of social status. He explored social promotion as one of the salient characteristics of the Bourbon Restoration. In 'Parisian physiog-nomies', the opening section of *La Fille aux yeux d'or*, Balzac described finely distinguished class differences of behaviour. There is, for instance, the small shopkeeper, working his way up, who

> takes his patriotism ready-made from the newspaper. . . . *He is always expert in miming mirth, grief, pity, astonishment, at producing conventional cries or remaining mute* [italics mine], as he stands by to take on any role at the Opera every other evening. . . . His children are recruited into the class immediately above. . . . Often the younger son of a small retailer aspires to a position in the civil service. . . . That kind of ambition brings our attention to the second of the spheres of Paris. There you will see the same result. Wholesale merchants and their staff, government employees, small bankers of great integrity, bailiffs,

28

solicitors, notaries, clerks; in short, the bustling, scheming, speculating members of that lower middle class.[37]

This portrait of the *moeurs* of the petit bourgeois derives in form both from Buffon's descriptions of animal species and the characterizations of La Bruyère. It is a report on the physiology, habits and inclinations of the genus. Typically, the petit bourgeois belongs to the National Guard, has a plot at the Père Lachaise cemetery, hires a carriage for a Sunday drive in the country with his wife and children, goes to the Théâtre Italien at night. At fifty, when their children are married, he and his wife get a third-tier box at the opera, go to the Longchamps races in a hired cab and wear somewhat faded clothes on the boulevard. At sixty-five, he is awarded the Cross of the Legion of Honour. His children meantime have risen to the ranks of the upper bourgeoisie. 'Thus, each social sphere projects its spawn into the sphere immediately above it. The rich grocer's son becomes a notary, the timber merchant's son becomes a magistrate. Not a cog fails to fit into its groove and everything stimulates the upward march of money.'[38]

On the next level, there are the business men, lawyers, barristers, bankers, traders on a grand scale and doctors. Here, Balzac agreed with Moreau's clues to physical, moral and aesthetic consequences of certain professions:

What countenance can retain its beauty in the debasing exercise of a profession which compels a man to bear the burden of public miseries, to analyse them, weigh them, appraise them, batten on them? . . . they no longer feel, they merely apply rules which are stultified by particular cases. . . . And so their faces present the raw pallor, the unnatural colouring, the lack-lustre eyes with rings round them, the sensual, babbling mouths by which an observant person recognizes the symptoms of the deterioration of thought, and its rotation within a narrow circle of ideas calculated to destroy the faculties of the brain and the gift for seeing things broadly, for generalizing and drawing inferences.[39]

Of the 'idle' rich he wrote:

Unrelieved boredom, this inanity of mind, heart, and brain, this weariness with the unending round of Paris receptions, all leave their mark on the features and produce these paste-board faces, those premature wrinkles, that rich man's physiognomy on which impotence has set its grimace.[40]

Balzac was explicit about the relation between type and environment. Temperament sets one's outlook but contact with urban society has major, usually corrupting effects. In *Une Fille d'Eve* he explained that social mobility has produced a world of 'infinite nuances'. Previously, 'the caste system gave each person a physiognomy which was more important than the individual; today the individual gets his physiognomy from himself'.[41]

29

The education of a provincial in Parisian society is the vehicle used by Balzac and his contemporaries, both novelists and caricaturists as we will see later, to present the effects of society on the individual: physiognomic adaptation is a recurrent device. The typical novels of mid-nineteenth century France – Stendhal's *Le Rouge et le noir*, George Sand's *Elle et lui*, Flaubert's *Education sentimentale* – all constitute a vade-mecum of types, people and situations to cultivate and avoid, appropriate behaviour and decorum in a variety of circumstances.

In Balzac's *Père Goriot*, Eugène de Rastignac is coached by the Mephistophelian Vautrin and becomes the picture of an unscrupulous climber, straining against the human sentiments and family feeling with which he arrived from the provinces. (The Vicomte de Beauséant also advises Rastignac never to reveal his true feelings.) Throughout *La Comédie humaine*, Vautrin is noted for his genius for disguise. There are recurrent references to the means of dissimulation, particularly masks and costume, and to its opposite, phrenology, whose evidence cannot be modified by training or disguise.

The study of cranial cavities and protuberances as indices to character was a popular branch of medicine. F. J. Gall's phrenological theories were translated into French in 1818 and were used by Balzac and other novelists and illustrators.[42] We have seen that Moreau's updated Lavater included sections on phrenology. Phrenological reference occurs throughout Balzac's work.[43] For instance: 'Foreheads which are high, but receding at the top, betray an inclination to materialism'; 'all domed heads are ideological'.[44] In *Théorie de la démarche* Balzac argued that one's walk and bearing – 'the physiognomy of the body' – is harder to disguise than facial expression.[45] Only actors are trained to manipulate their appearance thoroughly, convincingly to convey a character unlike themselves. In *Splendeurs et misères des courtisanes* even Vautrin, in an unguarded moment, reverts to his convict's *démarche* and is recognized by an old associate.

Théorie de la démarche is the text which most explicitly reveals Balzac's view of his own enterprise:

> Pushed also, no doubt, by a first love for a new subject, I yielded to this passion: . . . was it not necessary to analyse, abstract and classify?
>   To classify, so as to be able to codify!
> To codify, to draw up the code of *démarche* . . . so that progressive men, and those who believe in perfectibility, can study to appear amiable, gracious, well-bred, educated, instead of vulgar, stupid, boring. . . . And is this not the most important thing in a nation whose motto is 'All for display'?[46]

Balzac developed a set of axioms: the walk announces the man; gesture is thought in action, by which one can decipher vice, remorse, sickness; the look, the voice and walk are equal means by which you can know the

12 DAUMIER, 'The Cranioscope-Phrénologistocope: Yes, that's it I have the bump of ideality, of causality, of locality, it's a remarkability.' 1836. D.300

entire man; all our body participates in movement, but no part should predominate; when the body is in movement, the face is immobile; economy of movement is the means to render a noble and gracious walk; all jerky movement betrays a vice or bad education; grace favours rounded forms; rest is the silence of the body; work has its effect on our bearing, scholars, for instance, incline their heads; courtisans, actors, spouses and spies, the ambitious and vindictive, betray their disingenuousness in their walk and bearing.

Balzac's recognition of popular consciousness of decorum and pose can be seen in a Daumieresque description from *Grandeur et décadence de César Birotteau*: 'Almost everyone has a favourite pose, which they think will heighten their natural advantages; in the case of Crevel, this consisted in crossing his arms Napoleonically, setting his head at a three-quarters angle, and fixing his gaze on the horizon, as the painter of his portrait had shown him.'[47]

Balzac's vignettes on social types developed into an independent semi-journalistic genre – the *Physiologies* – which, under the leadership of the

31

editor Philipon, was taken up by other writers and illustrated by leading draughtsmen of the day. This literature began in the 1830s, reached its peak in the early 1840s and subsided in the 1850s.

The range of its audience, though still somewhat a matter of conjecture, can be inferred from novels, caricatures and illustrations which show people as consumers of this literature, as well as from the material itself. Their success depended on the authors' awareness of their readers' ambitions, fantasies, fears and uncertainties, and in its vernacular recognizability. The *Physiologies* had a precursor in the literature of decorum – the *Codes*. These were admonitory and humorous 'books of rules' for eating, for conversation, for love and marriage, and for the traveller. They were mostly published between 1825 and 1830, under such titles as: *Code Parisien. Manuel complet du provincial et de l'étranger à Paris, contenant les lois, règles, applications et examples de l'art de vivre dans cette capitale, sans être dupé et de s'y amuser à peu de frais.* This particular example, by Charles Rousset, was a satire of social life that contained practical advice for the tourist in Paris, with anecdotes dealing with customs, manners and bearing. The writer recommended to the visitor not to be too expressive about his impressions: don't gape; don't mime your impressions: follow the new manner of theatre audiences who don't applaud excessively; don't assume airs (head high, nose in the air): an honest and modest bearing is the sign of a good education; the object of a journey is to notice, not to be noticed, your costume will anyway identify you as a stranger; if you want a view of the 'petulant frivolity' of the Parisian population, go to the Tuileries in the afternoon; everyone should go to a café, but stay only half an hour; the fashionable thing to do at a ball is to stay at one's table, engage in general conversation, and not dance. And so on.

The descriptive *Physiologies* were more popular – little paperbound monographs on Parisian occupational and avocational types that flooded the bookstalls between 1841 and 1843. Their vogue in these years was spectacular. A verse in *Le Charivari* ran:

> *Semblable aux champignons*
> *Après une pluie*
> *On vit ces embryons*
> *La ville remplie!*
> *Chose étrange à concevoir.*
> *Chaque homme voulut avoir*
> *Sa physiologie*
> *O gué!*
> *Sa physiologie.*[48]

(Like mushrooms after a rain/one saw these lumps all over town/It's hard to understand/Everybody wanted to have his Physiologie/heigh-ho/his physiologie.)

32

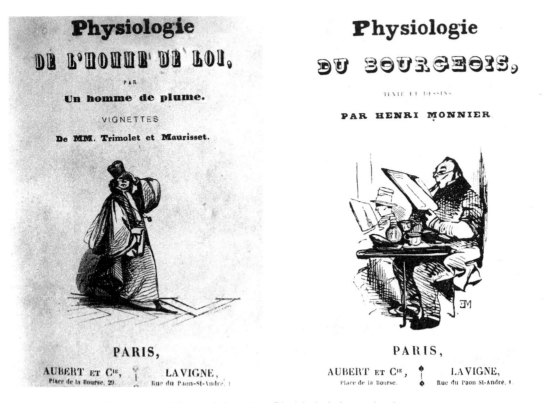

13 Frontispieces, *Physiologie de l'homme de loi*, 1841; *Physiologie du bourgeois*, 1841

Over 130 volumes, profusely illustrated, with 30 to 60 engravings to a hundred pages of print, were published primarily by the Maison Aubert, print-sellers and publishers of the illustrated newspapers *La Caricature* and its successor *Le Charivari* (to be discussed in more detail in Chapter Three). Philipon, Aubert's general editor, retained and guided a stable of writers, illustrators and caricaturists from the newspapers. Grandville, Daumier, Gavarni and Monnier were outstanding among the illustrators; others included Traviès, Joseph-Louis Trimolet and D.-A.-M. Raffet.

Balzac claimed paternity of the *Physiologies* as a genre – his own *Physiologie du mariage* had been published eleven years before the Aubert series appeared.[49] Balzac acknowledged Brillat-Savarin's *Physiologie du goût ou méditation de gastronomie transcendante* (1826) as a predecessor; but his own book certainly was the direct model for the genre.

Many of the *Physiologies* were first serialized in the daily *Le Charivari* before being issued as paperbacks. *Physiologies* were full of anecdotal accounts and contemporary allusions. As Benjamin observed, they were basically a petit-bourgeois genre.[50] At one franc each, they were cheap and portable.[51]

An ironic definition of the physiologist was offered in *Le Charivari*:

33

The physiologist is a kind of La Bruyère at so much a line, who takes on, in the newspapers, the observation and study of private and public manners. . . . The physiologist is above all a sceptic, and has never believed in virtue, least of all in the virtue of women; he says that he is paid to be like that. The physiologist is grave and dignified; when asked the reason for his sadness, he responds modestly that it is the mark of perceptive spirits and cites Molière and Deburau.[52]

The term *physiologie* suggested objective observation of a *type* rather than of an individual. The series dealt with the broad range of middle-class life according to profession, trade and avocation, diagnosed by habits, customs and manners. Besides the accounts of Parisian types, there were also physiologies of neighbourhoods and institutions, such as the press, the cafés, the balls. They described and illustrated where people lived, how they dressed, what they ate, where they went, what theatre and café they frequented, what they aspired to and the compromises they accepted. The roles were described primarily by social behaviour and interactions rather than by visual characteristics of the individual. The physiologies were classifications by stereotypes: the doctor, the lawyer, the investor, the soldier, the traveller, the student, the poet, the musician, the bluestocking, the married man, the robber, the tailor, the kept woman, the worker, the bourgeois and the spectator.[53]

Balzac's *Physiologie de l'employé* (1841), illustrated by Trimolet, sketched a bureaucracy that revolved around power and money. As with his *Théorie de la démarche*, Balzac articulated his descriptions with axioms such as: 'For employees, the office supplants nature.' Balzac depicted the office manager exuding such self-satisfaction that on passing him in the street one could diagnose with assurance, 'that's an office manager'. He described the social bearing of all office workers from secretaries to bosses. Monnier had covered the same ground in his series *Moeurs administratives* of 1828. Huart's *Physiologie de l'étudiant* (1841), illustrated by Trimolet, Alophe and Maurisset, is another early example that drew explicitly on the natural-history model for its imagery: students exhibit a variety of habits and an exuberant pretentiousness, they later undergo a metamorphosis more striking than nature's: 'The brilliant butterfly once he returns to the provinces, folds into a chrysalis for the rest of his days.' The profuse variety of characteristics found among students collapses into a single stereotype of passivity.

Half a million copies of the *Physiologies* were bought during the few years of their vogue. (The Paris population at this time was less than one million, and only half were literate.) The most popular volumes concerned diversions: the zoo, the theatre; and avocations: the spectator, the man of fashion, the traveller, followed by professions and trades. The popular theatre during this same period incorporated a number of themes from

34

Le salut est comme les caractères, il est altier, simple,

. . bonhomme, insultant, bienveillant, froid, humiliant, . . . bas, ...

. . . . . naïf, gourmé, ... orgueilleux, triste, ...

. . . . inquiet, misérable, ... audacieux. . . . .

14 'How One Greets in Paris: Salutation is like character, it is haughty, simple, good-natured, offensive, kindly, mortifying, base, naive, affected, arrogant, sad, apprehensive, wretched, bold . . . .' *Le Diable à Paris*, 1845–6

15 Frontispiece, *Les Français peints par eux-mêmes*, 1840–2

16 Frontispiece, *Le Diable à Paris*, 1845–6

these publications – a further indication of their success and of the close interchange between the theatre and the popular press of the time.

After the initial success of the inexpensive pocket volumes, several publishers invested in grander formats: bound omnibus volumes, to which the same group of writers and illustrators contributed, which appealed to a more affluent and 'settled' audience, and which typically would be displayed in the drawing room.[54] Such a publication was L. Curmer's eight-volume *Les Français peints par eux-mêmes* (1840–2).[55] A contemporary compendium of characters 'in the manner of La Bruyère', it depicted 'our persons, habits, customs, and tastes'. In his introduction, Jules Janin observed that in the past, when society had been more cohesive, a single person could engage in its analysis, as La Bruyère had done; but increasing complexity and diversity made it necessary to introduce 'this play of a thousand and one varied acts'.[56]

36

Janin gave clear clues as to the book's intentions and audience: it was based on the premise that, unlike the major events recorded by historians, the observation and history of everyday life normally went unrecorded. The purpose of these volumes, he explained, was to pass on 'what sort of men we were, and how we employed our time'. As Janin noted, 'not a year passed that would not furnish materials for a volume of characters'. The past seemed golden by comparison with the present: wealthy but cultured men had been replaced by the 'capitalist of 1840', a speculator and a social climber. It was, therefore, 'the duty of the writer of the present day . . . to describe the new roads to fortune: the Bank, the Exchange, advertisements, prospectuses, joint-stock companies, rises and falls, disaster and bankruptcies, the endless speculations on nothing, on the vacuum'.[57]

'France had become "the Grand Nation of grocers"', he continued;

37

the Charter of 1830 'created among us an entirely new set of characters, of strange and incredible manners'. The tone was one of intellectual disappointment and disaffection with society. Janin explicitly contrasted La Bruyère's types with contemporary ones: a more caustic form of description was now appropriate.

Another publication in this genre was a two-volume compendium of Paris and Parisian life illustrating 'our physiognomy, our gesture, and our costumes', *Le Diable à Paris, Paris et les parisiens* (1845–6), edited by Jules Hetzel. It carried the subtitle: 'Manners and costumes, character and portraits of the inhabitants of Paris; complete picture of their lives: private, public, political, artistic, literary, industrial, etc. etc.' Among the contributors were George Sand, Charles Nodier, Eugène Briffault, Balzac, Alphonse Karr, Gérard de Nerval, Arsène Houssaye, Théophile Gautier and Alfred de Musset. Gavarni drew a series of caricatures for these volumes, *Les gens de Paris*, including: *Philosophes* (Street Types), *En Carnaval, Presenteurs et présentés, Hommes et femmes de plume* (Men and Women Writers), *Bourgeois, Artistes, Petits Commerces* (Small Trades), and so on.

The narrative device used in this collection of texts is of the devil bored with hell, deciding to visit part of his empire, Paris. The book is hardly an exposé: it begins with straightforward accounts of the history and geography of Paris and ends with government statistics on population, finance, professions, criminality, schooling and poverty. The core of the book consists of entertaining, cynical accounts of customs and institutions, such as the Chamber of Deputies and the Palace of Justice (though carefully never crossing the line of censorship), the Jockey Club, the cemeteries, theatres, carnivals and balls. There is a song on indifference, and a satire of bourgeois marriage by Monnier. In an illustrated section entitled 'How one greets in Paris', B. Pascal noted: 'In France every conversation begins with a ballet', and suggested that one could write a history of Parisian society by providing a chronological account of forms of greeting.[58]

Six years later, a still more ambitiously illustrated two-volume work, Texier's *Tableau de Paris* (1852–3), was published with 1,500 engravings, some reproduced from the vignettes in *Le Diable à Paris*, and some from the various caricature journals and illustrated newspapers. The frontispiece shows a panorama of the city and, in his text, Texier punned on other popular uses of the suffix 'rama': the diorama, the panorama, the georama, the neorama, the navalorama. (In *Père Goriot* the students in Mme Vauquer's pension pun on the same lines.) *Tableau de Paris* is a panorama of the city; a detailed account of Parisian sites and institutions just before the city was redesigned and expanded by Napoleon III and Baron Georges-Eugène Haussmann, the prefect of Paris. Texier presented

38

a straightforward account of streets, neighbourhoods, law courts, medical and law schools, artist's ateliers, theatres, department stores, carnivals, prisons, cabarets, balls and parks. He delighted in the rich physiological detail of the city: 'Physiognomy and physiology, individual and collective, the mass and the details: this programme is continuously developing and always new, from the viewpoints of a thousand observers; every human being with eyes and judgment will make his own new and original discovery, but the exact plan will never be complete.'[59]

Paradoxically, when Haussmann and Napoleon began to impose their panoramic design on the city in 1854, the bird's-eye view lost most of its visual drama and became hardly more than official propaganda, revealing little more than what Haussmann had intentionally put there. Before then, it had afforded the Romantic pleasure of a privileged command over recalcitrant, unplanned material: Baudelaire's *fourmillante cité* and Balzac's 'organism'. The pleasures – 'demonic', rapacious, voyeuristic or scientific – of discovering *hidden* structures, like those of Nature, are lost when the spectacle is a deliberate artefact.[60]

17 Projected view of the Place de l'Etoile, after a drawing by M. Wibaille, architect, 1857

39

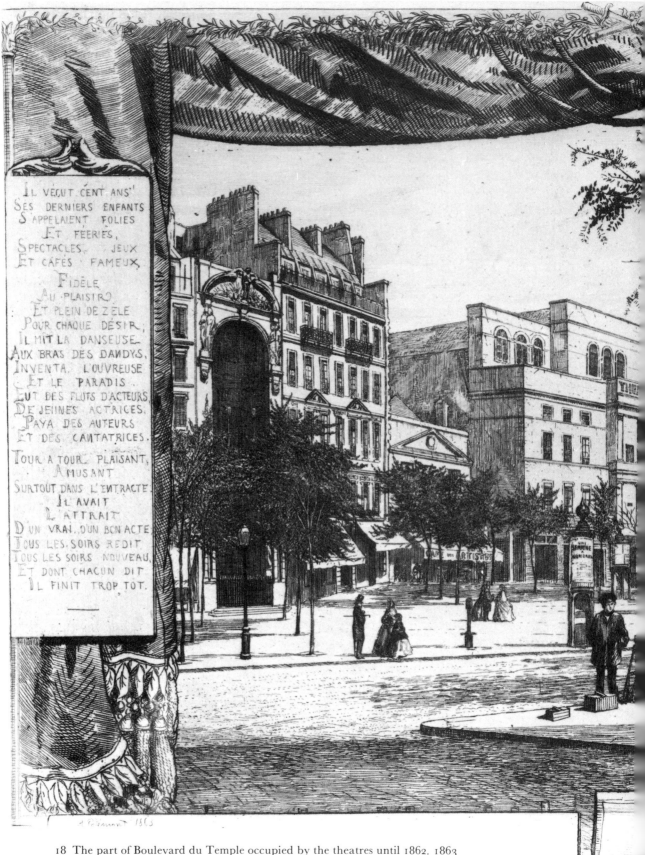

IL VÉCUT CENT ANS!
SES DERNIERS ENFANTS
S'APPELAIENT FOLIES
ET FÉERIES,
SPECTACLES, JEUX
ET CAFÉS FAMEUX,
FIDÈLE
AU PLAISIR
ET PLEIN DE ZÈLE
POUR CHAQUE DÉSIR,
IL MIT LA DANSEUSE
AUX BRAS DES DANDYS,
INVENTA L'OUVREUSE
ET LE PARADIS...
EUT DES FLOTS D'ACTEURS
DE JEUNES ACTRICES,
PAYA DES AUTEURS
ET DES CANTATRICES.

TOUR À TOUR PLAISANT,
AMUSANT
SURTOUT DANS L'ENTR'ACTE
IL AVAIT
L'ATTRAIT
D'UN VRAI, D'UN BON ACTE
TOUS LES SOIRS REDIT,
TOUS LES SOIRS NOUVEAU,
ET DONT CHACUN DIT
IL FINIT TROP TÔT.

18 The part of Boulevard du Temple occupied by the theatres until 1862. 1863

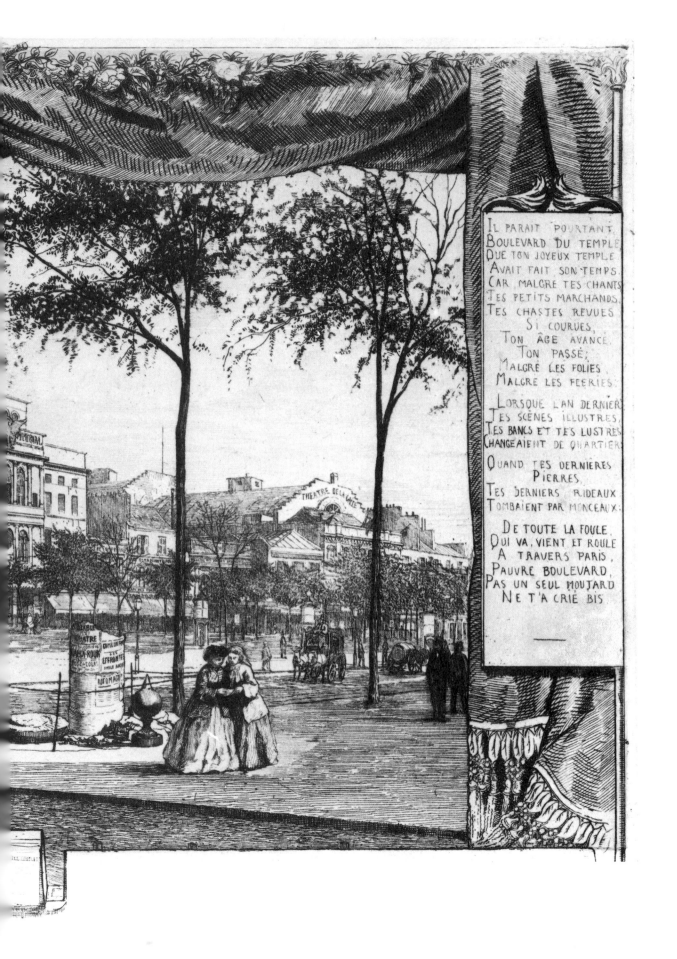

IL PARAIT POURTANT,
BOULEVARD DU TEMPLE
QUE TON JOYEUX TEMPLE
AVAIT FAIT SON TEMPS,
CAR MALGRÉ TES CHANTS,
TES PETITS MARCHANDS,
TES CHASTES REVUES
SI COURUES,
TON ÂGE AVANCE,
TON PASSÉ,
MALGRÉ LES FOLIES
MALGRÉ LES FÉERIES.

LORSQUE L'AN DERNIER
TES SCÈNES ILLUSTRES,
TES BANCS ET TES LUSTRES
CHANGEAIENT DE QUARTIER,
QUAND TES DERNIÈRES
PIERRES,
TES DERNIERS RIDEAUX
TOMBAIENT PAR MONCEAUX.

DE TOUTE LA FOULE
QUI VA, VIENT ET ROULE
A TRAVERS PARIS,
PAUVRE BOULEVARD
PAS UN SEUL MOUTARD
NE T'A CRIÉ BIS

Two Deburau and the Théâtre des Funambules. The literary marionettes

The pantomime is the real human comedy, and though it doesn't employ 2,000 characters like Balzac, it is not less complete: with four or five types it manages everything. THEOPHILE GAUTIER[1]

WRITTEN descriptions of human types, the codes and guides to physiognomy, bearing and gesture that have been our focus so far, were adapted to an urban society where people's identity was increasingly linked to profession and occupation; where daily mass printing was heightening self-consciousness among the urban public; and where the modern as such was becoming an explicit theme for art and criticism.

Two popular visual genres are considered in the rest of our study: mime and caricature, both addressed to a broad and daily audience and both supported and advocated by the same group of writers and critics. The classification of human types and the repertoire of bodily expression are at work in both.

Within our period, we can trace a double transformation in caricature and in mime: the updating and enriching of traditional canons, reflecting, even anticipating the structures and concerns of modern society, and the breakdown of the dividing lines between vernacular and high art.

Deburau's repertoire of naturalistic roles and scenes from working-class and lower-middle-class life was under way before the caricaturists Traviès and Daumier began to develop their depictions of daily life in the mid 1830s, and before the *Physiologies* of the early 1840s. Deburau's point of departure was Pierrot, one of the characters from the *commedia dell'arte* tradition, which had survived in France attenuated but unbroken.[2]

The Théâtre des Funambules, which opened in 1816, was at first hardly more than a collection of variety turns, the sort to be seen at fairs. It was based on the performances of travelling troupes, especially acrobats and tight-rope dancers, whence the name Funambules, and included in its programme trained dogs and fire-eaters. Also performing was a professional *grimacier* or *physiomane*, Leclerq, whom Baudelaire described: 'His act consisted in making faces; and by the light of two candles his face

42

19 The 'paradis' at the
Théâtre des Funambules.
Texier, *Tableau de Paris*,
1852–3
20 Interior of the Théâtre
des Funambules. Texier,
Tableau de Paris, 1852–3

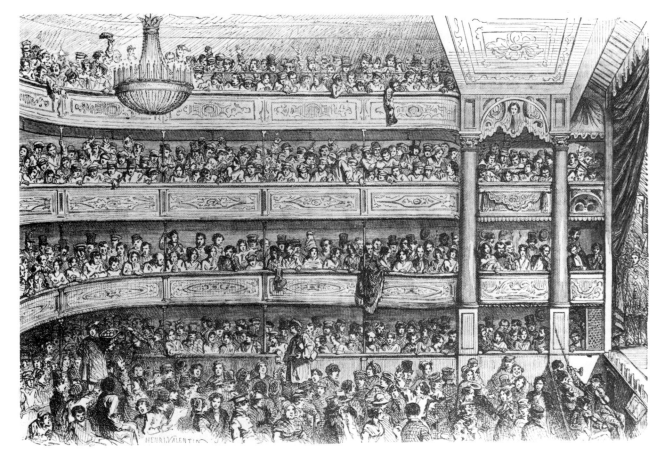

would depict all the human passions. It was like the notebook for *Les Caractères des passions de M. Le Brun peintre du roi.*'³

The Funambules was a small and squalid theatre which could only seat five hundred. It had its own particular regular audience, most of whom never attended other spectacles – at least those who sat in the *paradis*, or the upper gallery, the street urchins, the apprentices and the workers. A place in the *paradis* was cheaper than a newspaper or a loaf of bread.⁴ Located on the Boulevard du Temple, it was close to the working-class districts of St Antoine and St Denis. This street, established as an old fair ground, housed about thirty-three popular theatres, as well as cabarets and cafés and was something like the Times Square of its day.⁵ It was also called the Boulevard du Crime, because so much violence was depicted on the stages of its theatres.

The Funambules was a silent theatre. Legislation of 1806 obliged theatres to stay within their assigned genres: pantomimes were forbidden to use dialogue.⁶ At one time the Funambules circumvented this restriction by announcements spoken from the wings; they also, like silent films, used explanatory placards. In 1818, when the Funambules obtained grudging permission to show 'vaudeville' with three characters, each of the three had to cross the stage on a tight-rope, before the play itself began to establish the genre. These restrictions were not lifted until the Revolution of 1830.

The silence of this theatre became its trademark and strength. In the prolonged periods of censorship until 1830 and from 1835 to its demolition in 1863, it was able to introduce subversive notes through 'gait, glance, and gesture'.

The plays performed at the Funambules at this time had fairly standard *commedia dell'arte* plots, with the invariable stock of comic characters. Arlequin was always the suitor, in love with the beautiful and ideal Colombine, who in turn was courted by the crass rich Pantalon (or Léandre) with the support of Colombine's father, the avaricious and opinionated Cassandre. Pierrot was his downtrodden valet, the butt of anger and reprisal. With the arrival of Deburau, the *commedia* tradition became revitalized.

Deburau was born in 1796 in Neukolin, Bohemia. His father was French and had been a mercenary soldier and then a puppeteer and acrobat: the family performed as a travelling troupe of acrobatic mimes. In 1811 they arrived in Paris and in 1816 were engaged by the Théâtre des Funambules. Baptiste, as the young Deburau was called, was trained as an acrobat, the member of the troupe whose classic and physically demanding role it is to fail comically at every turn. He replaced the Funambules Pierrot at short notice, in 1819, and stole the show by his melancholy long features and his calm unpreparedness in the midst of the horseplay of others. Gradually, the give-and-take between Pierrot and Cassandre became the dominating element in the Funambules panto-mimes, which began to outshine the variety turns.

Deburau kept the role of Pierrot for life, transforming the white-faced clown of the *commedia dell'arte*, who had been a foil for the jokes and plots of others, into a wily and audacious character who got the better of his master. Around this new and successful Pierrot other changes transpired which gradually transformed the *commedia* into a theatre of contemporary types and situations. Deburau introduced naturalistic costumes and scenes and, above all, naturalistic gestures in his performances. His Pierrot portrayed various jobs and trades, particularly manual ones. Deburau and the Funambules troupe all had first-hand experience in manual trades.[7] As theatre critic for the *Journal des débats* and *Figaro* in 1832, Janin observed that Deburau 'made a society in his own guise. Pierrot is the people, in turn happy, sad, sick, well, beating, being beaten, musician, poet, simpleton, always poor like the people'.[8] And Gautier, a writer and leading theatre critic for *La Presse* who also wrote an occasional scenario for the Funambules, added: 'Pierrot, pallid, slender, dressed in sad colours, always hungry and always beaten, is the ancient slave, the modern proletarian, the pariah, the passive and disinherited being, who, glum and sly, witnesses the orgies and follies of his masters.'[9] Deburau's roles were like working-class *Physiologies* but sharper, more cunning and malicious and, at the same time, charming, with the appeal of the servant who deftly turns the tables on his master.

The Funambules pantomimes were never without slapstick and acro-batics: pratfalls, kicks in the seat, virtuoso leaps, often through counter-weighted trapdoors, and tumbling sequences frequently incorporated in the choreography of a fight. Deburau was a master of all this. He seems also to have made full use of the classic repertoire of theatrical gesture – the 'take' of surprise, the stance expressive of pride, the pointing finger of denunciation or singling out. He used this inherited, highly stylized, professional vocabulary in plays of increasing naturalism and contem-porary specificity. Contemporaries reported that he augmented and up-dated the gestural repertoire with new vernacular elements, often specific to one or another of the trades or working-class types: 'Deburau mimed *argot*'[10] (*argot* meaning both slang and professional jargon). His innova-tions had to pass the test of the *paradis*, with its audience of streetwise connoisseurs. George Sand described them: 'Go and see with what seriousness all these neighbourhood street children [*gamins*] watch the inimitable pantomime of their much loved Pierrot. They don't laugh much; they examine, they study, they feel the finesse, the elegance, the sobriety, the accuracy of effect of all his gestures, and the smallest change in that physiognomy so delicately drawn under his mask of chalk.'[11]

45

21 AUGUST BOUQUET, frontispiece to
Jules Janin, *Deburau : histoire du
théâtre à quatre-sous*, 1832
22 DÉSIRÉ VAUTIER, 'Deburau
Gallery' 1846(?)

Deburau's extreme facial expressiveness (based on extreme composure)
allowed his gestures to be understated. As a more effective foil for his long
face, he replaced Pierrot's traditional ruffled collar and floppy hat by a
tight black skullcap and a loose, collarless tunic. He also whitened his face,
making it a neutral mask on which the slightest change was legible.

There are engravings and lithographs of Deburau – though until compounded with written testimony, they hardly convey much of his distinction. The most informative depictions date from the time (at least after
1836) when Deburau varied his Pierrot's costume: a print by a fellow
actor Désiré Vautier, entitled *Galerie Deburau*, parades Deburau in the
costumes of his most popular roles – *Amour et désespoir*, *Le Billet de mille
francs*, *Noir et blanc*, *Les Jolis Soldats*, *Les Dupes ou les deux georgettes*, *Les
Epreuves* (The Trials), *Le Cheveu du diable* (The Devil's Hair), *Le Lutin
femelle* (The Female Elf), *Le Songe d'or* (The Dream of Gold), *Salade* (The

23 Deburau in *Le Billet de mille francs*.
Drawing by Patrice Dillon, after
Bouquet, 1833

Salad Vendor), *Pierrot en Afrique* and *Pierrette ou les deux braconiers* (Pierrette
or the Two Poachers).

   The prints of Deburau, except those drawn by the caricaturist Cham
(Amédée de Noé), all agree in one respect: the composure of his features,
the absence of emphatic grimace. Auguste Bouquet's lithographs of
Deburau in five different roles, illustrating Janin's *Deburau: histoire du
théâtre à quatre-sous* (1832), shows this composure rather more convincingly
than does Vautier's panorama.[12] In Vautier's version, the rag-picker
from *Le Billet de mille francs* is merely ragged, with a static pose and a life-
less glance. Bouquet's rag-picker, by contrast, has an eloquent stance,
burdened but rakish and assertive, with a hand braced at the hip and a
sour stare from a black eye. An aggressive elbow shows through a torn
sleeve; extravagant black corkscrew side curls, a tilted bonnet and a
dramatically raised collar set off the challenging face. The long delicate

47

lines of the curved nose and lantern jaw could be nobody's but Deburau's. In another portrait sketch of Deburau by H. Salmon, Pierrot is shown, in his classic skullcap, looking back over his shoulder at the spectator, black eyes agape, dark mouth ajar, the features and pale face accentuated.

Essential to the extraordinarily vivid impression that Deburau made was that he carried off both broad farce and naturalistic anecdote, not only with subtlety but somehow with elegance: on this all contemporary accounts agree.[13] George Sand focused most sharply on this transforming combination of 'low' motifs and high style: 'He is just, and when he distributes his kicks and blows, he does so with the impartiality of an enlightened magistrate and the elegance of a marquis. He is essentially a gentleman to the end of his long sleeves.'[14]

Paul de Saint-Victor, a contemporary writer, observed of Deburau's characterization: 'For petulance and brutal hilarity he substituted a mocking gravity and ironic stolidness. . . . His gestures were sombre, precise, caustic and malicious. The shrug of the shoulders, the snapping of fingers, the tripping up were done with nonchalant elegance. His roles were free, rough, even obscene.'[15]

The most informed guide to Deburau's pantomimes was Champfleury (Jules Husson, 1821–89), journalist, art critic, novelist and leading theorist of Realism, who was also among the first to write appreciatively about Courbet and Daumier. Much of Champfleury's life was dedicated to the study of popular arts: caricature, popular imagery and

48

24, 25 The costumes of Deburau. Texier, *Tableau de Paris*, 1852–3

26 H. Salmon, Jean-Baptiste Deburau

pantomime. He first saw Deburau in 1844 in Laon, just before coming to Paris. Champfleury was involved with the Théâtre des Funambules from his first evening in Paris to its closing in 1862.[16] He wrote nine pantomimes for the Funambules between 1846 and 1851 and became its director in its last year. In *Souvenirs des Funambules* (1859), Champfleury described the types of pantomime developed there. In *La Bataille réaliste* (1913), the historian Emile Bouvier observed that the sequence of pantomime between 1820 and 1850 seems to parody the literary development of the same period.[17]

Following the *commedia* with which the Funambules began, the mimes and their authors developed the *pantomime mélodrame*, presenting standard Romantic themes, brigands, tyrants and damsels in distress rescued by young heroes. Frédérick Lemaitre, who began his career as the juvenile romantic lead at the Funambules, became one of the greatest popular actors of this period. There were miraculous escapes from dungeons, thunderstorms and a variety of other dramatic effects.[18] In the midst of all this (even after July 1830 when the regulation restricting speech was lifted) Deburau as Pierrot remained mute and white-faced. And to his audience – and to Champfleury – this silent mime was ideal.[19] It was said that at the Funambules 'on écoutait la pantomime' – one listened.[20]

Another type of pantomime evolved at the Funambules was the magic or enchanted pantomime, *pantomime féerique* or *pantomime à trucs*, which

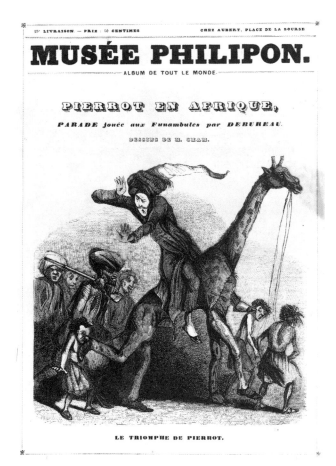

27 CHAM, 'Pierrot en Afrique',
Musée Philipon, 1842

used the *commedia* characters but with a complete disdain for any rules. Good and bad fairies and sorcerers presided; people were cut into pieces and magically restored to life. The motivation for the special effects was flimsy or non-existent. They relied on rapid set changes, known as *trucs*, to convey a sense of fantasy.[21] One of the most popular plays of this genre was *Le Boeuf enragé* (1827), written, anonymously, by Charles Nodier (director of the biggest theatre collection in Paris, the Bibliothèque de l'Arsenal) and performed about two hundred times.[22]

Of this type of pantomime, the contemporary playwright Théodore de Banville observed: 'In the Funambules, the pantomime ran its course among a series of exceptionally clownish incidents to carry us away from our prosaic cares and worries, but at the same time, it expressed life, simplified, idealized by a powerful mercurial fantasy.'[23]

Highly popular in this genre was *Pierrot en Afrique* (1842), a pantomime in four acts, exceptional in Deburau's repertory for its contemporary historical and political reference. It was performed at the time the French

et qui finit par danser à la grande jubilation de Pierrot, qui,
d'abord, se contente d'admirer les pas de la statue, et finit par
les imiter, les dépasser même, et se livrer à une cachucha parisienne tellement légère et *intempestive* que l'autorité se voit
forcée d'intervenir dans l'intérêt des mœurs.

Arlequin le délivre; et, par reconnaissance, Pierrot délivre Arlequin du diable, en brûlant le contrat synallagmatique.

Soit l'effet de la danse excentrique, soit l'effet du violon, le
dîner de Cassandre tourne sur le cœur du pauvre Pierrot, les gaz
se dilatent et son *ventre prend du corps*, comme disent les bonnes
femmes. Un habile vétérinaire le guérit par un remède propor-
tionné au volume abdominal.

Le marquis est chassé; Arlequin et Colombine sont unis par
Pierrot, qui leur promet un bonheur sans nuages.

Mais la guérison ramène la gloutonnerie, et bientôt Pierrot,
qui a encore dérobé à quelqu'un son repas, se remet à manger
et boire. Deux singuliers convives viennent lui demander leur
part du festin.

Imprimé par Bethune et Plon, à Paris

were fighting against Abd-el-Kader after the occupation of Algeria, and contained a number of quasi-patriotic scenes ridiculed by Pierrot's clowning.[24] But, as Péricaud, the leading historian of the Théâtre des Funambules observed, it was the most incomprehensible and foolish of all their pantomimes. Cham illustrated this play for the magazine *Le Musée Philipon*, giving us some sense of its pratfalls and slapstick style.[25] The Romantic writers De Nerval and Janin were attracted to enchanted pantomime and wrote scenarios in this genre. Even the Realist champion Champfleury confessed to a weakness for this somewhat frivolous and illogical form, and he considered the *Songe d'or* (1828), attributed to Nodier, the most complete and poetic example of the *pantomime féerique*.[26]

Champfleury credited to Deburau the beginning of the *pantomime réaliste*, the fourth type of pantomime, in which Deburau left off his Pierrot costume and appeared as a soldier, grave-digger, cobbler, and so on. Champfleury wrote of the *pantomime réaliste*: 'In general it is short: the action sticks to scenes of popular life. I belong body and soul to this school [of pantomime] which I have crystallized, developed and made capable of effects of serious comedy which had not been approached before.'[27] Even in this new naturalistic genre, Champfleury's ideal pantomime was improvisational, and as far as possible mimed, not spoken.

All these types, the *commedia*, the melodrama, the magic pantomime and the realistic pantomime, coexisted at the Funambules by the time of Deburau's death. They all included a stylized cast of *commedia* characters and some elements of slapstick.

Contemporary writing about Deburau illustrates the intersection between his inherited genre, the development of his distinctive role and talent, and the artistic ideologies of the 1820s through to the 1840s. Everyone described Deburau's Pierrot according to their own predilection. The first published recognition from the world of high culture was an enthusiastic article by Nodier, which appeared in 1828 in the daily newspaper *La Pandore*;[28] in it he encouraged all of Paris to come to the Funambules. It seems to have been Nodier who first brought to the Funambules Balzac, Gautier, De Nerval and Janin. As we have seen, George Sand and Baudelaire were early enthusiasts. In 1832 Janin published his two-volume *Deburau: histoire du théâtre à quatre-sous*, that did much to establish Deburau's reputation. More a Romantic polemic than a biography, it emphasized the 'common man' aspect of Deburau's Pierrot: 'It is the people Deburau represents in all his dramas. He knows what makes people laugh, what amuses them, what makes them angry. He knows at heart what people admire, what they like, what they are. He is an actor without passion, without words, and almost without a face; who can say all, express all, and mock all; who can play without a word all of Molière.'[29]

Unlike Janin and George Sand, whose Deburau is relatively benign, both Baudelaire and Champfleury, the *poète maudit* and the Realist, could see his cynical and dark side.[30] Baudelaire observed in Pierrot's character as portrayed by Deburau, 'unconcern and detachment, and in consequence, the satisfaction of every greed and rapacious whim'.[31] And Champfleury noted his 'brutal joviality, he is to Arlequin what Mayeux is to Don Juan, vice in passion, cynicism of spirit'.[32]

There was an echo of this disconcerting character in an episode of Deburau's private life. On a day off in 1836, while strolling in a park, Deburau was repeatedly accosted by a heckler. Finally, the mime raised his cane and, with one blow, killed his adversary. The trial attracted much attention, in large measure because of the public's great curiosity to hear Deburau speak. Under this spotlight, Deburau was acquitted, on the grounds that he acted without premeditation or intent to kill. The theme of violent death appears in a number of Deburau mimes, both before and after the accident. In *Le Marchand d'habits* (The Old-Clothes Man), first performed in 1842 – one of Deburau's most significant roles, as Gautier commented – Pierrot murders an old-clothes merchant in order to attend a society ball. Champfleury contributed to this macabre genre his *Pierrot, valet de mort* (1846), *Pierrot pendu* (1846) and *Pierrot marquis* (1847).[33]

The Funambules represented the revitalization of a popular art, capable of accommodating contemporary types and situations. Both Romanticism and Realism advocated a poetry of modern urban life, and seized upon themes and forms hitherto marginal or beneath the dignity of the fine arts. Deburau met both these ideals. The formal canon of pantomime was in itself an aesthetic transformation which appealed to the Romantics, while Deburau's precise naturalistic vocabulary, his *argot*, fulfilled Realist demands for the literal depiction of life. While Champfleury fought the 'Realist battle' as a critic and scenario-writer, Deburau embodied his programme.

Popular enthusiasm for the Funambules and for Pierrot continued for about a decade after Deburau's death in 1846. He was succeeded by his son Charles (1829–73) who, though acknowledged and appreciated, added little to the repertory of pantomimic expression and was less subtle in his technique. He played his father's roles and Gautier and De Nerval continued to compose scenarios; he performed seventy-four roles in a period of ten years.[34] We have a record of his expressions in the photographs taken by Adrien Tournachon, Nadar's younger brother, in a series, *Têtes d'expression de Pierrot* (exhibited at the Exposition Universelle of 1855).[35] In these half- and full-figure poses we see broad grimaces and gestures. He is shown winking, gaping, smiling and frowning, but his body lacks tensile alertness and must have required larger movements to register expression.

Baptiste Deburau had the necessary quality of a great mime – a sustained line of force to his body; the highly charged composure that the great twentieth-century mime and teacher, Etienne Decroux, called 'present zero'. Baptiste was a compelling presence at the centre of the space he commanded; by contrast, as revealed in the Tournachon photographs, Charles was always slightly off axis. The most appealing of the photographs shows him as Pierrot the photographer. Here the sense of captured movement is conveyed by the shift of weight, the raised and open-fingered hands. But he looks downward and, in doing so, loosens the tension between himself and the viewer. In other photographs he is shown shrugging his shoulders, pointing coyly off camera, in an expression of mock surprise, mouth drawn in, eyes agape, brows raised, the gaze vaguely off centre, perched forward and buffered by raised shoulders.

The exaggeration of grimace may in part be explained by the genre: the *Têtes d'expression* can be seen in the tradition of the *grimaces*, facial exaggerations triggered by emotion or external stimulus to the senses. We must assume that Charles might have exaggerated the expressions for the photographic series as he would not necessarily have done on stage. And long studio exposures may also have taken their toll.

Still, the falling off of the public confirms that with Charles, Pierrot became a clown again. Baptiste's Pierrot, as Baudelaire described him, 'as mysterious as silence, as flexible and mute as the serpent activated by strange springs', could not be evoked by another actor.[36] Champfleury and others tried to carry on Baptiste's tradition but it was impossible to maintain through scenario alone his poetic paradox of simplicity and mastery. Baptiste's modesty of plot and complexity of performance had drawn an audience both high and low. With more high-flown plots and less subtle performances, both audiences were lost. Gautier claimed that the old pantomime was being replaced by comic opera and vaudeville, that 'the crowd had lost the meaning of these high symbols and profound mysteries which make the poet and philosopher dream'.[37]

When Champfleury took over as director of the Théâtre des Funambules in 1862, he intended to reinforce the Realist commitment of the theatre, but it was too late. In 1863, the Théâtre des Funambules came down, along with the rest of the Boulevard du Temple, a casualty of the redesigning of Paris.

There was, however, an after-life for Pierrot. As a poetic motif, he persisted from the 1850s to the 1880s in the paintings of Thomas Couture, Manet and Cézanne.[38] The theme of the *saltimbanque*, the acrobatic street performer, was also carried on in the drawings, watercolours and lithographs of Daumier and, as we shall see, with poignant autobiographical overtones, Baudelaire too, in 1861, in his poem 'Vieux Saltimbanque', reflected on the misery of the life of the old clown.[39]

29, 30, 31 Charles Deburau.
Photographs by Adrien Tournachon,
*Têtes d'expression de Pierrot, c.*1855

In 1861 Daumier dedicated a portrait drawing of a mime to Charles Deburau; it was his only non-caricatural portrait.[40] Typically of Daumier, the emphasis is less on the features than on the expression captured in the process of formation; repeated contours and agile lines evoke the sense of movement. Pierrot's open mouth, raised eyebrows and sideward glance convey total attention – a moment of performance rather than a static pose. Although the drawing is dedicated to Charles, it was not necessarily of him; it could have been a portrait of Baptiste, offered and inscribed to his son.[41] Daumier always drew from memory, and he must have seen Baptiste perform. Daumier's drawing was done in 1861, at a time of difficulties for both Daumier and Charles Deburau: the year before, Daumier had been dismissed from *Le Charivari*; in the next year, the Théâtre des Funambules would shut down. This common jeopardy could well have created sympathy between them and, in drawing on Baptiste, Daumier may have been extending to Charles something of his father's strength in adversity without needing to distinguish between them; his subject was a role and, perhaps, its analogies with his own.

The puppet theatre was similar to the pantomime in many ways. Since the seventeenth century, puppeteers and mimes had been relegated to the same status and locations – both thrived on the fairgrounds along with acrobats and sideshows. Both were Italian imports and were essentially non-verbal. Both managed, for the most part, to escape censorship; they were not perceived as a direct threat to the established theatres.

In mid-seventeenth century England and Germany, when spoken theatre was banned, it was the marionette theatre that preserved the drama and its tradition.[42] In *Wilhelm Meister* (1795–6) Goethe described the effect on him as a child in 1771 of seeing Faust in the puppet theatre – he was impressed by the puppets' gestures, reduced to the indispensable, and the strength and simplicity of character and plot.[43] Heinrich von Kleist, in 'Über das Marionettentheater' (1810), analysed the structure of gestural expression in string puppets. To Kleist, the stylization of the puppet was an idealization which could represent conditions of the spirit. Since the puppet is inanimate, it is capable of unaffected expressive gesture; it is without ego or prejudice:

> With the marionette, each movement has a centre of gravity, and it is enough to control the motion of this point in the interior of the figure. . . . On the other hand, this line represents the path of the dancer's soul. . . . The technician places himself in the centre of gravity of the puppet, in other words,

32 Daumier, portrait of Deburau, 1861(?). Maison, I, 144

he dances. . . . The marionette doesn't give itself airs. Affectation, in dancing, shows itself when the soul is in any other point than the centre of gravity of the movement.[44]

In nineteenth-century Paris, the character and appeal of the marionette theatre had a particular place as a popular art form, appealing both to children and to men of letters; it was simple and profound, traditional and flexible. Puppet theatres, like pantomime theatres, had established themselves on the Boulevard du Temple. By the 1840s there were about forty free-standing puppet theatres (like the English Punch and Judy Show) in the public parks of Paris; their audience was mainly children and their attendants.[45] The fairground and park setting together with the improvisational tradition of the puppet theatre offered an opportunity for conveying contemporary messages.

A distinctive strain of 'literary' French marionettes was developed by a few writers who were also admirers of pantomime, or at any rate of Deburau, and who advocated the popular arts as vehicles for contemporary comment. This group included Nodier, Gautier, De Nerval, and Maurice and George Sand. For them, the puppet theatre was also a way

57

of modelling or sketching new dramatic and literary tendencies, whether fashionable or experimental. Three of them actually set up puppet theatres: Maurice Sand, Edmond Duranty and Lemercier de Neuville. The one who produced the most consistent and elaborate performances was the amateur Sand, who set up his Théâtre des Amis in his mother's house in Nohant in 1847. Performances continued there until 1872, with 120 works and with a stock company of 125 characters. The plays ranged from the fantastic to the contemporary, with themes from and parodies of fashionable plays, such as Dumas' *Dame au camélias*.[46] His principal character was Pierrot, based on the characterization of Deburau.[47]

Maurice Sand himself, together with a fellow student from the atelier of Delacroix, Eugène Lambert, sculpted many of the marionettes' heads; George Sand made all the costumes.[48] Among the voices for the puppets were several who went on to have significant roles in the Parisian theatre: Thiron, an actor at the Comédie Française; Borel, director of the Théâtre Odéon; and Bocage, one of the great actors of the nineteenth century. The audience consisted of the Romantic writers in the circle of George Sand and various children of guests. After George's death and the dispersal of the family from Nohant, Maurice moved his theatre first to a house in Berry where it remained until 1880, and then, for the last nine years of his life, to Passy where he had a theatre that held fifty people, and where it was reported all fashionable Paris came.

In her foreword to Maurice's history of *commedia dell'arte*, *Masques et bouffons* (1860), George Sand wrote that the puppets met the need to personify diverse naïve instincts and treacheries through such types as Arlequin and Pierrot. The puppet also provided instruction in mores, 'drawing together all classes by their gaiety and simplicity'.

Maurice Sand wrote of his glove puppets:

If I showed you a fine German marionette, highly painted, shining, covered with sequins, and moving on springs, you would not be able to forget that it is a doll, a mechanical device, whereas my *burattino*, floppy, obeying all the movements of my fingers, comes, goes, turns his head, crosses his arms, raises them to heaven . . . beats on the wall in joy or in despair. And you believe you see all his emotions expressed in his face, isn't it true? How is it that a head so sketchily indicated, so ugly seen at close quarters, can suddenly assume, under the play of light, a reality of expression which makes you forget its real scale? . . . This apparently impossible marriage, of a head the size of my fist and a voice as strong as mine . . . do you know where this magic comes from? It comes from the fact that the burattino is not an automaton, that he obeys my whim, my inspiration, my verve – from the fact that all his movements are the outcome of the ideas that come to me and the words which I lend him, that he is *me*, in short, that is, he is a being and not a doll.[49]

58

LE
THÉATRE
DES
MARIONNETTES
DE
MAURICE SAND
déssiné d'après nature
par
lui même.

FONDÉ
EN 1847
RESTAURÉ
EN 1854.

33 Frontispiece, *Le Théâtre des Marionnettes de Maurice Sand*, 1876

34, 35, 36 The marionette theatre of
Maurice Sand

37, 38 *Right*, Two marionettes of
Duranty
39 *Far right*, A puppeteer in Sand's theatre

40 MAURICE SAND, a performance in the atelier of Maurice Sand, at Passy. *L'Illustration*

Maurice Sand's account of the expressiveness of the puppet is a counterpart to Kleist's. There are intrinsic differences between Kleist's jointed marionette and Sand's less articulated glove puppet. More importantly, Kleist's puppeteer is a technician, though 'not without feeling', who puts himself into the puppet and is at its service; Sand's puppeteer is a poet – the puppet is an expressive extension of himself. The eighteenth-century soul as source of action has been displaced by nineteenth-century imagination – 'caprice'.[50]

In the same year that Champfleury took on the directorship of the Théâtre des Funambules, Duranty, his friend and colleague, set up a marionette theatre in the Tuileries garden. Duranty was editor of the short-lived journal *Le Réalisme*. In *La Nouvelle Peinture* (1876), he advocated contemporaneity, stressing that the arts should not embellish but present things as they are; and he emphasized the communicative effect of gesture.[51] (Champfleury was called the Corneille of pantomime, Duranty, the Molière of marionettes.)[52]

Duranty saw the two enterprises – his own and Champfleury's – as analogous, and he looked for support to the same group of critics, artists and audience, but largely in vain. On Duranty's behalf, Baudelaire contacted Gautier about writing a preface for the opening play. From a broadsheet posted in 1860 we learn that Duranty hoped to have Courbet paint sets for his theatre and that Champfleury would be writing a scenario.[53] Courbet never did participate; but Nadar provided an engraved illustration for the prospectus, which was dedicated to George Sand. Duranty approached Daumier to sculpt the puppet heads, but he, like many others, was busy with the Exposition Universelle of 1861 and declined.[54] Finally, Duranty had to act largely as his own sculptor and architect, librettist and puppeteer. His commitment to his theatre and its message was more than programmatic: he staked his livelihood and his credit with his friends.[55]

Duranty claimed that a microcosm of modern society could be found in his puppet plays, such as *Les Plaideurs malgré eux* (The Litigants Despite Themselves), *Les Voisines* (The Neighbours), and *Le Mariage de raison*: lawyers, commissioners, policemen, doctors, apothecaries, 'in general, all professions without pleasure are subjected for all time to the execrations of comedy – especially in the mime and marionettes'.[56] In fact, however, Duranty's plays have a bitter pessimism and a lack of poetry which are more reminiscent of Monnier than of Champfleury who, in Baudelaire's words, was 'more of a poet than he knows'.

Whereas Deburau at the Funambules had an established audience for traditional pantomimes, Duranty had to face the difficulty of a new beginning. Moreover, he lacked Deburau's discipline as a trouper and his transforming style. He hoped for a broad appeal through the use of scenarios of daily accidents and incidents, but he failed to hold the attention of the children and their attendants in the Tuileries, or to attract the enthusiasm even of those who sympathized with his Realist programme.[57]

Overleaf
41 DARJOU, The staff of *Le Charivari*, headed by Daumier, *Current Events*, 1867

63

Three Caricature: newspapers and politics

The truth is that remarkable relentlessness and cohesion were displayed in the operation, and however dogged the reply of the authorities, it is a matter of great surprise today, when we look through these archives of buffoonery, that such a furious war could have been kept up for so long.

CHARLES BAUDELAIRE *writing about Philipon's campaign against censorship and the regime of Louis-Philippe*[1]

IN 1830, when the leftist caricature newspapers *La Silhouette* and *La Caricature* were first being published, France underwent its second Revolution. The government of Charles X was weakened when the liberal opposition won the majority of seats in the Chamber of Deputies in the June–July elections. Shortly after that, Charles X prohibited publication of any journal or pamphlet of less than twenty-five pages without official authorization.[2] The journalists, led by Thiers, a moderate Republican, issued in the newspaper *La Nationale* a manifesto calling on France to resist. The caricaturists in *La Silhouette* and *La Caricature* contributed to the cause with vitriolic portrayals of the king and his government. A caricature of Charles X as a Jesuit led to the suppression of an issue of *La Caricature*, and the impact of the image was only increased by the court case that followed. On 28 July there was rioting in the street. In three days of fighting, *les trois glorieuses*, the monarchy was overthrown.

A coalition of Republicans and anti-Bourbon monarchists proposed the Duke of Orleans, Louis-Philippe, as 'lieutenant-general', with the Marquis de Lafayette, the old hero of the great Revolution, as president of the Republic. But to those who held power, landowners, financiers and politicians, Lafayette was too radical. A compromise was found in Louis-Philippe who was declared king in 1830: he had fought under the flag of the Revolution at Jenappes, he was not of the Royal Bourbon line and he seemed agreeable to a constitutional monarchy.

In the Charter of 1830, a declaration of rights of the Republic, Catholicism (which had regained political influence under Charles X) was no longer to be 'the religion of the state'. The power of suspending or revoking

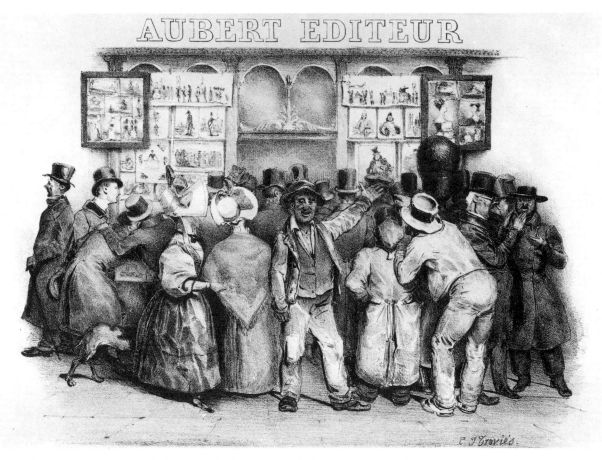

42 Traviès, 'You have to admit the head of government looks pretty funny.' 1831

laws was removed from the king to the elected Assembly, and censorship was abolished 'forever'. Political journals, however, still had to deposit substantial amounts of money (*loi de cautionnement*) against convictions for offence to the king or government.

But soon the limitations of Louis-Philippe's constitutionalism became evident.[3] Behind the habits of bourgeois propriety which he had acquired in exile, Louis-Philippe was ready to exploit his position. His government served the interests of the wealthy bourgeoisie with open lack of scruple. The result was turmoil and dissatisfaction in the early years of Louis-Philippe's reign. And as it became clearer that the 1830 Revolution had been hopelessly betrayed, an informal opposition of Parisian *gens d'esprit* developed, whose critique of bourgeois *moeurs* and culture was inseparable from their political disappointment.

Political caricature had become programmatic in the first caricature journal, *La Silhouette*, founded in 1829 (and folded in 1831), which brought together many of the caricaturists and journalists who set the tone for the

67

43, 44 NADAR, photographs of Daumier (1855) and Philipon (1853–4)

next thirty years. Illustrators and caricaturists, Republican by conviction, who had been issuing individual prints and series of prints on Parisian customs, manners and habits, came together to launch an attack on the monarch. This generation of caricaturists came of age around 1830; their parents had lived through the great Revolution of 1789. For the most part, they were born into artisan families from outside Paris: they had experienced political, social and geographic displacement.

By the 1830s caricature had become a way of carrying out a political discourse particularly adapted to the technical and social emergence of mass daily illustrated newspapers. Caricature was a visual commentary on its time whose vehicle was the human figure; it was a vernacular art, drawing on the expressive conventions of painting, but unhampered by academic precept. Censorship, which started creeping back from 1831 and became official in 1835, feared political images more than words.

The pressure of prosecution on the caricature press provoked the caricaturists to ingenious use of their visual training, forcing the traditional visual repertoire to yield up indirect political and social meaning.

Charles Philipon was the founder and director of the two most important caricature newspapers, *La Caricature* and *Le Charivari*, and for thirty years the leader of the journalistic and caricatural campaign on behalf of betrayed Republican principles. He was the son of a wallpaper manufacturer in Lyon, acquainted with printing technology and popular imagery. He spent a year in Paris in the studio of Antoine Jean Gros, apparently in preparation to work as a designer in his father's business; he returned briefly to Lyon in 1823, but came back to Paris and found work among the publishers of popular prints, trade cards, children's picture stories and rebuses.

In the 1820s, Romantic artists had started exploring the new techniques of lithography. The most notable example was Delacroix's illustrations for Goethe's *Faust*, which were published as a series of lithographic prints in 1828. The young Philipon experimented with decorative lithography and with lithographed caricatures for *La Silhouette*, where Daumier was also to make his first appearance. Philipon also drew many individual prints and series on fashions and social manners and habits. His career as the impresario of the graphic publication world began as an enterprise intended to help his brother-in-law, Gabriel Aubert, out of financial difficulties. In 1829 they set up a print publishing business, the Maison Aubert, in the new and elegant Galerie Véro-Dodat. Philipon had a sense of the market and realized that, even when the stock was meagre, it was worth having a good shop window which could draw the spectators to see the daily production of lithographs. Here Philipon first began to assemble a repertory of prints, illustrations and caricatures, lithographs and wood-cuts, including books, pamphlets, prints, individually and in series, in a range of popular formats.[4]

Baudelaire described something of the character of this pictorial domain:

> For sketches of manners, for the portrayal of bourgeois life and the fashion scene, the quickest and the cheapest technical means will evidently be the best. The more beauty the artist puts into it, the more valuable will the work be; but there is in the trivial things of life, in the daily exchange of external things, a speed of movement that imposes upon the artist an equal speed of execution. As soon as lithography was invented it was quickly seen to be very suitable for this enormous task, so frivolous in appearance. We possess veritable national records in this class; the works of Gavarni and Daumier have been accurately described as complements to *La Comédie humaine*.[5]

Philipon's first collaborators had been his colleagues on *La Silhouette*, most of whom joined the weekly journal *La Caricature* which began publication in 1830 with Balzac as editor in charge of text and Grandville as its most distinguished illustrator. Daumier joined a few months later, at about the time when Philipon shifted from social comment to political satire and polemic. In 1832 Philipon, foreseeing increased difficulties because of censorship fines, established a sister publication and eventual successor, *Le Charivari* (*charivari* meaning a loud clatter of pots and pans at the windows of unpopular people). One large sheet folded into four pages, this paper included a full-page lithograph by Daumier, Gavarni

69

or others and smaller engraved caricature vignettes interspersed throughout the text. Published daily, it gave caricature a larger audience than
ever before. From the start it covered social as well as political subjects.
Philipon set the editorial policy and tone.

Philipon was not a caricaturist of the first order himself, but he was a
generous discoverer and sure-footed guide and animator of the talents of
others. In his little study on Daumier, Henry James spoke of Philipon as
having 'a suggestive share in any enterprise in which he had a hand'.[6]
Daumier is reported as saying that without Philipon's prodding he 'would
never have done anything'.[7] Philipon had the instinct of the publicist: a
sharp awareness of the realities and the potential of his milieu. In his
obituary for Philipon, Nadar spoke of his great sense of the public.[8]

Balzac and Philipon, the man of letters and the *imagier*, friends and
collaborators, each took city life as his source material and as his field of
struggle. Although their political stances were widely different, their
common enterprise was the understanding and portrayal, through visual
clues, of a new urban society. In a short article written in the form of a
manual for caricaturists, *Le Dedans jugé par le dehors* (The Inside Judged by
the Outside), Philipon left an explicit document of the contact between
the caricaturists' art and the literary tradition of *moeurs*.[9] This is strikingly
close in tone and focus to Balzac's *Théorie de la démarche*. But Balzac's piece
is cast in the form of a guide to behaviour, whereas Philipon's little treatise,
intended for the novice caricaturist, is a witty, vernacular take-off of Le
Brun's classic guide to the expression of the passions and emotions, gesture
and painting, the textbook that had been most familiar to every art
student since the seventeenth century. Most of Philipon's examples were
taken from the life of the street and the boulevard – vignettes as seen by a
passerby, a non-participant. One section deals with how people greet one
another when they meet, and what can be inferred by eye about their
relationship: 'Two men who despise one another greet each other with
great deference, very affectionately, for they fear one another'; in another
example: 'the husband greets the lover with a protective air: the lover
smiles as he returns his greeting; two rival lovers greet one another with
pinched lips; the creditor greets with embarrassment, the debtor with
lightness'.[10]

Philipon's description of 'detestable' behaviour is very close to Theophrastus' 'Tedious Man' in La Bruyère's translation. According to
Philipon:

> Among detestable gestures, in the first line, is that of unbuttoning and re-
> buttoning the interlocutor's waistcoat, of taking the auditor by the front of
> his coat and shaking him from time to time, of stopping him every three paces,
> letting him go and stopping him again, until he is falling over with impatience
> and lassitude.[11]

An observer who wrote like this must, indeed, have been good company for Daumier.

Champfleury wrote of Philipon that he

personified in himself – I was about to say that he created – political caricature, one of the liveliest forces of argument, which pierces when it touches, against which no shield can protect; it is all the more redoubtable under its apparent harmlessness, like the barbs of an arrow. . . . Its incisive art of memory, which argues and preaches to the eye, equips it with a force which governments could not be slow to understand and to repress . . . The man of unique talent who took up this terrible weapon and used it dazzlingly was a man of virtue and conviction.[12]

From 1831 onward the explicitness of caricature was hampered by intensifying prosecution. *Ad hoc* censorship was building up: repeated fines were levied by the government of Louis-Philippe on Philipon and his caricaturists, bringing *La Caricature* to the brink of closure as a result of increasing debts.

However, censorship of explicit caricature merely encouraged more subtle means, and from 1830 to 1835 political caricature continued to flourish. There was an escalation of devices for the submersion of words into silence: puns, emblems, allegories and typifications. Philipon developed a vernacular code as a form of guerilla warfare against Louis-Philippe and his censors. He invented the most famous and effective single political emblem, the *poire*, or pear, as a representation of Louis-Philippe. It was simple to draw the analogy between the king's body and the image of the pear: the monarch was puffy and paunchy, so he was shown as a pear head on a pear body. But the pertinence – or impertinence – of this image came from its linguistic hint: in slang, *poire* means fat-head. The pear became the standard pun, a visual constant, with an extraordinary capacity for specificity and variety. First, the pear in all its variants and combinations was established as an emblem for the king himself; then, by extension, it began to be used for his courtiers and ministers and, in general, for the rapacious money-grubbing speculators who profited under his Gargantuan regime.

Baudelaire noted: 'The symbol had been found, thanks to an obliging analogy. From then on, the symbol was enough. With this kind of plastic slang, artists could express and convey to the populace anything they like, and it was, therefore, around this tyrannical and cursed pear that the large mob of yelling patrons collected.'[13] The pear openly teased the censors and provoked them to more convoluted regulations, which in turn the caricaturists bypassed with increasing inventiveness.

The pear, which appeared frequently in caricature, in popular literature and imagery, became a cause célèbre between the caricaturists and the government. The *loi de cautionnement* made it easy for the government

71

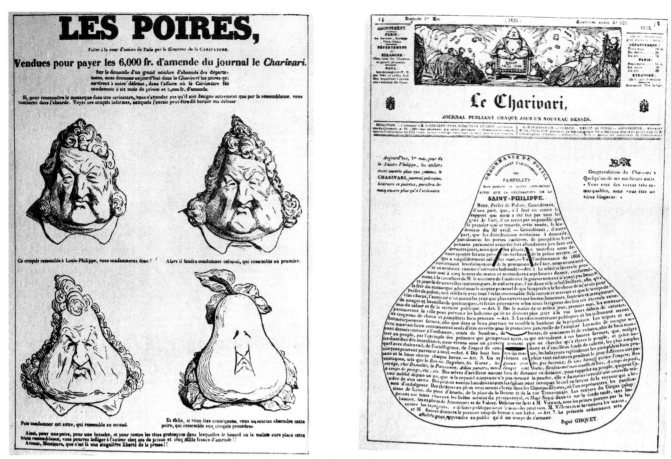

45 PHILIPON, 'The Pears', *Le Charivari*, 17 January 1831
46 Police ordinance concerning the seizure of satirical pamphlets, published in the
shape of a pear. *Le Charivari*, 1 May 1835

to fine newspapers: it depended on the daring and budget of the paper
to test the limits. After several attempted prosecutions, *Le Charivari* was
accused of 'offence to the person of the king' because of a caricature showing him as a pear. On 14 November 1831, Philipon, appearing for the
defence, claimed his right, under the Charter, to criticize the government
openly; he described how he had decided to dedicate *Le Charivari* to
political polemic because of the government's reaction to an early cartoon
showing Louis-Philippe blowing soap-bubbles, each of which was a
promise made at the setting up of the July monarchy.

Pencil in hand, Philipon showed the court the contradictions that
followed from condemning the pear motif as an offence to the king's
person. He drew four heads: the first was a representation of Louis-
Philippe; in the second, he slightly reduced the distinctiveness of the
features; the third emphasized further the shape of a head, pointed at the
top, rounded at the bottom; and the fourth was a pear. To be consistent,

72

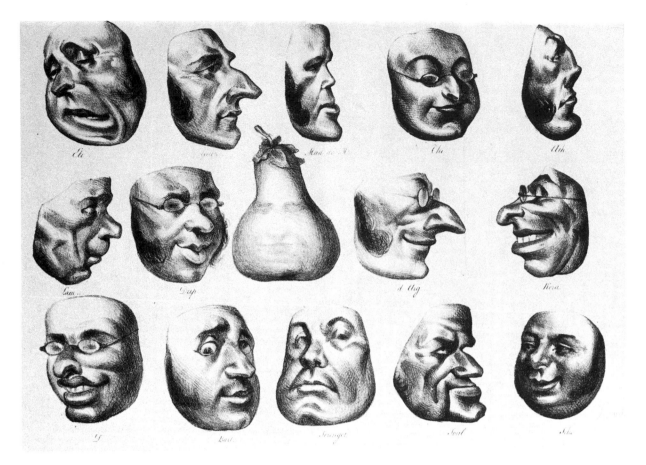

47 DAUMIER, 'Masks of 1831': *left to right*, Etienne, Guizot, Madier de Montjau,
Thiers, Athalin, Lameth, Dupin, roi Louis-Philippe, D'Argout, D. de Keratry, Barthe,
Lobau, Soult, Shonen. 1832, D.34

Philipon claimed, the court would have to prosecute any drawing of a
pear-shaped object in any context. Philipon did not pretend that his pear
caricature was *not* political; he defended the paper's right to use a symbol
of the king as a visual means, recognizable to everyone, of making critical
statements about the regime. Philipon described how the government's
harassment of the press 'held back his pen and his tongue' so that he 'tried
by signs, by sketches, to make the regime understand that it is deceiving
itself and going wrong'.[14] *La Caricature* printed the judgment that went
against Philipon in the typographical form of a pear.

Over the next four years, the pear appeared frequently in popular
imagery and literature. In an article published in *La Caricature* in 1832,
'L'Envahissement de la poire' (The Invasion of the Pear), a journalist
observed that the image of the pear was so pervasive that the mayor of
Auxerre, a town 170 kilometres from Paris, added to the post-no-bills sign
'nor any pears'. Bouquet illustrated this point in a lithograph for *La*

73

48 DAUMIER, 'Mr Thing, First Saltimbanque of Europe', 1833. D.161

Caricature showing a group of children drawing Louis-Philippe pear heads on a wall.

One of the first *Physiologies* that was published was Peytel's *Physiologie de la poire* in 1832, a parody of a naturalist's taxonomic description, listing the varieties of pears including the *Roi-Louis*:

> One of those pears of destiny which ripen around the end of July or the beginning of August. The *Roi-Louis* was imported into France in the year of grace 1830. Since then it has been a large, broad fruit, puffy and ill-formed. Abroad, it had already produced abundant seeds, and although it was not certain that the stock would do well on French soil, the variety was purchased here at high cost, 500,000 Parisis.[15]

In one caricature, a pear is shown being raised as a central monument in the Place de la Concorde with the inscription: 'The *expiapoire* [*expiatoire* = expiatory] monument is raised on the site of the Revolution, exactly in the place where Louis XVI was guillotined.' Daumier showed Louis-Philippe as a pear perilously crossing a tight-rope. Grandville and Forest depicted a reception where all of the figures in Louis-Philippe's court are pears. Bouquet's *Les Favoris de la poire* (The Favourites, or Side Whiskers, of the Pear) shows two censors with scissors snuggling up to a huge pear.

74

In *La Poire et ses pépins* (The Pear and its Pips), a double-page spread of an open half of the huge fleshy fruit shows in its dark womb Louis-Philippe's ministers huddled around a pot marked 'budget' from which they feed.

The censors in despair finally adopted Philipon's doctrine of consistency and forbade the caricaturists to draw *any* pear-like objects. This in itself became a subject for satire, as the caricaturists teased the censors with animals and objects that approximated pear-shapedness. The censors' obsession with pears led them to overlook other disguised political references and the journalists and caricaturists teased the censors on this point. A writer for *La Caricature* noted: 'It's fortunate that the censors didn't see in the hunter with his cap, an allusion to the censorship firing at sparrows – and didn't recognize some great personage of the court in the fox, emblem of cunning.'[16] It is quite likely that such retrospective gibes were often made even when the original drawing had in fact had no particular political implication.

In *Censeurs*, Grandville depicted the censors as bug-headed with crossed bulging eyes, pawing over pages; one of them is clipping his nails with a large pair of shears, recalling a demon in Goya's lithograph *Fate*. Grandville's caption read: 'Ah, this is too much, we, the censors, rendered in caricature, we owe a lesson to these artists. Cut!' The accompanying text explained:

49 GRANDVILLE, 'Censors', November 1835. s. I, 275

75

Few qualities are necessary for the censor! It's enough if he hasn't the vaguest idea, in order to be able to judge the ideas of others; that is the sole condition of impartiality required of him. . . . You may be astonished by the indulgence they have shown toward this picture of themselves, but rest assured, it is more stupidity than magnanimity. The artist has so flattered their portraits, that these gentlemen, no doubt, don't recognize themselves.[17]

In *Liberté de la presse*, Daumier showed a strong and noble printer, a man of the people, standing firm in defence of his press, contrasted with the figures of monarchy, church and a group of politicians who hover and lurk in the background. This was published as one of thirty-six extraordinary prints issued monthly by Philipon's Association Lithographique Mensuelle, in order to raise revenues to pay the fines.[18]

Earlier political caricatures, such as Goya's *Caprichos*, and the work of Hogarth, Gilray and Rowlandson, had been issued as self-contained series or individual prints. With the use of lithography in the newspapers and the mechanization of the popular press, caricature could be integrated with journalism and reach a much wider audience on a daily basis.[19] Over the next twenty years there was a continual growth of illustrated newspapers and journals.[20] The newspaper channelled back images, often daily, into the texture of city life from which they were drawn. The caricaturists became a current conscience for the urban population.

Nineteenth-century French caricature had a traditional predilection for formal exaggerations, mutations, transformations, sets of variations and, as we have seen, puns, emblems and analogies; among the precedents were Louis Boilly's *Grimaces* of 1823–8.[21] The generation of caricaturists led by Philipon, who faced the new opportunities of daily lithography and the new constraints of censorship, inherited a well-stocked formal armoury. Explicit caricatures appeared of Louis-Philippe in allegorical situations that reveal his attitudes and policies, such as Daumier's depiction of him as a clown posed before a stage, pointing derisively to a gagged and blindfolded personification of France; or standing by the bed of a dead Republican exclaiming: 'It is safe to release this one.' In one of the most virulent caricatures of Louis-Philippe, Daumier depicted him as Gargantua sitting on a commodious throne, being fed bribes by small courtiers and defecating medals and money; this referred to Louis-Philippe's distribution of insignia of the Legion of Honour, ennobling bureaucrats and shopkeepers loyal to Napoleon's military glory. This caricature, published in 1832, led to a six-month imprisonment for Daumier.

Another distinct branch of political caricature was the *portraits charges*, exaggerated portraits of recognizable political figures such as Louis-Philippe and his ministers (Dargou, Dupin, Persil and others). Daumier

50 LOUIS BOILLY, 'Smokers and Snuff-takers', *Les Grimaces*, 1823

51 DAUMIER, 'Lower the Curtain,
the Farce is Over.' 1834, D.86

52 DAUMIER, 'Gargantua', 1831. D.34

53 DAUMIER, 'The Legislative Body (or Paunch): Aspect of the ministerial bench in the prostituted chamber of 1834.' 1834. D.131

was the most practised, skillful and imaginative caricaturist of this genre both in drawing and in sculpture (see Chapter Five).

There were also group *portraits charges*. In *Le Ventre législatif* (The Legislative Paunch), published by the Association Lithographique Mensuelle, Daumier represented each member of the Legislative Body, varying the predominant characteristics of each deputy – fat, big-paunched, heavy-jowled, thick-lipped, small-eyed – each in a state of stupor, indifference or arrogance, while the deputy Dr Prunelle presides over them with Machiavellian alertness.

Analogies between animals and humans were another form of political caricature. Daumier, for example, represented Dupin, the attorney-general, exaggerating his simian skull.[22] But the animal analogy was more often used in caricatures of type than of public individuals: and mostly to convey moral categories. This type of caricature was practised primarily

79

54 GRANDVILLE, 'Projected Shadows', 1830. s.62

by Grandville, a master of transformation. In his *Ombres portées* (Projected Shadows) of 1830, the shadows cast by parading politicians and clerks betray their sinister animal equivalents, owls, serpents and lizards; he also depicted politicians as strutting roosters.

In August 1835, official and comprehensive censorship laws were declared in an attempt to silence the caricaturists' continual barrage against the king and his government.[23] In July there had been an assassination attempt on the king.[24] The *loi de cautionnement* was increased from 30,000 to 100,000 francs. Administrative authorities were encouraged to interfere with the press in day-to-day activities. There were new press offences: one could not attack the king directly or indirectly in any of the following forms – any criticism of the king, any censure or blame of the king for any act of government, any attack against the character or form of the government established by the Charter, any act of disloyalty, any use of the name 'Republican', any desire or wish that the constitutional monarchy might be destroyed, and, on the 'rightist' side, any wish that the legitimist Bourbon might be restored. Such offences could be classed as treason. Furthermore, any reporting of libel or slander trials, even the names of witnesses in such trials, was forbidden.

The major innovation of the new law was prior censorship: no drawings, engravings, lithographs or prints of whatever nature (even decorative vignettes) were permitted to be publicly exhibited or placed on sale without the prior authorization of the Minister of the Interior or by authorization of a Prefect in the provinces. If any were objected to, they

80

could be confiscated and the publishers would be tried, not by juries but by 'correction tribunals' presided over by the king's magistrates. Fines and terms of imprisonment were doubled or even quadrupled. Theatres and plays were also subjected to prior authorizations and regulation. All street performers who were known for subversive skits had to submit their songs and acts to government officials in advance of their performances.

All in all, the laws of 1835 effectively brought the explicit pictorial treatment of political subjects to a halt. And although the Charter proclaimed that 'Frenchmen have the right to circulate their opinions in published form', it added that: 'when opinions are converted into actions by the circulation of drawings, it is a question of speaking to the eyes. That is something more than the expression of an opinion; it is an incitement to action not covered by Article 3.'[25]

La Caricature folded on 27 August 1835. On 16 September, the day after the censorship laws were officially announced, *Le Charivari* published a blank page surrounded by a funeral border. The missing drawing was described in words, an expedient which ridiculed the anomaly of the new laws, more fearful of images than of words. This provocative device was repeated over the next months. The guerilla warfare of Philipon and his troupe of caricaturists was mobilized with new imaginative devices.

On 17 September, *Le Charivari* addressed its subscribers 'concerning the evil designs [*desseins*] of the censor against the drawings [*dessins*]', explaining that the publication of drawings would be affected by the censor but that they would still do everything they could to assert themselves on political issues; they were as concerned and committed as ever. They stated their position in verse: 'You can gag me, oh hostile doctrine!/But force me to change, never! – I defy you/No, *Charivari* will not change.' This was followed by verses obviously set to the tune of the *Marseillaise*:

> *La censure en vain nous dévore!*
> *Elle enfante des traits nouveaux;*
> *Sous les ciseaux, voyez éclore*
> *Croquis, pochades et tableaux.*
> *Méprisons cette vaine injure!*
> *Laissons couler leur encre impure!*
> > *En avant, croquons!*
> > *Et que nos crayons,*
> *Bravant ses ciseaux, ses grattoirs, ses torchons,*
> > *Embêtent la censure!*

(Censorship in vain devours us!/She brings forth new traits;/Under her scissors, see sketches, scribbles, scenes unfold/We despise this futile insult!/ Let their foul ink flow!/Onward, sketching!/ And let our crayons/defying her scissors, erasers and wipers/ continue to harass the censorship.)

Legitimist and Republican journalists informed their readers that cunning and hypocrisy would be needed, and that readers should become accustomed to looking for innuendos.[26] Their defiant irrepressibility became a recurrent motif with political force in itself, and generated a wealth of alternative codes for making political points. The journalists established a new level of highly articulate subversive silence. Such inventiveness, involving the complicity of the audience in the same way as a rebus or a puzzle would, was a great part of the appeal of the caricatures of that period.

At the same time a deeper transformation was taking place: the caricaturists were beginning to shift their focus from public events, individual politicians and specific laws and policies, to their sources and consequences in social conditions. In this shift, Daumier, in collaboration with Philipon, played the major role. How Daumier made this transition will be followed in detail in Chapter Five. This new strain of caricature was more resistant to censorship. The individual political *portrait charge* and explicit political caricature were replaced by the representative or symbolic type, which stood for a recognizable category of protagonists, beneficiaries or victims of the regime. The classification of people by types became part of the caricaturists' armoury.

One version of this device was the 'emblematic type', a fictional character with a proper name and set of characteristics with whom the public could gradually develop an involved acquaintance. Once created and established in the public's imagination, such types, like Deburau's Pierrot, were put through a variety of contemporary situations and stresses and given different professions. Sometimes these figures were explicitly political in their activities; sometimes only the accompanying text would spell out the political reference; sometimes they reflected the attitudes and cultural effects of the regime. The sources of these popular types were found in illustrations, literature, fables, theatre and popular songs. Inevitably, the depiction of such types tended to represent weaknesses and faults rather than merits and good qualities.[27]

Four principal emblematic types were evolved in caricature between 1830 and 1870; they reflected a political progression. They were Mayeux, from 1830 to 1833 (the same time as the *poire*); Robert Macaire from 1835 to 1838; Ratapoil from 1850 to 1852; and Joseph Prudhomme from 1852 to 1870.[28] As types for caricature, Macaire, Ratapoil and Prudhomme are Daumier's, although both Macaire and Prudhomme were taken over from the theatre.

Mayeux was the creation of Traviès, who reportedly based the physical type on Leclerq's impersonation of a hunchback, partly pathetic, partly querulous.[29] Traviès' inspiration was to adapt this image to a political type who, at the height of the patriotic fervour of July 1830, personified a

82

55 TRAVIÈS, 'Out of the question, my dear, I'm on duty now . . . Later, perhaps . . .'. 1831

56 TRAVIÈS, 'She's a smart bit of work, by God.' *The pranks of Mr Mayeux*, 1831

57 *Right,* Frédérick Lemaître in his role as Macaire. After a photograph by Carjat

58 *Far right,* DAUMIER, 'Bertrand, I'm in love with finance . . . if you want, we'll open a bank. Yes, a real bank! Capital 100 million, million shares, 100 milliard milliards. We'll sink the bank of France, we'll sink the bankers, we'll sink the mountebanks, we'll sink everybody! – Yes, but what about the police? – Don't be a fool, Bertrand, no one arrests a millionaire.' *Caricaturana,* I, 1836. D.354

whole ominous aspect of the 1830 Revolution: the figure of the small self-seeker who had chosen the revolutionary side and who, as a member of the National Guard, was in a position to exercise petty tyranny and exploitation, not least over women. He remains a small shopkeeper, but he has naïve ambitions to positions of influence under the new regime. His hunchback associates him with Punch or Polichinelle, traditionally a cynical outsider, the butt of mockery and himself a mocker. The *Gazette de Paris*, in a note on Mayeux in 1833, put him in the tradition of Thersites and Aesop, malformed outsiders and mockers of society. The force of the character comes from the fact that this outsider, without social ties or responsibility, is in a position of arbitrary (though petty) social power. As soon as he appeared in Traviès' cartoons, he was generally seized upon as a current reference in political and social commentary,[30] as 'the figure who summed up our angers, our enthusiasm, our credibilities, the type of 1830 and 1831'.[31] Mayeux's reign was shortlived. He was declared dead in 1833, of ennui and disappointment, a 'devouring and indeterminate malady which the doctors . . . have named "ingrown revolution"'.[32] The *Gazette de Paris* reported: 'Mayeux disappears and Robert Macaire takes possession of the street . . . the hunchback dies at the hour when illusions are no longer possible; the rascal Robert Macaire . . . says to Mayeux: "Ah, die, naïve buffoon. Naïveté is dead".'[33]

84

Robert Macaire, the quintessential con-man, was a satire on the July
Monarchy and its financial oligarchy. Macaire had his origins in the
theatre, the creation of the actor Lemaître in his free interpretation of a
bland melodrama of Benjamin Antier, Saint-Amand and Paulyanthe,
L'Auberge des adrets, first performed at the Théâtre Ambigu-Comique in
1823. The plot concerned a criminal who was shot and died a repentant
sinner. Lemaître introduced comic elements in his characterization so
that by the early 1830s the play had become a satire. In the final scene
Macaire and his side-kick Bertrand stand in front of the *Bourse*, the stock
exchange, about to be admitted to the Panthéon des Voleurs, the Robbers'
Hall of Fame. Daumier rendered this scene in caricature.[34]

In 1834 a new comedy was written around Lemaître's Macaire, *Robert
Macaire, ce cynique scapin du crime*, clearly a satire on the July Monarchy.
In the last performance of this play, when it was banned in 1835, Lemaître/
Macaire appeared made up as Louis-Philippe.[35]

Daumier adopted Lemaître's Macaire for caricature. On 13 November
1834 he first depicted Macaire and Louis-Philippe embracing while picking one another's pockets. In the background are Thiers and Persil, the
Attorney-General. The hundred lithographs of Daumier's Macaire series,
Caricaturana, were published in *Le Charivari* between 1836 and 1838, in
collaboration with Philipon who wrote the legends. Macaire, manipula-

tive, corrupt, dissembling, represented politics on the citizenry level; as a financial and social operator, he was a political phenomenon. He came to life in an age of feverish speculation, a supporter of the monarchy in his own financial interest. *Le Charivari* noted that while Macaire had been banned from the theatre where he had his origins, 'his type persists as the most complete personification of the period. Because of censorship we can't stigmatize the political Robert Macaire, so we look to the business-man Macaire.'

Baudelaire noted:

> Macaire was the clear starting point of the caricature of manners. . . . The political pamphlet gave way to comedy. . . . And so caricature took on a new character, and was no longer particularly political. It became the general satire of the citizenry. It impinged on the domain of the novel.[36]

59 DAUMIER, 'We are all honest men – let us embrace, and put an end to our disagreements.' *Caricaturana*, I, 1834. D.95

60 DAUMIER, 'Robert Macaire, Attorney: Gentlemen, the contract in question is manifoldly null and void, fraudulent and without force in law. (The President interrupting M. Macaire) But you are arguing against your own client. (Robert, aside) The Devil! It's true, I'm in trouble. (Aloud) This is no doubt what my colleagues will try to tell you. . . . But in fact, this contract is certainly sound, legal, and completely binding, etc., etc. (He pleaded 5 hours without stopping to spit and lost his case).' *Caricaturana*, 77, 1837. D.399

61 DAUMIER, 'Robert Macaire, Attorney: 'My dear Bertrand, give me a hundred écus and I'll have him taken care of right away. – No, I've no money. – All right, give me a hundred francs. – I haven't a penny. – You don't have ten francs? – Not a farthing. – Then give me your boots, and I'll plead extenuating circumstances.' *Caricaturana*, 9, 1836. D.362

62 DAUMIER, 'The Lion's Share: Quiet gentlemen, please! We have 100 louis; 80 for me, 18 for M. le Compte de S. Bertrand, remainder, 2 . . . and 15 of you asking for them. . . . Really, these endless demands. . . . People ought not to deceive themselves like this! Well, gentlemen, we're all honest men, arrange it among yourselves how to divide these 2 louis. Let's not make trouble!' *Caricaturana*, 22, 1837. D.376

Macaire was depicted in numerous different professional guises, but 'money was the common denominator':[37] banker, chairman of a stock company, shareholder, speculator, lawyer, industrialist, political candidate, editor of an industrial journal, proprietor. Also among his professions was medicine: he was represented as doctor, surgeon, dentist, oculist, hypnotist, magnetizer, pharmacist and dispenser of quack medicine. His depiction as journalist and editor without scruples led one English contemporary to speculate that Macaire was in part a parody of Emile de Girardin, who, after his days at *La Silhouette*, became a conservative and establishment figure.[38] Balzac described his Baron de Nucingen, an exploitative hard-hearted banker who appeared in many of his novels, as 'ce vieux Robert Macaire du Nucingen'.[39] And Marx directly linked Macaire to Louis-Philippe, observing: 'The July Monarchy was no more than a joint stock company, for the exploitation of French national wealth . . . Louis-Philippe was a director of this company, a Robert Macaire on the throne.'[40]

There are no moral claims in Macaire's world. Gautier noted his 'audacity and his desperate attack on the social order and against people'.[41] His bearing is a matter of manipulation, a dramatic device. Daumier expressed this attitude through his depiction of Macaire based on Frédérick: he wears an eye-patch, and a cravat hitched high to mask his mouth, obscuring his most revealing features.

With Macaire, Daumier first developed his particular syntax of bearing and gesture, the modification of conventional gestures by individually observed traits which amend and sometimes reverse our reading of the figure's intentions: we can tell from Macaire's pose what he is really up to. He took on the lawyer's outstretched accusatory arm, the landlord's proprietary stance. Macaire was also often presented in a gentleman's pose, but exaggerated to the point of charlatanry. The pose itself had been conventional, at least since the Renaissance, and was adopted consistently in artistic representations from Poussin and Le Brun to David and nineteenth-century academic painting. In *The Art of Painting and All Its Branches* (1838), Gerard de Lairesse described this pose aptly: 'In an erect posture, the feet must make a right angle, to wit, the heel of the one with the inner ankle of the other.'[42] This is what is known in ballet as the fourth position. Daumier used this pose in depicting politicians, lawyers, the bourgeois, anyone with power or pretension. Lavater had described moral traits deducible from this pose:

> Ridiculous affectation of superiority exercising its empire over a humble and timid character. . . . Presumption of every kind supposes folly at bottom and one meets both in every disproportionate and gross physiognomy which affects an air of solemnity and authority. . . . Theatrical affectation of man is destitute of sense and meaning and used to give oneself airs.[43]

88

63 DAUMIER, 'Monsieur Daumier, your Robert Macaire series is delightful! It's an
exact picture of the thievery of our times . . . the faithful portrait of innumerable
crooked characters who turn up everywhere – in business, in politics, in the bureaucracy,
in finance, everywhere! everywhere! The rascals must bear you quite a grudge . . . But
you have the good opinion of decent people . . . You haven't been given the *croix
d'honneur* yet? . . . That's really shocking!' *Caricaturana*, 78, 1838. D.433

64 DAUMIER, 'Messrs Victor Hugo and Emile Girardin attempting to raise Prince Louis on the shield of battle – a not too firm support.' *Current Events,* 1848, D.1756

A contemporary writer of theatrical gesture, Henry Siddons, in his *Practical Illustrations of Rhetorical Gesture and Action* of 1822 (based on Engel's *Ideen zu einer Mimik*, 1785–6, which is reprinted in the Lavater 1806 French edition), described the pose as indicative of pride and conceit, pretentiousness and arrogance.

Macaire, who personified the exploitative opportunities of the July Monarchy, disappeared with the downfall of Louis-Philippe in 1848.[44] The new Republican government was helpless in the face of the economic crises which followed the Revolution of 1848.[45] Distrust and tension built up between the masses and the middle class.[46] It became clear that economic conditions under the Republic were worse than under Louis-Philippe. Six 'June days' of bitter street fighting between working class and bourgeoisie ensued. In December Louis-Napoleon was named President of the French Republic. The conflict and instability of this new appointment was expressed in Daumier's lithograph of Hugo balancing Louis-Napoleon on a see-saw. In 1852 the new French constitution gave the president monarchical powers.[47] Two weeks later Louis-Napoleon proclaimed himself Emperor Napoleon III. This 'Second Empire' lasted until September 1870.

In the period between 1848 and 1852, the censorship laws were lifted, and Daumier and other caricaturists returned to political caricature. It was in 1850, when Daumier felt that the Republic was doomed, that he invented his new emblematic character, Ratapoil, who first appeared in individual lithographs in *Le Charivari*. A hired bully and agent of the secret police, who had begun his rise to power in 1848, Ratapoil gathers votes for Louis-Napoleon by threats and bribes. Ratapoil was first conceived as a sculpture: Daumier's only free-standing, full-length single figure, 17 inches high. In the lithographs of 1851, he took on his typical look: angular, skeletal, a battered hat resting on a broken nose.[48] Ratapoil appeared in forty Daumier lithographs between 1850 and 1851. The writer and art critic Gustave Geffroy called him 'the resumé of an epoch, the agitator who prepared the coup d'état'.[49]

Daumier's sustained indictment of this figure was a cry of warning, part of a campaign against Louis-Napoleon's claims to sovereignty. As Jules Michelet, the prominent anti-Bonapartist historian, remarked, Daumier did more for Republicanism with Ratapoil than all the politicians put together.[50]

By the time of the establishment of the Second Empire (1852), whether because of renewed censorship or because the battle was now lost, Ratapoil was dropped from Daumier's repertoire. He reappeared in a few lithographs in 1871, after the Franco-Prussian war, where he was depicted trying to rouse peasants to the cause of the deposed emperor. Ratapoil's political successor in Daumier's work was to be the apolitical Prudhomme, who is discussed in Chapters Four and Five.

Along with typical and recurrent emblematic characters like Macaire and Ratapoil who have a name and continuity through all their guises, *Le Charivari* also developed broader strategies for expressing political attitudes in social satire. After the censorship laws of 1835, satirical

65 DAUMIER, sculpture of Ratapoil, 1851

66 DAUMIER, 'Ratapoil Making Propaganda: If you
love your wife, your house, your field, your heifer and
your calf, sign, you haven't a minute to lose.' *Current Events*,
1851. D.2117

representations of professions flourished. The first and most important of
these series, *Types français* (1835), was a collaboration between Traviès
and Daumier, at the time when they were also drawing Mayeux and
Macaire respectively. The introductory text stated that the series

> reproduces the types of physiognomy, the bearing, and the costume particular
> to the different classes that form the ornament of society. This series along
> with Grandville's *Grotesques parisiens* and Bourdet's *Béotismes parisiens* [Parisian
> Follies] forms in *Le Charivari* a complete physiognomy of the Nation known as
> the most witty and gracious in the world.

This editorial provided a specific link between one of the occupational
types and two named public figures, *Le Charivari's* special enemies:

> The La Bruyère who is responsible for tracing in our contemporary pictures
> a moral portrait of the little clerk, the brook-jumper [message-runner], has

only forgotten to add that above all he is not afraid of getting his hands dirty. It is from the number of the brook-jumpers that two actual censors come, MM. Jules de Wailley and Pierrot.[51]

While each figure in *Types français* bears the attributes of his trade there is something suspect about each of them. In contrast to the noble emblematic workers whom Daumier represented in *Liberté de la presse*, *Mort pour la liberté* and *Rue Transnonain*, and the politically neutral earlier types of the 'Cries of the City', these rag-pickers, letter-writers, boot-blacks and clerks are portrayed in a way which provides a bitter insight into their corrupting or degrading circumstances.

For example, *L'Ecrivain public* (The Public Scrivener) is shown as a poor and mean-looking old man huddled in a small hole-in-the-wall, his office, which, we are told, reeks of alcohol and tobacco. We also learn that he serves as the neighbourhood confessor, and as confidant for the messenger,

67 DAUMIER, 'Freedom of the Press. Don't meddle with it.' 1834, D.133

the water-carrier, the valet and the lady's maid. He might once have been an apprentice to a notary, or an ex-procurer of the monarchy, or an author of novels successful thirty years ago. All the same, no secret is safe with him, because he is the chief informer for the prefect of the police. The text warned:

> Journalists, authors, draughtsmen, engravers, caricaturists, editors, librarians, all you to whom the new law concerning the liberty of the press applies, when you pass before this miserable shop of the public scrivener, doff your hat.[52]

The implication may be: because this is where you too may end; or perhaps it is an expression of his power to compromise his neighbours.

Daumier's depictions of the banker bear a close resemblance to the pear-like figure of Louis-Philippe: 'nothing but a container, a coffer exclusively fit for finances'. The accompanying text read:

> This is the banker-lynx [lynx: an epithet for 'greedy capitalist']: robber and croupier of the stockmarket, a politic speculator, a deputy who gravitates to the centre. In his physique he is large and fat; morally he is even more gross. He is the prototype of egoism, presumption and pride. He loves luxury, and apes the aristocracy which he aspires to displace. He keeps his carriage, livery, and Opera dancer, as the nobility do, but he lacks their tact, manners and taste. In his air, manner and language, he shows his usurious origins. He is attached to the established power. Patriotism, liberalism, national dignity, are utopian chimeras at which he smiles pityingly. Politically he has good sense; he is eligible, often he is elected, he always keeps silent in the House – that is, he does not speak; but he roars ah! and oh! and hi! according to the needs of the minister, whose feudal dependent he is.
>
> Any country where the banker gains government power is liable to become the most cowardly, the most materialistic, the most debased in the world.[53]

This character also bears close resemblance to Lavater's description of a type to be avoided:

> Large bulky persons, with small eyes, round full hanging cheeks, puffed lips, and a chin resembling a purse or bag; who are continually occupied with their own corpulence, who on every occasion consult their own ease without regard to others, are, in reality, frivolous, insipid, powerless, vain, inconstant, imprudent, conceited voluptuous characters, difficult to guide, which desire much and enjoy little – and whoever enjoys little, gives little.[54]

The banker embodies exploitation, as did the similar characters of Gobseck and Nucingen in Balzac's *Père Goriot*. In Daumier's caricatures, lawyers stand for injustice and bankers for speculation, corruption and greed. Caricatures of professional types continued throughout the nineteenth century. However, by the mid 1840s they became increasingly characterological, with only occasional political innuendo.

94

68, 69 *Left*, DAUMIER, 'The Public Scrivener: 'The public scriviner is the confidant of the chamber maid, the poet, the cooks, the love interpreter of the soldiers and the consultant of the porters. His status is the last refuge of the missed education and for the invalids of literature.' *French Types*, 1835. D.262. *Right*, 'The Banker: Called financial capacity, because he is nothing but a recipient, a coffer exclusively fit for finances.' *French Types*, 1835. D.263

Caricatures of other non-professional urban types appeared regularly in *Le Charivari*, alternating with the *Types français*. Daumier's *Flibustiers parisiens* of 1835 depicted different kinds of thieves and petty criminals. The editorial explained that Daumier proposed to represent the different ways in which the inexperienced provincial was fleeced by crooks, as well as by the foolishness of the local citizens. The series had the double appeal of putting the public on guard and of offering a physiognomic guide to that category of the population of Paris.

A. Bourdet's *Béotismes parisiens*, published in *Le Charivari* on 12 August 1836, provided comment on politics, caricature and the bourgeois, censorship and economics. In one scene a politician is depicted requesting a lithographic portrait to distribute to his constituency, while the accompanying text explained: 'Thanks to the excellent type of the Parisian bourgeois, the caricaturist/artist, sentenced to inaction by the September Laws, can still find work.'

70,71 *Left*, Travìès, 'Titi, the plasterer's mate . . . at the Funambules Theatre',
Physiognomic Gallery, No. 26, 1837. *Right*, 'The Man who lives by his wits: operative
in charge of apple-cores at the Funambules Theatre.' *Physiognomic Gallery*, No. 28,
1837

Throughout this period the caricaturists were elaborating their basic techniques of physiognomic expression beyond the scope of Le Brun and Lavater. After intensive collaborative political caricature between 1830 and 1835, the individual stylistic gifts of the caricaturists began to emerge with greater clarity. Their work developed in two directions: civilian satire in the caricature journals, and book illustration, less subject to day-to-day pressures and bordering on contemporary genre painting. (Some genre themes of Impressionist painting – café scenes, street scenes, casual encounters – are directly anticipated in this material.)

After 1835 Travìès (1804–59) attempted the transition to social caricature in his lithographs for *Le Charivari*.[55] He depicted Parisian working-class types living on the squalid outskirts of the city, demeaned by their work or lack of work and usually broken down by drink. His *Tableau de Paris* and *Politesse française* were as unappealing as Hogarth's *Gin Lane* had been in the previous century and, like Hogarth, he included in his panorama of demoralization a rogues' gallery of 'reputable' citizens: the consumer, a rich fat man; the industrialist holding a purse and a ledger; the 'honest' solicitor depicted as a robber. His style was literal and unrelenting. His proto-naturalism and pictorial social conscience were out of step with his time: a prefiguration of the novels of Zola.

96

A competent draughtsman, he drew several series of satirical physiognomic studies in the manner of Boilly, including *Les Contrastes* (1829) which pairs off independence and servitude, ferocity and compassion, and *Les Petites Grimaces* (1830–1). Traviès employed animal-human analogies in his *Histoire naturelle* of 1830, a parody of Buffon applied to contemporary reprehensible types. He also contributed illustrations to the *Physiologies* of the Maison Aubert, *Les français peints par eux-mêmes* and Texier's *Tableau de Paris*, as well as a few series on Parisian *moeurs*, for example, *Scènes de moeurs*, *Les Plaisirs parisiens* and *Les Rues de Paris*.

But nothing further developed along these lines: Traviès' work with its edge of brutality did not survive long in the milder world of social satire. Little is known about his remaining years. Champfleury, in his history of caricature, cites an article recounting Traviès' end: poor, alone and forgotten.[56]

Grandville (Jean Isidore Gérard, 1803–46) was born in Nancy, where his father was a miniaturist painter. Even in his political days he had operated on a different axis from his colleagues – more fantastic, more abstract. He had turned mainly to book illustration by the late 1830s, occasionally contributing a print to one of the published albums of

72 TRAVIÈS, *The Little Grimaces: Left to Right*, – satisfaction, blubberers, smokers, *portraits charges*, pot-bellies, fear, masks, success. 1832

individual caricatures.[57] There are approximately 3,000 prints, lithographs and engravings in his oeuvre. Grandville's work in the 1830s extended the formal vocabulary of feature and expression. His morphological reduction from Apollo to a frog follows studies by Giacomo della Porta, Le Brun and Lavater. Physiognomic variations in response to a common stimulus, such as snuff-taking or smoking, are also in the tradition of Boilly's *Grimaces*. In *Formes différentes du visage* (1836), he paired heads with their reduction to basic shapes: circular, square, triangular, and so on. Such analogies had also been made by Lavater.

It was Grandville who provided the frontispiece for Peytel's *Physiologie de la poire* in 1832, and he also drew vignettes for the 1845 edition of La Bruyère's *Les Caractères ou les moeurs de ce siècle*. For *Les Français peints par eux-mêmes*, he illustrated the stockholder, the man of letters, the pharmacist, the writer and the surgical orderly. Social roles, customs and habits are depicted in *Chaque âge à ses plaisirs* of 1827 and *Types modernes: les dedans de l'homme expliqué par le dehors* of 1835.

73, 74 GRANDVILLE, 'Heads of Men and Animals Compared', 1844. s.307. 'Man Descending towards the Brute', 1843. s.304

98

75 GRANDVILLE, 'Varieties of Snuff-sniffers', *Critical Observations*

76 GRANDVILLE, 'Different Cranial Forms', 1836. s.283

77, 78 GRANDVILLE, *Left*, Visitors are recommended not to annoy the new inmates at the zoo.' *Right*, 'The Carnival is the one thing that raises Man above the animals – one can't claim that invention for them.' *Scenes of the Private and Public Lives of Animals*, 1842. s.1076, s.934

As Grandville distanced himself from daily comment, he moved away from speaking silence into silent silence. He became obsessed with fantastic cosmology outside social reality. His cosmogothic romanticism anticipated the fantasy genre of science fiction. He returned to his earlier interest in physiognomy, bearing and gesture, and became fascinated by the 'physiognomy' of inanimate objects and in animating them. He drew morphogeneses and metamorphoses: animals turned into humans, inanimate objects to animate ones, geometrical forms to organic shapes. Above all, he developed animal-human analogies. Working within the long tradition of expressing moral issues through animal fables, from Aesop to La Fontaine whom he illustrated, Grandville greatly extended the traditional range of characterological traits associated with animals. Such analogies recur throughout his oeuvre. One of his first series, *Les Métamorphoses du jour* (1830), consisting of seventy-two lithographs, was reprinted in *Le Charivari* in 1832 with the title *Métamorphoses du jour ou les hommes à têtes de bêtes*.

Grandville's most complete study of animal-human analogies appeared in *Scènes de la vie privée et publique des animaux : études des moeurs contemporaines* (its projected but unpublished title being: *Les Animaux peints par eux-mêmes et dessinés par un autre*). This consisted of illustrations for a collection of short stories by Balzac, De Musset, Janin, Nodier, George Sand, Louis Viardot and La Bédollière, published in a hundred installments between 1840 and 1842. The preface made it clear that in this case the book was conceived as a satire on government and society.

The framework of the story is a revolt initiated by the animals (anticipating George Orwell's *Animal Farm*) in the Paris zoo, the Jardin des Plantes. The revolutionaries elect Grandville as an honorary animal and enlist him to illustrate the history of their republic. Each animal contributes a tale. As in his earlier journalistic work, there are references to politics and professions. This is how he described the theatre critic:

> As it was the first night of a representation, I left the box at once with the air of one burdened with thought; and making my way to the green-room, joined a group of theatrical critics walking about with a supercilious pedantic air. One had the sting of the wasp, another the beak of the vulture, a third the cunning of the fox. Birds of prey were there, hungering for helpless victims. Lions were proudly showing their teeth.[58]

Un Autre Monde (Another World), of 1844, with 188 wood engravings, is the culmination of Grandville's work; it was subtitled *Transformations, visions, incarnations, ascensions, locomotions, explorations, peregrinations, excursions, stations, cosmogonies, fantasmagories, reveries, games, buffooneries, caprices, metamorphoses, zoomorphoses, lithomorphoses, metempsychoses, apotheoses and other matters*. This work was initially issued in thirty-six installments: the author's name was given as Taxile Delord, a pseudonym for Grandville. The story tells of three travellers who explore the modern world from three points of view: under the seas, from a balloon in the sky and from the land. It is about the world turned upside down, with fish luring humans from the water with bait of jewellery, money and liquor, and animals visiting a human zoo. There are also metaphors taken from carnivals and puppet theatres: the puppets act out the mechanical conformities of social life (variations on the *Vanity Fair* motif). In the chapter called 'The Best Form of Government', people's heads are being hammered and tagged and the inscription reads: 'Applying the discoveries of the phrenologists' society will eliminate crime and encourage virtue by physically altering the bumps on people's heads.' Grandville also used inanimate objects as characters in this book, such as the chisel sculpting a human thumb of huge proportions.

Grandville also brought the spectator theme into sharp focus. In 'Venus at the Opera' Grandville presented the viewers as heads of eyes, the stare epitomized.

Grandville's imagery was not to find its true audience until the times of Symbolism and Surrealism. Baudelaire wrote:

79 GRANDVILLE, 'Venus at the Opera', *Another World*, 1844. S.1232

Grandville . . . wanted his pencil to elucidate the law of association of ideas. . . . There are certain superficial people whom Grandville amuses; for my part, he alarms me. . . . When I step into the world of Grandville, some sort of disquiet takes hold of me, as though I were going into an apartment where the disorder was systematically organized. . . . It is by the lunatic side of his talent that Grandville is significant.[59]

Whether or not his eccentricity was clinical, his end was tragic. His book illustrations brought him a moderate livelihood but, by 1847, after the deaths of several of his children, he was a broken man. His wife and eldest son destroyed his original drawings after his death. He provided his own epitaph: 'Here lies Grandville; he gave life to everything and made everything move and speak. The one thing is, he didn't know how to make his own way.'[60]

A third major caricaturist, Gavarni (Guillaume Chevalier, 1804–66), a Parisian from an artisan family, had been in practice since the late 1820s as an illustrator, costume designer and elegant satirist of manners. In 1830 he was hired by De Girardin as principal illustrator for *La Mode*. His work was less prominent than that of Daumier, Grandville or Traviès in Philipon's newspapers between 1830 and 1835 when political caricature

80 GRANDVILLE, 'The Fish of April', *Another World*, 1844. S.1210

81 GAVARNI, 'Women Painters'. Texier, *Tableau de Paris*, 1852–3

was in the ascendant. After 1835 he emerged as one of the principal social caricaturists of Philipon's stable; with Daumier, he is the best-known and the most technically accomplished of the caricaturists of the mid-nineteenth century, producing over 10,000 lithographs and wood engravings in his forty-year career.[61] Like Daumier, Grandville, Monnier, Traviès and others, Gavarni contributed to the *Physiologies* of the Maison Aubert, *Les Français peints par eux-mêmes, Muséum parisien* as well as *Le Diable à Paris*, and *La Grande Ville*.

The theme of most of Philipon's caricaturists at this time was the solid core of the bourgeoisie; the world of Gavarni, a Romantic, is the demimonde of erring wives, flirtatious shop girls (*grisettes*) and tarts (*lorettes*), students and artists.[62] His flowing, *chiaroscuro* style lent itself to the theme of social mutability through the elegant costume of social theatre. What Romantics and Realists had in common, as we noted in relation to their enthusiasm for Deburau, was a commitment to 'being of one's time', and a sense of opposition to the bourgeois and to the status quo in the official arts with their bourgeois clientele.

However, Gavarni's wide popularity depended on his ability to show people as they liked to see themselves, on display at the foyers and boxes of the theatres, at their leisure, at balls and carnivals, rather than defined by their work. Gavarni was the illustrator of women *par excellence*. His

104

82 GAVARNI, 'Men and Women of Letters': *A smell of cooking mingles with the myrtles,/ And trails the unkempt muse, even in her verses./In these – so sensitive – amorous games,/How many tears fall in the rabbit stew,/How love partakes of onions!/Illusion, followed soon by sour regret! Ah, Poesy, where will you hide your crown, Tomorrow, when Expedience puts on sale/ The lover's portrait (and the rabbit-skin?).* People of Paris, from *Le Diable à Paris,* 1845–6

83 GAVARNI, 'Metempsychoses & Palingeneses: Ruins of Elleviou.' (François Elleviou was a celebrated singer who died in 1842). *People of Paris*, from *Le Diable à Paris*, 1845–6

84 GAVARNI, 'The Little Sarcasms: The lady looks well, but the hat is badly worn.' *People of Paris*, from *Le Diable à Paris*, 1845–6

85 GAVARNI, 'Salomeon, known as Pigeonneaux, claque manager, controls all bravos, encores, hushes, laughs and tears, and in general everything that contributes to success. (His headquarters is in the wineshop.)' *People of Paris*, from *Le Diable à Paris*, 1845–6

satire lay in his choice and presentation of a situation rather than in physiognomic caricature. In the series *Les Gens de Paris*, published in *Le Diable à Paris* in 1845, class distinctions are conveyed by the decorum of the pose.

By means of bearing, situation and costume, Gavarni distinguished between amateur and professional dissipation from the shop girls of easy morals to kept women. His women are languorous and laconic: there is little action or reaction. The contours are static, the facial expressions muted. Edmond and Jules de Goncourt, Gavarni's biographers, commented that his applied physiognomics was worthy of Gall and Lavater.

According to the De Goncourts he presented

> the modern body in its melancholy, fatigue, estrangement, informality, nonchalance, the looseness of it at ease and in movement . . . a full length portrait for which the nineteenth century posed as it was in the street, in one's room, without assuming a pose.

In 1837, when Daumier's series on Robert Macaire was coming to an end, Philipon suggested to Gavarni a series on 'une Mme. Robert Macaire'. Gavarni rejected the idea and in its place Philipon and Gavarni launched a series on *Fourberies de femmes en matière de sentiment*, a Balzacian profusion of deceits, hypocrisies, ruses, outrages and duplicities of all sorts. For instance, an enraged husband catching his wife in an illicit amorous scene is restrained by her with the words: 'Would you harm the father of your children?' It was with this series that Gavarni introduced his own brand of social satire.

In 1848, when revolution was brewing and his 'frivolous' social scenes were in disfavour with fervent Republicans,[63] Gavarni moved to London where his work had already attracted a particularly appreciative audience: Queen Victoria and Prince Albert were said to be collectors of his prints. Once in London, rather than the elegant world and the court, he drew everything that struck him as picturesque: scenes of the professions, new industries, but also the Dickensian poor of the London streets, hardly less abject than in Hogarth's time. These prints were published in the *Illustrated London News*, *L'Illustration* in Paris, and in a set of prints entitled *Gavarni in London*. Gavarni complained that he was weary of making images to amuse the bourgeois.[64] Soon he lost interest in his work and started to drink. He frequented only a few English friends with whom he could discuss mathematics, inventions and his growing obsession with a new system of astronomy which would supersede Newton and 'dethrone the sun'.[65]

It is paradoxical that while in France, Gavarni only occasionally showed scenes of low life, but was taxed with social irresponsibility; and yet once in England, where the *beau monde* was eager to see itself in his mirror, he was drawn instead to picturesque exposé.

107

86 GAVARNI, The Loge. Texier, *Tableau de Paris*, 1852–3

Back in Paris in the early 1850s, Gavarni heartened and applied his new social concern. Among his best series of the 1850s was *Masques et visages*, verbal and visual vignettes on Parisian types and situations in which he developed a new emblematic figure, the ragged street philosopher, Thomas Vireloque, who has 'a bitter eloquence of uncultivated wisdom', and was born in one of the old working-class neighbourhoods of Paris, like Gavarni himself. Vireloque is a bestial-looking character 'with a skull like Socrates and a monkey's mouth'.[66] He wears the Phrygian bonnet, attribute of the *chiffonnier* or rag-picker, which appears in Bouquet's engraving of Deburau in *Le Billet de mille francs*. The *chiffonnier* was a popular image in the 'Cries of the City'. The theme of the down-and-out street philosopher was taken up by Manet in the early 1860s in his *Buveur d'absinthe* (Absinth Drinker) and *Le Vieux Musicien*.[67] The drunken and loquacious rag-picker is also the protagonist of Baudelaire's poem, *Le vin du chiffonnier*.[68]

Vireloque, the opposite of Gavarni's fashionable character, became his spokesman, free, able to speak his mind, sharpened by years on the street and with nothing to lose. Like Gavarni in later life, Vireloque was proudly misanthropic. Gavarni himself wrote that Vireloque had a 'vigorous hatred of all wickedness, translated into a bitter sarcasm'.[69]

Gavarni, a Romantic in subject-matter and style, became increasingly embittered in his last years, sick of his audience and of his profession. In 1857, when his young son died, he entered a final period of profound depression which lasted until his death in 1866.

There is a pattern in the lives of all these caricaturists: and many of the emblematic figures they devised are woven into this pattern. Traviès is the adversary of his creature, Mayeux: he saw himself as the defender of those whom Mayeux exploits. In contrast, Gavarni's Vireloque sardonically represents his author in late life. Except for Daumier, all the caricaturists discussed here lived their lives in increasingly tense and abrasive relations with society and ended in isolation and despair. Daumier, exceptionally, was supported in old age and adversity by the strength of his talent and conviction, and by the ties of family and friendship. Henry Monnier, the subject of the following chapter, represents an extreme case of an author's identification with his principal character, Joseph Prudhomme; this identification with his anti-hero encapsulated his whole life story.

87 GAVARNI, Thomas Vireloque.
'People going into the Opéra ball.'
Texier, *Tableau de Paris*, 1852–3

Four Henry Monnier:
Joseph Prudhomme

Every age has its gait, glance, and gesture.

CHARLES BAUDELAIRE[1]

HENRY MONNIER'S Joseph Prudhomme is an emblematic type who emerged in the theatre at the same time as the *poire* and Robert Macaire in caricature. Prudhomme represents a whole class, the bourgeoisie; he is the most enduring of the emblematic figures; he prevailed through three governments: the July Monarchy, the Republic and the Second Empire.

Prudhomme played a pivotal role in caricature. Champfleury observed that 'the bourgeois never found their portraitist, only their caricaturists'.[2] The portrait of the bourgeois would have been a portrait of a generality; the ultimate caricature of the bourgeois was a clear-cut personality who yet has nothing to distinguish him from his fellows.

Henry Monnier (1799–1877), actor, writer and caricaturist, first introduced Prudhomme in 1830 in a play, *La Famille improvisée*; Monnier himself played all four characters, including Prudhomme.[3] Prudhomme became a lifetime creation – Monnier's principal role as an actor and the most frequent protagonist in his plays and satirical writings, with occasional appearances in his drawings, watercolours and lithographs. But Prudhomme's active life in caricature was forwarded mainly by Daumier, in parallel with Monnier's verbal development of the character. Monnier's *Les Mémoires de Monsieur Joseph Prudhomme* was published in 1857, and Daumier portrayed Prudhomme in more than sixty caricatures between 1852 and 1870.

Monnier wove instances from his own experience into the character of Prudhomme, on more than one level. Prudhomme begins his career as a copy clerk in a government office, a milieu which Monnier knew well from his father's post as a Parisian civil servant and his own apprenticeship as supernumerary to a notary. Monnier had satirized office life in detail in his caricature series, *Moeurs administratives*. These were offices where, as Champfleury described, 'everyone is asleep, but with one eye open', and where 'profound and unceasing studies of colleagues are made by Lavaters

88 DAUMIER, 'Henry Monnier in the role of Joseph Prudhomme', 1852. D.2347

full of bad intentions'.[4] Prudhomme goes through a whole gamut of bourgeois professions: office manager, stockbroker, theatre owner and manager, and finally newspaper editor for which he is selected because he has no opinions and because he sees the newspaper as a commercial enterprise 'like the distillery, or a sugar refinery'. As Prudhomme rises through the hierarchy, he remains unchanged, the perfect bourgeois who genuinely respects institutions and conventions.

Prudhomme is a stolid and benign character. Monnier based his description on a mild exaggeration of his own person; on stage he had only to impersonate one side of himself. Daudet, who as a young poet had some contact with Monnier, described his almost schizophrenic character: on the one hand, a clear-eyed observer, comedian and practical joker; on the other, a narrow and stodgy stereotype, set in his bachelor ways, unmitigated by his exceptional insight into his own type.[5]

Physically, Prudhomme also resembled Monnier; his trademarks were a single tuft of hair, double chin and hawk-like nose, a high white false collar and spectacles. He appears in the classic pose of the gentleman, feet at right angles, and evenly planted, paunch protruding. His head is pulled back on his shoulders, so that he looks down his nose. He is formal and pretentious and does not accommodate himself to circumstances: he never

89 'Henry Monnier in '*The Improvised Family*', *Théâtre du Vaudeville*, 1831

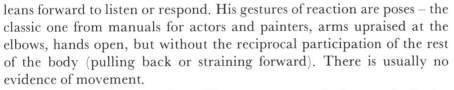

90 MONNIER, Monnier as Prudhomme.
Watercolour, 1873

leans forward to listen or respond. His gestures of reaction are poses – the classic one from manuals for actors and painters, arms upraised at the elbows, hands open, but without the reciprocal participation of the rest of the body (pulling back or straining forward). There is usually no evidence of movement.

This rigidity of posture is a telling comment on the bourgeois. It also marks an expressive restriction of caricature compared with the drawings of Daumier, Gavarni or Grandville, who conveyed movement in a variety of ways. Monnier's interest was in the still image: the pose rather than the captured moment of action. To draw Prudhomme, he used first to have himself photographed in the appropriate pose.

91 DAUMIER, 'I intend to leave an imperishable monument of our visit to this cliff. I shall add your name, too, Adelaide; the respect that I profess for the fair sex obliges me'. *The Good Bourgeois*, 1854. D.2599

Prudhomme's composite personality portrait – theatrical character, caricature, protagonist of the written *Mémoires*, and self-portrait – was underwritten also by his particular use of language: when he appeared in caricature, the accompanying captions were almost always direct speech. Unlike his predecessors Mayeux and Macaire, Prudhomme was known as much for his characteristic sayings, his *Prudhommeries*, as for his look and behaviour. Much of the strength of this character came from Monnier's implacable grasp of the banalities and rigidities of bourgeois conversation. Monnier anticipated Flaubert's *Bouvard et Pécuchet* and *Dictionnaire des idées reçues* in his masterly use of cliché to express his characters' *ennui* and their lack of contact with reality, especially reality of feeling.[6]

The *poire* represented an individual in power; it was a *portrait charge* of Louis-Philippe, reduced and abstracted so far that it could become a key term in a silent language. Prudhomme, on the other hand, was a generic figure arrived at by an opposite development: a summing up of a class into an emblematic individual who was a political symptom rather than an operator. His empty prolixity powerfully conveyed the oppressive stagnation of the times.

116

The name Prudhomme, like *poire*, also derived from a verbal pun, this time drawn from standard speech rather than slang. In the seventeenth and eighteenth centuries *Prudhomme* meant a man of probity and sagacity, a prudent adjudicator. Still earlier, the etymology of the term involved the word *preux*, meaning valiant and galant: a *Prudhomme* was a valiant knightly man. Monnier ironically repositioned this figure into the dead-centre of the middle class and transposed the man of wisdom into a parody of practical sagacity, of *prudence* and *pruderie*, who is only capable of uttering received ideas. *Prudhomme* took on new meaning and re-entered standard

92 DAUMIER, 'Sir, I will willingly pay a new franc . . . if you will do me the extreme favour of extricating me from this turnstile!' *The World's Fair*, 1855. D.2693

117

speech by way of Monnier's character: *Prudhommerie*, *Prudhommesque*, *Prudhommade*, even *Josephprudhommiser*; the name became generic for sentenious and banal attitudes and statements. Thus, at a banquet given in his honour Prudhomme said: 'This banquet is the most beautiful day of my life.' Elsewhere he commented: 'Take a man out of society and you isolate him'; in his role as theatre director he offered a toast to 'Dieu et Molière'; after losing a fashionable Realist director he had hired, he tried to woo him by closing his letter: 'Je vous en prie, Monsieur et cher auteur, d'agréer l'assurance de ma considération et de mon réalisme les plus distingués. p.s. mon épouse se joint à moi pour vous prier de croire à son parfait réalisme.'[7] ('I beg you to accept, honoured sir and dear author, the expression of my highest consideration and most distinguished realism. P.S. My wife joins me in asking you to believe in her complete realism.')

Monnier was a master of the telling detail. He captured the turn of a phrase or a lapel, as signifiers of character, attitude and social status. Monnier's comedy of manners was meticulous and acid, more so than that of Gavarni. Gautier called Monnier's mimeticism 'intellectual photography'.[8] Monnier's themes and methods were consistent and continuous in the three parts of his activity – caricaturist, writer and actor. A theme developed in theatrical improvisation would be carried over into a text or drawing; the same detailed observation of costume and facial expression informed his lithography and his theatrical performances.

After watching Monnier applying make-up before a performance, Gautier wrote in *La Presse*:

> Each touch is thought out, placed where it belongs, as if in a picture; the characteristic lines and wrinkles are incredibly right; that red spot near the nostril might have been put there by Balzac; Meissonier alone could find that puce coloured dressing gown which contains the whole 18th century; for the smallest detail has its importance in Monnier's roles: the writer observes, the painter sketches, the actor executes. Hence, that perfect harmony, that absolute illusion.[9]

Gautier pointed out that Monnier had been a Realist twenty years before there was a movement by that name. Monnier shared the Romantic disdain of the bourgeois. And yet, wilfully, he chose them as his material; he based a lifetime's work, observation and creation on a generalized anti-heroic class portrait in an extreme realist mode. He was motivated by distaste and melancholy (not by political and social conviction as with Daumier); his tragedy was that he could not separate himself from what he hated.[10]

Reflecting on Monnier's unique control of Realist technique, Gautier asked 'why in that case is he not the greatest painter, the greatest writer and the greatest actor of the epoch?'[11] The answer was that Monnier, by his obdurate and extreme literalism, parodied and undermined the

93 DAUMIER, 'There's no doubt about it, it certainly is my profile; but I shall always regret that the artist had the obstinacy to omit my spectacles.' *The Public at the Exhibition*, 1864. D.3316

94 MONNIER, 'The Dissatisfied: Regrets of the past, disappointed hopes, errors and prejudices.' *Impressions de Voyage*, 1843

Realist ideal: 'His bourgeois – and nobody has painted them justly, not even Balzac – bore you just as real bourgeois do, by unstoppable waves of commonplaces and solemn stupidities. It's no longer comedy, it's stenography.'[12] In the end, according to Gautier, Monnier's realism itself becomes a kind of *Prudhommerie*, which says nothing.

Monnier's 'intellectual photography' as Gautier called it – his determination to record rather than transform – went beyond the tragic/comic figure of Prudhomme in his descriptions of other social types. *Les Industriels, métiers et professions en France* (1842), was part of a twenty-year collaboration between Monnier as illustrator and La Bedollière who wrote the text. Its stated purpose was to

> put the well-to-do class in rapport with the poor class, to initiate the public to the existence of artisans who are too misunderstood and unknown – that group of street merchants, criers, artisans who are called in the second half of the nineteenth century 'the people'.

Les Industriels opens with a quotation from Jean-Jacques Rousseau: 'The sole means to know the true habits [*moeurs*] of a people is to study private lives in the most populous classes; for to stop at those people who are always represented, is to see nothing but actors.' La Bedollière commented that 'the people' are rarely shown in the theatre except in

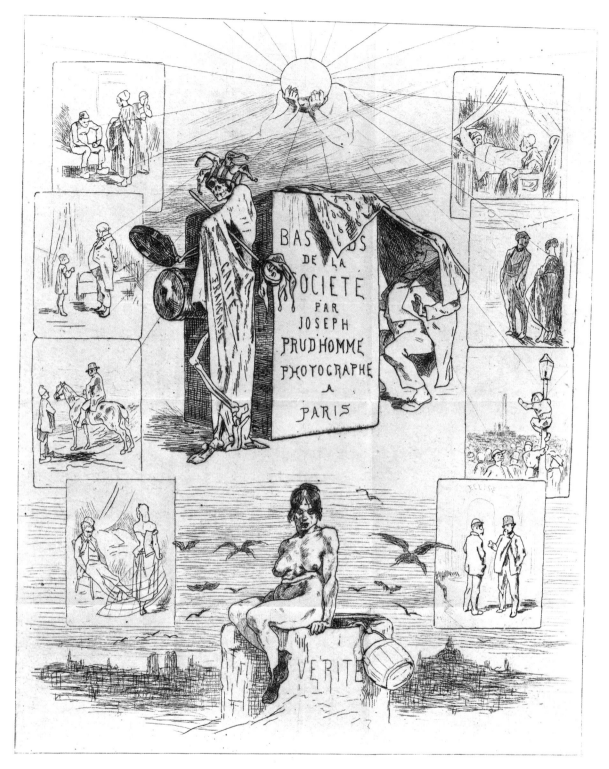

95 FÉLICIEN ROPS, frontispiece to Monnier, *Les Bas-fonds de la société*, 1862

96 MONNIER, 'A Bourgeois Parisian Marriage'

stereotype. In fact, he wrote, there is greater variety of costume, manner and character among 'the people' than among the monotonously uniform upper rungs of society. The approach of Monnier and La Bedollière was to depict as accurately as possible the look, pose, habits, costumes and implements of different trades. They sought to show how the nature of the work affected the look of the worker – 'the transforming influence of habitual occupations'.[13]

Monnier's text, *Les Bas-fonds de la société*, published in an edition of two hundred in 1862, is a document of social types in a narrative form, with the intention of raising consciousness. Monnier used the metaphor of the pen as a surgical scalpel; his written sketches (the only illustration is the frontispiece by Félicien Rops) were intended to prick social conscience.[14] Gautier also used this metaphor of Monnier's work: 'La Bruyère and La Rochefoucauld, those pitiless anatomists, do not plunge their scalpel into a human nature more deeply.'[15]

Monnier's recognition and merciless portrayal of boredom as a predominant feature of the time was a significant innovation in the characterization of a class. By the conspicuous absence of physiognomic variety and change he registered the inability to feel, the unconscious counterparts of Baudelaire's concept of 'spleen', the predominant state of the conscious city-dweller.

From his earliest drawings of the bourgeoisie in the period 1827 to 1830, Monnier showed bored married couples turning away from one another, silently, in contrast to the period of courtship in which the same couples are shown in animated conversation. At a ball organized by Dumas in 1835, Monnier himself appeared in the guise of 'one who is bored to death', simulating 'the sleepy stodginess of a respectable shopkeeper or small business man'.[16]

In his *Physiologie du bourgeois* (1841) Monnier attempted an explicitly generic description of the whole class, and he again made boredom its salient characteristic. Nothing, he wrote, is worse than sitting next to a bourgeois at the theatre. Either they laugh in the wrong place or wait for everyone else to laugh, or they don't laugh at all. This is a class that either does not know its true feelings or has none.

The theme of boredom intensified in the last period of Monnier's work. Between 1866 and 1877 Monnier did a series of watercolours with the title *Les Diseurs de riens* (Those who Say Trifles). When his play of the same title was to be published in *Le Bourgeois de Paris* in 1854, the editor proposed cutting three-quarters of it – banal events, countless details, mixed metaphors – because it was in itself tedious. Monnier retorted that if the characters said anything interesting they wouldn't be *diseurs de riens*.

In the watercolours and drawings, fat people are shown sitting in stuffed chairs in dark salons doing nothing and saying nothing. In some of these the theme of boredom is fused with the figure of Prudhomme and his lack of expression. The theme of boredom is an extension into social circumstances of Prudhomme's stolid physical being.

Although he portrayed boredom, Monnier did not venture to explore its causes and his critics attacked him for not doing so. Duranty complained that Monnier's reality consisted of isolated fragments: he gave no picture of society as a whole, only its shell.[17] But this criticism overlooked Monnier's substantial contribution in mapping out whole areas of society in his caricatures. Between 1827 and 1830 and then again from 1840 to 1847 Monnier scrutinized the ways of the city in a series of prints on petit-bourgeois neighbourhoods, trades, shops and theatres with nearly obsessive persistence.[18]

In the spirit of precise description – and satire – he illustrated many of the popular codes and manuals of the period 1828 to 1830, all of which revealed a keen sense of social hierarchy and decorum. There were manuals for married couples, for godparents, for lovers and for employees, such as: *Manuel de l'employé de toutes classes et de tous grades, precédé de l'art d'obtenir sûrement et facilement des places, de les conserver et de se procurer de l'avancement. Code indispensable à tout employé qui veut parvenir aux honneurs et à la fortune* (1830). (Manual for employees of all classes and grades, preceded by the guaranteed and easy way to obtain and keep employment and to gain promotion. Indispensable code for every employee who wishes to achieve honours and fortune.)

Bourgeois Types and Situations

97 MONNIER, 'Office Chief',
Administrative Mores, 1828

98 MONNIER, 'The Marais', *Six
Quartiers of Paris*, 1828

99 MONNIER, 'A Lesson in
Declamation', *Theatrical Galley*, 1829

100 MONNIER, 'Indiscretion',
Parisian Sketches, 1827

Monnier was among the most frequent contributors to the *Physiologies* of the Maison Aubert, primarily as illustrator, occasionally as writer. Not surprisingly, his most notable contribution was his *Physiologie du bourgeois*. For *Les Français peints par eux-mêmes*, he drew one hundred illustrations, most of them taken from the lower orders: a waiter, a maid, a type-setter, a messenger and an old soldier. Other collections of types appear in his *Cris de Paris* (1845–6) on the street criers, and his *Code civil illustré* (1846–7).

Criticism of Monnier by his colleagues reached its full height at the time that the Realist movement came into full force, around 1850. He had influenced Duranty, Champfleury and Daudet. All three now rejected him. Reviewing Monnier's play *La Grandeur et décadence de M. Joseph Prudhomme*, in 1852, Janin wrote that twenty years before, at the début of Prudhomme, Monnier had been extraordinary and original. Now he was

a sad shadow, an echo, a memory . . . so meticulous about the form, so irresponsible in the foundations of his comedy! Such an able draughtsman, so misguided as a writer, who never recounts anything but the miseries and embarrassments of his subject.[19]

101 MONNIER, 'The Prison', 1842

102 MONNIER, 'Imprisoned
Types (Men)', *Les Français
peints par eux-mêmes*, 1840–2

One of Monnier's biographers drew attention to Balzac's description
of his own character Bixiou, presumably based on Monnier:

> witty, but in a monkeyish way, without consequence or continuity. . . . He
> attacked weak people for preference, respected nothing, believed neither in
> Grace, God nor art . . . insulting especially what he didn't understand at all.
> . . . His lively mind, his abundance of ideas, made him sought after by people
> used to the display of intelligence . . . but none of his friends was fond of him.[20]

Various contemporaries were critical of what they perceived to be
Monnier's sole capacity – mimicry. Baudelaire contrasted Monnier with
Daumier thus: 'Instead of grasping wholly and at once a complete statement of a figure or subject, Henry Monnier would proceed by a slow and
successive examination of details.'[21]

Baudelaire equated Monnier's characterizations with daguerreotypes:
Monnier 'can create, idealize, compose nothing . . . Monnier has one

JOURNAL AMUSANT
JOURNAL ILLUSTRE,
Journal d'images, journal comique, critique, satirique, etc.

LES CONTEMPORAINS DE NADAR.

HENRI MONNIER.

103 Caricature of Monnier, *Le Journal amusant*, 1859

104 MONNIER, ink drawings, 1871: *Right*, Joseph Prudhomme; *left*, 'I have said for a long time and I repeat it, Napoleon III is nothing but ambitious. If he remained a plain representative of the people, he would still be on the throne.'

unusual faculty, but only one, the cold clarity of a mirror that does not think, and contents itself with reflecting the passers-by'.[22]

Gautier saw Prudhomme as Monnier's revenge on the bourgeois: 'He recoups himself for all the boredom, contrariness, humiliations, and all the other little sufferings the bourgeois cause the artists (and not only the artists) often without even knowing it.'[23] Balzac was more critical:

> With him, everything is surface. He presents as a person, our period, unbelieving, mocking, sceptical, and oblivious. Without direction, without criteria, without goal, when he mocks M. Prudhomme, he doesn't realize that he is mocking himself.[24]

In the same years when Monnier's Romantic and Realist colleagues lost interest in his work, his play, *La Grandeur et décadence de M. Joseph Prudhomme*, established a new level of popularity for his character. This was reinforced by the publication of his *Mémoires* which quickly sold 20,000 copies, a very high figure for the time.

As a boy, Monnier had been fascinated by the *grimacier*, and by the *mystificateur*, the practical joker who plays on the credulity of others for amusement. He was clearly fascinated by dissimulation. Prudhomme is incapable of dissimulation, but Monnier was a master of it. But as Prudhomme became a more complete personality, and a more famous one, his identity with Monnier became more stifling – until through an awful intensification of his mimetic skill, the two became inseparable. In 1873 Monnier drew a double portrait, *Joseph Prudhomme et Henry Monnier*; they are almost identical twins.

There is an inverted Romanticism in Monnier's self-creation, and self-destruction, as anti-hero. Monnier/Prudhomme did not in the end transcend convention but consciously and helplessly epitomized it. The contemporary critic Paul de Saint-Victor summed up his tragedy: 'Le masque avait mangé le visage.' (The mask had consumed the face.)

Overleaf. 105 DAUMIER, 'The Parisians in search of pleasure – two hours in line at any theatre.' *Good Parisians*, 1855. D.2652

Five Honoré Daumier:
strategy and style

Daumier is a moralist with the suppleness of an artist and the accuracy of Lavater.

CHARLES BAUDELAIRE[1]

DAUMIER, unlike Monnier, never became trapped in a character of his own invention, nor in narrow limits of style or social viewpoint. The first impression from a review of Daumier's caricatures is one of spectacular variety, both 'linguistic' and pictorial. Just as Daumier included not one but many physiognomic types within the category 'lawyer', though all of them show vanity and inhumanity, so he had not one graphic formula for outrage, but a range of finely discriminated indications – the surprised and helpless outrage of the lawyer's victim, the outrage of offended bourgeois decorum, or the righteous outrage of the liberated woman asked by her husband to sew on a trouser button; moral variations conveyed by facial expression, by bearing and gesture and by context. He specified the tone with which a gesture is assumed – the adverbs of his syntax – reluctantly, eagerly, deliberately.

The effect of Daumier's unprecedented completeness of information about character and social interaction, as Baudelaire pointed out, is moral – not at a personal but at a political level. His vignettes of social encounters, conflicts or collusions are not isolated: cumulatively they tell us (as they told their contemporary public) about a social fabric, determined by specific political and economic conditions.

What was unique was not Daumier's social insight or political commitment, but the combination of these with his mastery of traditional problems of figure drawing and figural composition, and with his enlargement of the pictorial repertoire of facial and bodily expression. Degas was not capricious in taking Daumier as seriously as he did Ingres or Delacroix. And Balzac reflected that Daumier 'has something of Michelangelo under his skin'.[2]

Honoré Daumier (1808–79) was born in Marseilles, a city of exuberant gestures. His father, a glazier, was an aspiring poet and playwright, whose ambitions brought the family to Paris in 1815, and whose poverty led

132

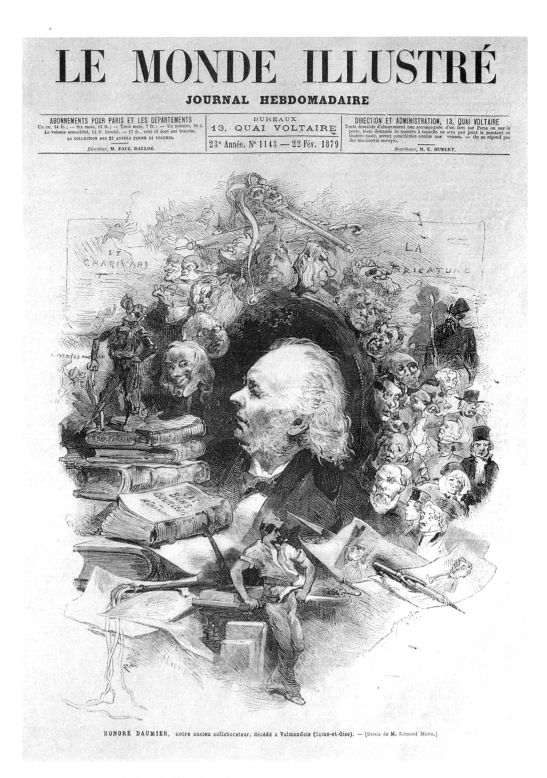

106 Frontispiece, *Le Monde Illustré*, 27 February 1879

them to move repeatedly within the city. Daumier did not fit clearly into any defined social class. His family was essentially artisan turned bohemian, in the double sense then current: artistic on the one hand and, on the other, poor and marginal. Daumier grew up detached, involved, and on the alert.

He began work as an errand boy for a legal firm and went on to apprentice to a lithographer (Charles Ramelet) and a publisher (Z. F. J. Belliard) who also made lithographic portraits. In 1828 he attended informally the studio of Boudin, an academic artist. There he met other young sculptors and painters: August Préault, Philippe-Auguste Jeanron, and Narcisse Diaz de la Peña who became one of the Barbizon painters. Alexandre Lenoir, founder of the Museum of French Monuments, befriended Daumier in his late adolescence, and Daumier became familiar with his collection of portraits, chosen for their diverse facial expressions.[3] In the late 1820s Daumier began to draw caricatures and *portraits charges* of political figures.

Daumier's first caricatures, all political, were published in 1830 in *La Silhouette* and in *La Caricature*. In that same year of the July Revolution, Daumier's father went mad.[4] Daumier's attacks against the government became the family's principal means of income.

His work almost immediately began appearing two to three times weekly in *Le Charivari*. Five of the most lastingly effective political caricatures of this period, *Rue Transnonain, Gargantua, Lafayette, Liberté de la presse*, and *Le Ventre législatif* were his, drawn while he was in his mid-twenties.

Daumier produced nearly 4,000 lithographs and 1,000 wood engravings, setting the standard and scope for political and social satire in the period 1830 to 1870, in both newspapers and illustrated books, including the novels of Balzac and Eugène Sue, as well as numbers of the *Physiologie* of the Maison Aubert and chapters in *Les Français peints par eux-mêmes*.

Baudelaire wrote of Daumier as:

> A man who every morning gives the Paris population a laugh, who every day supplies the need of public gaiety, and gives it something to feed on. Honest burgher, businessman, youngster, fine lady, one and all laugh, and often go their way – the ungrateful creatures! – without looking at the signature![5]

The details of daily situations that Daumier drew were in the service of his social outlook, Republican, egalitarian and domestic. The strength of his underlying ideology distinguished his work from that of Gavarni, Monnier and Constantin Guys.

Daumier's work, like that of Deburau, was often compared to Balzac's *La Comédie humaine*, for the range and depth of its portrayal of Parisian society. Balzac's title claims completeness: as *La divina commedia* was a complete spiritual cosmology (in vernacular narrative), so *La Comédie*

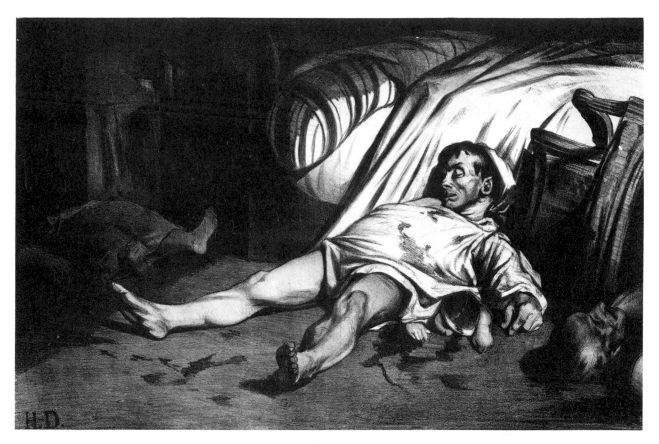

107 DAUMIER, 'Rue Transnonain', 1834. D.135. Working-class families in Lyons massacred by the police in retaliation for an incident on their street.

humaine was meant to be a complete social description.[6] When contemporaries applied the same title to the oeuvre of Deburau or of Daumier, completeness is what they meant.

The structure of the *comédie humaine* necessarily differed according to the medium. Whereas Deburau created a working-class repertoire by way of the single figure of Pierrot, an 'everyman', and Balzac developed hundreds of named individuals through narration, Daumier presented discrete and instantaneous situations. With few exceptions, the figures are anonymous; not strongly individualized, but careful variations within clearly communicated types. Daumier grasped the professional structure of the expanding bourgeoisie – from the small shopkeeper and concierge, to the politician, lawyer and banker – and interwove its distinguishing traits with those of a moral characterology drawing on the traditions of Le Brun and Lavater.

135

108 'The View', *Parisian Types*, 1839. D.595

The caricatural series, many of them planned by Philipon and Daumier together, are given broad and straightforward categories – *Les Beaux Jours de la vie*, *Les Baigneurs* (The Public Baths), *Les Bas bleus* (The Blue-stockings), *Monomanes* (Monomaniacs), *Les Gens de justice*. But Daumier's true recurrent themes are moral: wishful thinking; role-playing; affectation, sometimes pathetic and sometimes arrogant; wariness of cultural novelty; ambition, resentment, envy, vanity; powerlessness and indifference to the powerless; complacency and complaisance towards the status quo; embarrassment and obsequiousness; snobbery, self-righteousness, dissimulation, disingenuousness and hypocrisy. Daumier explores these themes between the upper and lower limits of the urban bourgeoisie. To quote from Baudelaire again:

> No one better than he has known and loved (in the manner of the artists) the bourgeois . . . this type at once so commonplace and eccentric. Daumier has lived in close contact with him, has watched him day and night; he has learned his intimate secrets, has made the acquaintance of his wife and children,

knows the shape of his nose, the structure of his head, he knows the sort of spirit that gives life to the household, from top to bottom.[7]

In comparison with Hogarth, perhaps the only social caricaturist of comparable stature and effect, Daumier's freedom from misanthropy or generalized disgust allows a much wider and more finely discriminated range of moral observation.

The bourgeoisie, Daumier's principal subject and audience, was not only typically preoccupied with social ambition; it was a class coming to terms with its own increased political power. Louis-Philippe's epithet, 'the bourgeois king', indicated not so much his personal style as his power base. The caricaturists and the bourgeois are adversaries: new forms of privilege, corruption, speculation, the betrayal of the Charter, the disappointment of democratic hopes, were all associated with the alliance of the monarchy and the bourgeoisie.

The political dimension of Daumier's portrayal of the bourgeoisie becomes clear when his work in the Louis-Philippe years is viewed together. Each individual caricature can often be seen as purely social, and many of them are benign: domesticity, simple diversions, natural affections, are shown with sympathy as well as irony. Daumier's political stance emerges as he repeatedly presents situations of conflict and dissonance: between people's origins and their circumstances; between traditional bourgeois values of family stability, caution and frugality, and new opportunities for self-serving and display; between power of office and powerlessness. These political implications gain in strength because his attack, in its *cumulative* effect, is not on individual moral turpitude, but on the social dislocations which engender pomposity and embarrassment as well as cruelty, dishonesty and corruption.

By symptomatic moments, he mapped the fault-lines of his society, the lines of shift and strain. Where Monnier presented the static manifestations of the petit-bourgeois, Daumier succeeded in describing the dynamic of an entire class. This required a development of the caricaturist's armoury far beyond anything attempted before. If one leafs through Daumier's earliest caricatures, which are derivative in manner and content from his more experienced contemporaries, one sees how he developed an increasingly articulate style that could carry moral and political satire forward.

Daumier's early work was within the framework of physiognomic tradition: there are even some indications that he was interested in current phrenological theories. In 1832 Philipon commissioned him to make a series of thirty-six sculpted *portraits charges*. There had been a successful precedent in the late 1820s with the figurines of public figures by the sculptor Jean-Pierre Edouard Dantan – caricatures of Dumas, Hugo,

137

Liszt and others.[8] It is not clear what Philipon's intended use of the sculptures was – they were not cast in bronze until well after Daumier's death.[9] One story relates that Daumier made them surreptitiously in the gallery of the Legislature at a time when illustrators were not admitted. Their exaggerated bumps and hollows may be simply a sculptor's natural form of caricature, or they may consciously respond to the phrenological fashion.[10] These busts preceded the lithographic series, *Célébrités de la caricature*, published in 1832–3, in which he used the same politicians as his subject. The sculptural modelling is carried over to the prints in the emphasis on the three-dimensional structure of the head and nose – the use of light and dark planes, rather than line, to define form. Such an example is *D'Arg*, the 'portrait' of the Count d'Argout, who was the censor for the July Monarchy, as well as Minister of Commerce, Public Works, Fine Arts and the Interior.[11]

After 1835, when legislation forbade caricature of political figures, Daumier began to explore the caricature of social types and situations for

109 'The Coalman', from a late 18th-century *Cries of the City*

110 DAUMIER, 'The Tailor: He walks with his shoulders like a coat-hanger and his elbows out. His clothes are of the latest cut, but often at odds with his boots and hat. He nearly always has a very euphonic name such as Watenkermann or Pikprunman.' *French Types*, 1835. D.261

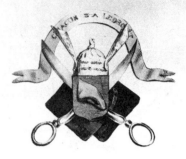

111 DAUMIER, Harle, 'Old Fool', Deputy of Calais, 'Fossil of the Centre', Gobin No. 32, 1832
112 DAUMIER, 'D'Arg . . .'. Censor for the July Monarchy, and minister of commerce, public works, fine arts and the interior. D'Argout's emblems were the scissors and his large nose which got into everything. 1832. D.48

the first time. In Chapter Three I discussed the first series in this mode, the *Types français* – social types based on classification by professions, accompanied by legends that were explicit in their reference to the relationship of the types to the regime, whether as victim or as accomplice.

Daumier's emphasis began to shift from the shape of the head, characteristic of the individual portrait bust, to bearing and play of features. The *Types français* are still in the popular print tradition of the 'Cries of the City', expressive but static; each stands alone with his attributes or implements, and a minimal indication of city setting, indoor or outdoor. The style is more graphic, less sculptural, than that of the *portraits chargés*, but still far from the calligraphic strength of his later work; shading is blended rather than cross-hatched, and line follows form rather than creating it.

In 1836 *Le Charivari* published the *Galerie physionomique*, also shared between Daumier and Traviès, which is more directly related to Boilly's *Grimaces* (1823–9). Here, single male figures are depicted, static and tightly delineated, smoking, eating, drinking, bored, surprised, shocked, frustrated, uncomfortable, dissatisfied; the pleasurable savouring of a Bordeaux-Lafitte is contrasted with the reaction to a bad-tasting medicine; the heavy features of the oyster-slurper are paired with the fine-lipped connoisseur of ices. There is no longer any political reference in the legends that accompany the prints.

139

113, 114 DAUMIER, 'Oh! my wife's dead.' *Physiognomic Gallery*, 1836. D.328.
'Oyster Lover', *Physiognomic Gallery*, 1836. D.329

115 DAUMIER, 'So I'm a rogue? – No – no – on the contrary.' *Sketches of Expressions*, No. 11, 1838. D.476

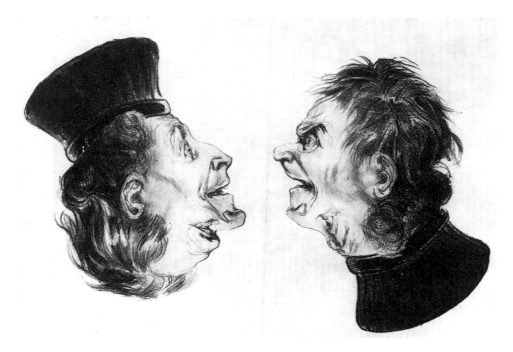

116 DAUMIER, 'Double Faces'. *Lower legend*: 'Your case didn't have a chance/You should have told me that before.' *Inverted legend*: 'You must plead, your case is excellent/ plead! plead!' No. 2, 1838. D.540

In *Double Faces* (1838), Daumier showed two profiles on each page; when the page is held upside-down the profiles read as the same two characters but in contrasting moods. This is the only instance where Daumier explicitly distinguished physiognomics (innate expression of character) from pathognomics (transient expression) by showing the same face with two expressions.

Daumier's mastery of the caricaturist's traditional vocabulary was already established in 1838. In *Croquis d'expressions* (1838–9), for the first time in his work, we clearly begin to see physiognomy in action, expression occasioned by urban encounters and confrontations. When Daumier presented two or more figures, their given facial features are in marked contrast to one another. Nose, chin and brow are articulated. Eyes are rounded with surprise, compressed with anger or suspicion or drooped in boredom. Eyebrows have an important place in the expressive repertoire of the face. Le Brun had already demonstrated that eyebrows could express all the emotions. Daumier enriched their expressive repertory further. Usually sharply angled, they can indicate attention, response, surprise, scepticism, fear or unexpected pleasure. Often the angle doubles, a circumflex which conveys the moment of their sudden rise. Full lips are rare; they are encumbrances in the line of profile and reserved for some affluent bourgeois, profligate and pouting. A mouth is more usually a thin

141

117 DAUMIER, 'Yes, an attempt is being made to destitute this orphan, whom I will not characterize as a young orphan, since he is fifty-seven years old, but an orphan nonetheless . . . but I am confident, gentlemen, in any case, for the eyes of justice are constantly open to all such culpable manoeuvres!' *Men of Justice*, 1845. D.1347

single line, but a line very specific and subtle in its expression – often set in boredom or determination. Sometimes boredom, like stupor and sleep, is shown by a lapse of control – as in the open flaccid mouths of the sleeping judges 'presiding' on the bench. There is an occasional yawn and several yells of rage.

Noses vary: sharp (critics, connoisseurs, and some politicians); long, full and bulbous (gluttonous types); hawk-like (Prudhomme); and the rarer stub found in workers more often than the bourgeoisie. Foreheads come in all shapes: receding, predominant, short, evenly curved, indented; the lower classes have shorter foreheads.

However, the play of expression takes precedence over given features in the lithographs from the late 1830s on. The fixed features are constants around which expressive lines play. It is the plane of the cheek between eye, ear, mouth and jaw, particularly difficult to activate and articulate, that predominates in Daumier's expressive heads. The three-quarter view is the most common one in his drawings, allowing maximum exposure of this neglected and revealing area.

The poor and modest worker, spare and lean, is typically shown with cheek bone casting its shadows on the hollows, in contrast with the well rounded jowl of the bourgeois. Ratapoil, sharp-edged and bony, has a hollow traced by the line of the movements of speech. By contrast, the worker into whose ear he whispers has a set cheek and downward turning fold, like the corners of his mouth, closed and sombre.

Series titles in the late 1830s and the early 1840s remained in the genre of physiognomics and typology. *Croquis d'expressions* depicts bourgeois pleasures, tribulations and aspirations. The emphasis is on social and domestic situations. Daumier introduced the theme of bourgeois self-image in scenes of people and their portraits, and painters, a version of the theme of the disparity between reality and wishful projection that appeared throughout his work.

118 DAUMIER, 'God, what a nose you've made me!' *Sketches of Expressions*, 1838. D.474

143

119 DAUMIER, 'Good lord! . . . Dazzling! . . . Ye gods! . . . superb . . . it speaks! . .'
Around the Studios, 1862. D.3246

Spectators

120 DAUMIER, *Above left*, 'Don't you think my dear, a person must be a bit touched to have her portrait done like that?' *The Public at the Salon*, 1852. D.2298

121 DAUMIER, *Above right*, 'Amateur classicists more and more convinced that art is lost in France.' *The Public at the Salon*, 1852. D.2295

122 DAUMIER, 'Delighted to find that he is exhibited, the original – seen here – escorts his spouse to the Salon and positions her in front of his likeness, to savour the opinions of the public. Look, say some, it's Lin, the Chinese envoy. No, say others, don't you see it's an illustration in natural history? A gentleman in possession of a catalogue corrects them: it's the portrait of Mr. D. insurance broker. Well, with a mug like that, he doesn't need to insure himself. Nobody's likely to steal him. Madame, the wife of the sitter, is extremely gratified.' *Current Events*, No. 52, 1841. D.918

123, 124 DAUMIER, *Left*, 'At the Porte St Martin: By God . . . that's a good scene . . . talk about a good scene . . . that's a good scene.' *The Best Days of Life*, 1846. D.1171 *Right*, 'Two gentlemen anxious to be recognized as connoisseurs of the highest comedy.' *The Parisians in 1852*, 1852. D.2227

In two series published between 1839 and 1842, *Types parisiens* and *Emotions parisiennes*, Daumier turned to more public confrontations. This preoccupation can perhaps be seen as reflecting the conflict of class interests that eventually led to the Revolution of 1848. Here we have scenes of personal injustice, confrontation and inconvenience, such as the poor man in front of a well-stocked shop window, the poor and dishevelled father running into his foppish son who refuses to recognize him, and so on. *Ouvrier et bourgeois* (1848) are two juxtaposed types: the worker looking after his class interests (avidly reading a newspaper while walking), the bourgeois looking after his individual interest (gazing at the food displayed in a shop window).[12] In the Salon, there are representations of the classes reacting differently according to their interests: farmers appraise a painted cow, and painters examine a rival's work. The contrast of roles and social positions became more acute: between employer and employee, lawyer and client, bureaucrat and petitioner, landlord and tenant. These contrasts are expressed primarily through bearing, the assertive versus the deferential.

146

125 DAUMIER, 'For three months his highness always posed like that . . . .'. *Whatever You Like*, 1848. D.1686

126 DAUMIER, 'Take it easy, guv'nor, I'll get you there as gently as if you were in a coffin.' *Parisian Types*, 1842. D.603

147

127, 128 *Left*, DAUMIER, 'A Dissatisfied Litigant', *Men of Justice*, 1846. D.1362
Right, 'If you would be good enough to take my case, I can assure you of my lifelong
gratitude.' *Physiognomies of the Law Court*, 1852. D.2303

Underlying each series were some broad correlations of character with
occupation which existed already, especially in the theatrical tradition,
and which Daumier developed further, both socially and politically. A
variety of individual physiognomies was played against a set of traits
characteristic of the occupation as a whole. Lawyers were linked with the
attributes of arrogance, greed and cunning; bankers with gluttony;
doctors with self-satisfaction and ambition; teachers with ineptitude;
landlords with obduracy; and so on.

Daumier depicted lawyers – prosecutors, defending counsels and judges
– more frequently than other professional groups. They inherit many of
the attributes of the politicians in this phase of social caricature. They are
always arrogant, avaricious and cunning. Robert Macaire appears as a
lawyer twice between 1836 and 1838. The first major legal series, *Les Gens
de justice*, was published in 1845–8, followed by *Les Avocats et les plaideurs*
(Lawyers and Litigants) in 1848–51, and *Physionomies du palais de justice*
(Physiognomies of the Law Court) in 1852.

129 DAUMIER, 'A trial lawyer visibly inspired by the deepest conviction . . . that his client will pay him well.' *Men of Justice*, 1845. D.1342

Daumier's attitude toward lawyers stemmed in part from their political complicity: the number of attorneys allowed to practise in Paris was limited: every nomination had to have the sanction of the government. Disinterestedness under these conditions was rare. *Les Gens de justice* is replete with exaggerated gestures as keys to insincerity and self-seeking. The cloaked advocate is leaving his client behind bars. His raised shoulders, cocked head, stealthy glance and grimacing smile give him a heavily disingenuous, surreptitious air. He is contrasted with the clear-contoured jailer and, more dramatically, with the prisoner, whose head alone is visible, eyes wide open. Although we do not know the full situation, the bearing and juxtaposition of the figures indicate clearly that the prisoner has cause to worry, the lawyer has little to lose. In another example, a worker, descending the stairs, turns and points accusingly at the lawyer on the landing above. The lawyer, in gentleman's pose, turns his head, but not his body, in the direction of the accuser; the accusation clearly perturbs him very little. He fingers his scarf, looks down his nose, thin

149

mouth pulled tight, jaw set with a sneering smugness, in contrast to the worker's irate, mobilized face – open mouth, open eyes. Their respective bearings reflect both class and feeling.

Daumier posed his lawyers in court like actors on the stage, with a highly stylized delivery and choreography of movements and gestures, but also with a wealth of physiognomic 'asides'. Many of the captions refer to the lawyer's pride in his oratory: 'So, you've lost your case. At least you've had the privilege of hearing my defence.' The gestures his characters use are pronounced, the accusing finger pointing more emphatically as the case being presented becomes more questionable. Daumier also used the conventional accusing gesture of the outstretched arm and pointed finger in his depictions of politicians, actors, bluestockings, Macaire and Prud-homme. This gesture was also commonly found in contemporary theatrical illustrations, and is still standard today in cartoons.

Daumier drew over a hundred lithographs of the medical profession: doctors, surgeons, dentists, pharmacists, oculists, homoeopaths and hypno-tists. Political implications were also characteristic of the medical pro-fession: a large percentage of the Chamber of Deputies were doctors. Of 1,550 doctors in Paris in 1848, 300 were decorated with the Legion of Honour.[13] As late as 1867 Daumier allegorically linked medicine and politics, showing members of the International Congress of Medicine armed with hypodermics in reference to the threat to France by the armament of Prussia.

Daumier's doctors are thinner, less prosperous and less gluttonous than his lawyers. They are more alert – their eyes emphatically open – but less self-assured: their stance is more tentative, without the aggressive, pom-pous paunch which is typical of his lawyers.

Most doctors, in fact, had meagre incomes which they frequently augmented by selling medicines. Daumier caricatured doctors as pur-veyors of quack remedies and questionable treatments. Again, Macaire is depicted offering free consultations and charging heavily for the medicine he supplies. In one of his earliest series, *L'Imagination*, done in collabora-tion with Grandville, Daumier presented a physician and his fantasies of cures. The doctors are a less scheming lot than the lawyers but Daumier attacked their methods: their use (whether in good faith or not) of quack remedies, leeches, cures by pure water, dieting, 'clyster pumps' and dromedary ointment. His doctors are solidly bourgeois by origin and con-viction: pedantic and indifferent, motivated only by self-interest.[14]

Another form of political power in the hands of the bourgeoisie was control of land use and habitation: this was an age of feverish housing and land speculation. The series *Locataires et propriétaires* (Tenants and Land-lords), published in *Le Charivari* (1847–8 and 1854–6), shows the power wielded by the landlord, and by his unofficial agent, the concierge. Pub-

130 DAUMIER, 'The Physician: Why the devil is it that I lose all my patients? . . .
However much I treat them, I purge them, I drug them . . . I don't understand it at
all!' *Scenes of The Imagination*, 1833. D.40

131, 132 *Left*, DAUMIER, 'Speak to the Concierge. . . . But the problem is to find the Concierge . . . that's the difficulty.' *Current Events*, 1853. D.2361. *Right*, 'Look, our nuptial chamber, Adelaide . . . these workers don't respect anything. They don't have the cult of memory!' *Parisian Sketches*, 1853. D.2429

lished a few years after the reinstatement of the censorship laws by Napoleon III, this was a direct attack on the government, but one that could pass the censors.[15] Beginning in 1850 Daumier exposed the effects of the demolition and reconstruction of Paris – the displacement of people, the inconvenience, the housing shortage and inflationary rents, the new speed of traffic and the danger to the pedestrian. Neighbourhoods were destroyed and landlords of new housing would not allow children or dogs. Daumier emphasized the destructive effect of such developments – and the prosperity of the builders: in January 1851 he showed Thiers and Louis-Napoleon as demolition workers.

The years immediately before the Revolution of 1848 were in some ways those of Daumier's greatest strength.[16] He had moved to the Ile St Louis in the early 1840s; in 1846 he had married. He was the unchallenged leader among the caricaturists – Grandville had died in 1845, Traviès had stopped publishing in the mid 1840s, Gavarni was turning away from his own success, Monnier was writing and acting Prudhomme and was hardly drawing. Cham, the next caricaturist in line, had just begun to publish in *Le Charivari* and as yet was openly Daumier's imitator.

It was in 1847 that Daumier first submitted a painting to the Salons – a mark of his *engagement* as a painter. And at about the same time, certain elements emerged in his caricatures which derived from the painting of earlier centuries, and which increased not only his graphic mastery but his narrative and satirical range. The poses of the individual figures became more varied and dynamic (as if he had been making sets of figure studies according to the practice of Leonardo, Pollaiuolo or Raphael) and he showed full mastery of the foreshortening of limbs and faces which these poses entail. He seemed to make a special point of varying the angle at which each face in a scene is shown. When he set faces in parallel it was deliberate, to convey mindless attention or haughty inattention.

Even more impressive is his increasingly dramatic treatment of the interactive stances of figures. Except where his principal characters are embedded in a crowd, there is never any doubt about where the feet of each are planted; and the line of interaction between two figures is almost never parallel with the picture plane (as it was in the earlier series) but subtly or dramatically oblique. There is pictorial depth – even aerial perspective – between them, though they may touch or intersect. The

133 DAUMIER, 'Paris at 6 p.m.: I don't believe that even at Limoges one encounters as many Limousins.' (An inhabitant of Limousin, also a stone-mason.) *Parisian Sketches*, 1854. D.2585

153

series *Les Femmes socialistes* (1849) is a set of virtuoso studies in the negative space between two figures (a concern carried on by Degas in many of his interior domestic scenes). The effect of this sculptural control of spatial relations is informative; it adds, to the bearing and facial expression of the individual figures, unmistakable evidence of their feelings towards one another. As Baudelaire wrote: 'All his figures stand firmly and are faith-fully portrayed in movement . . . it is all the logic of the scholar trans-planted into a light and fleeting art, which competes with the mobility of life itself.'[17]

Combined with Daumier's acute grasp of pose and gesture was his sense of timing, a sense which was directly linked to his developing mastery of drawing. Compare Daumier's theatrical scenes with those appearing in contemporary theatrical magazines, such as *Le Magasin théâtral*. One of the artist's classic challenges has always been the capture of the sense of movement. Leonardo, for instance, suggested that the artist should depict the moment immediately before the climax of a movement, so as to indi-cate the action leading up to that moment and to imply what will follow. Daumier used this device and added another in the very manner of his drawing: his rapidly drawn line and repeated contour indicate the figure

134 DAUMIER, Drawing, 'Heads of Two Men.' Maison I, 139

135 Comédie-Française, *The Fourchambault*, comedy
by M. Emile Augier, drawings by M. Adrien Marie.
Left, Mme Bernard to her son: 'You shall save him!
It is my wish; it is your duty'. *Right*, Mlle Letellier
to M. & Mme Fourchambault: 'I withdraw; but it
is I who dismiss you!'

136 DAUMIER, 'Insurrection against husbands is
proclaimed a sacred obligation.' *Socialist Women*,
1849, D.1918

without fixing it, and this conveys a sense of movement. We do not see the
exact placement of an arm in a lawyer's dramatic gesture, or the set of the
features in a grimace; what we see is how it comes into being. There is an
aspect of bravura performance in Daumier's draughtsmanship. The
crayon stroke clearly conveys the vigorous and assured motion of Daumier's own hand, and it is this dynamic inflected line that gives movement
to the figures portrayed – the tensely concave back of a woman hurrying
in tight shoes, or the admonitory arm gesture, constrained and inflated at
the same time, of Prudhomme instructing his small son.

One of Daumier's most constant devices was to juxtapose conventional
and spontaneous bearing and gesture. This contrast is carried over to
scenes of social confrontation: composure and the stylization of self is a
function of class. The disparity of social positions, the self-consciousness of
hierarchy is conveyed through juxtaposition of poses – as we have seen,
between lawyers and clients, landlords and tenants. The powerful adopt
conventional poses; the powerless do not conceal their apprehension or
dismay. In the series *Croquis parisiens* (1856), there is a drawing of two
janitors. One explicitly rehearses the pose of authority – feet together,
weight forward, chest protruding, one hand tucked into his vest, the
other hand behind his back, head perched back, looking down his nose.
The other stands by with mixed bemusement and scepticism.

155

138, 139 DAUMIER, *Left*, 'Oedipus at the Sphinx', *Ancient History*, 1842. D.967. *Right*, 'That's my wife! Outrageous! While the barber gives me a shave, she gives me the slip!' *Conjugal Manners*, 1839. D.645

137 DAUMIER, 'A queen preparing an especially demanding speech.' *Dramatic Sketches*, 1856. D.2897

140, 141 DAUMIER, *Left*, 'Scene in front of a minister's front office under any government.' *Whatever You Like*, 1849. D.1706. *Right*, 'Posed as a member of the Agricultural Board in his county.' *The Good Bourgeois*, 1865. D.3416

142 DAUMIER, 'Photography. A new procedure, used to ensure graceful poses.' *Parisian Sketches*, 1856. D.2803

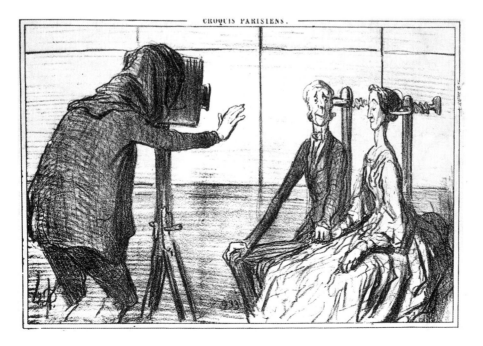

143 DAUMIER, 'Smiling practice before meeting the electorate.' *Current Events*, 1869. D.3706

The motif of the photography studio lends itself to the depiction of self-consciousness. In a scene of contrasting poses before the camera we witness some typical stylizations of self-image: 'civilized man' turns his body haughtily away from the camera, glancing back in its direction, affecting bare acknowledgment, but tense and ready for quick adjustments. By contrast, 'natural man' sits face forward, stable, with feet parallel, neither subtle nor seductive. Daumier contrasted the basic structure of their poses – the spiral and the block.

The theme of posing before a mirror was used by Daumier to show how a person confronts his own image, and to play with the disparity between the two: sometimes this shows the effort of simulating decorum, as with the politician rehearsing his bow and smile; sometimes the face reveals the state wished for and the wish or uncertainty itself, as with the woman looking coyly in the mirror.

Hypocrisy was a politically fruitful motif for Daumier. He used two basic strategies: explicit situations where the true intention is seen in action, for instance, Louis-Philippe and Robert Macaire embracing while picking each other's pockets, or the lawyer and defendant, or the con-man and his victim. More subtly, he juxtaposed rhetorical gesture with a theatrical 'aside', whether of face or bearing, that reveals the real intention. *Après vous* presents two generals before a door marked 'Disarmament'. Each invites the other to be the first to enter; but the expression contradicts the official meaning – the exaggerated gesture of deference and obsequious smiles convey mistrust.

It is not simply a question of traditional exaggeration used in order to achieve dramatic focus, but of disjunctive exaggeration used to reveal conflict or dissonance. For instance, a face attempts a noble expression but all the features are gross. This is true of Louis-Philippe and most of the *portraits charges*, particularly from *Les Représentants représentés* (1848–9). Where there are mixed signals of nobility and ignobility (decrepit, pot-bellied, middle-aged actors playing noble parts in classical plays), one is simply led to regard the nobility as empty.

Daumier used exaggerated theatrical pose to satirize the artificiality of an arcane style in a theatre unresponsive to contemporary realities. He also used canonical theatrical gesture – in scenes outside the theatre – to signify artifice and affectation. He employed the formal language of

144, 145 DAUMIER, *Left*, 'The promenade of an influential critic.' *Sketches at the Salon*, 1865. D.3448. *Right*, 'Ah, my dear sir, allow me to say that this year you have exhibited, quite simply, a masterpiece.' *Sketches at the Salon*, 1865. D.3441

LES BŒUFS

La force pesante des gens «de la paroisse de Saint-Pierre-aux-Bœufs, le patron des grosses bêtes».

146 LE BRUN, Oxen. Le Brun likens them to the inhabitants of the parish of Saint-Pierre-aux-Boeufs.

147 DAUMIER, 'Interior of a bus. Between a drunk and a butcher.' *Parisian Types*, 1839. D.566

presentation, declamation and reaction to underline pretentious, arrogant and dishonest characters. And almost always he counterpointed the standard mannerism with some revealing unselfconscious move or grimace.

Obviously, however, not all formalized dramatic gestures imply false appearances. Daumier used certain formal poses and movements as indicators for an immediately recognizable, easily read emotion or reaction. One of the most common poses used by men and women of all classes indicates surprise or fright: the figure 'taken aback', legs apart, knees bent, chest and head thrust forward, arms bent upward at the elbow, hands open. This pose was used by painters, caricaturists, actors and mimes. A gesture from antiquity through post-Renaissance theatrical prints and painting, it persists up to contemporary film animation.

Le Brun's schemata – recombined and updated – underlay some of Daumier's characterizations.[18] The pose and expression of esteem and veneration, shoulders raised, knees bent, body inclined forward, was used in an exaggerated form by Daumier for obsequious members of the court

LES CHATS-HUANTS

La tournée des grands-ducs : hibous, hulottes, chouettes : les rapaces nocturnes au hulul

148 LE BRUN, Owls. The envious man, with his pointed nose and pinched mouth, is likened to a sinister owl

149 DAUMIER, 'Mr Prudhomme, Philanthropist: It is precisely because I am philanthropic that I consider it my duty not to give encouragement to mendicancy. Man must supply all his needs by his labour. Have I ever been seen to mendicate?' *Current Events*, 1856. D.2828

in *La Cour du Roi Pétaud* (1832). Daumier's visitors responding to unfamiliar painting at the Salon drew on Le Brun's illustration of aversion, combined with the attributes of surprise. Anger was expressed in the same ways in the seventeenth and the nineteenth centuries: the forehead is creased, the nostrils dilated, the corners of the mouth turned down. Daumier added a caricatural touch – the hair stands on end.

Physiognomic comparisons of animals and humans codified by Le Brun were also used by Daumier. The owl, which Le Brun associated with misers, and with deceit and concealment, is clearly present in the features of Prudhomme refusing to give alms. Daumier's faces of clergy and government officials are directly compared with Le Brun's 'cheats, tricksters, and predators', their features based on the crow. Clergy were also depicted by Daumier as a cross between Le Brun's donkey (boorish) and his ram (stupid). Butchers resemble oxen. And the stone-marten, noted by Le Brun for its cunning and greed, was used by Daumier to depict the avaricious.[19] In addition, Daumier added new analogies to his bestiary – politicians as ravenous beetles.

161

150 DAUMIER, 'The Parisians are increasingly coming to appreciate the advantages of macadamized roads.' *Current Events*, 1854. D.2586

In the first major article on Daumier, published in 1878, Duranty referred to the repertory of fixed types and traits available to artists and pointed out that Daumier provided a true encyclopedia of types: 'the scientific or instinctive infallibility [of expression], a certitude in the expression of movement, an inexhaustible truth in the appearance of his figures'.[20]

Of all Daumier's types, the spectator is the most developed and expressive. The more skilled the caricaturist, the more carefully the individual spectator is scrutinized. The caricaturist's art, like that of the mime, consists in finding the salient clues of character and points of exaggeration that trigger a quick and accurate reading. The caricatured spectator, like the mime, indicates what is going on around him by his gestures and expressions of reaction. The spectator motif has a double aspect: it comprises two contrasted but intimately related types. One is the isolated and conscious observer, the *flâneur*, who is an analogue of the artist's own activity. (Alexandre called Daumier 'the spectator par excellence'.) The other is the undiscriminating (or at any rate, undiscriminated) member of an audience or a crowd of bystanders, the passive gaper, the *badaud*. There are political implications in underlining citizens' acceptance of their role as passive observers of an empire's reconstruction.

162

Hardly fifty years after the storming of the Bastille, Balzac reported in *Ferragus* that 'in Paris everything is a spectacle: no other people in the world have had such voracious eyes'.

Daumier developed the motif of the spectator with greater variety and intensity than any other caricaturist. He depicted spectators over 230 times (this represented 5 per cent of his graphic work and 10 per cent of his paintings). He first introduced the spectacle as a subject in his repertory of social caricature after the censorship laws of 1835: not only theatre audiences and spectators at the Salon, but people on the streets, turning the slightest event into a spectacle. A typology of audiences, of *badauds*, becomes in the censorship years a staple of the caricaturists' repertoire. Between 1835 and 1851, Daumier depicted spectators nearly 50 times. The subject became still more frequent between 1852 and 1868, when Paris was undergoing reconstruction: the upheaval of the city is shown through the spectators making their way across freshly macadamized streets or dodging past workers carrying beams. We also see the effect of the new scale and grandeur of the city: women strolling in wide crinolines

151 DAUMIER, 'These are no longer women, these are balloons.' *Current Events*, 1855. D.2627

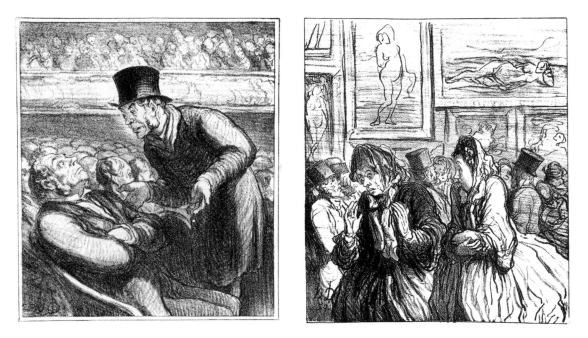

152, 153 DAUMIER, *Left*, 'For the seventh time, will you give me my seat? . . . if not . . . '.
'If not, what?' 'If not, I'll be obliged to go and that would displease me very much.'
Difficult Moments in Life, 1864. D.3274. *Right*, 'More Venusses this year . . . always
Venusses! . . . as if there were any women who look like that! . . '. *Sketches at the Salon*,
1865. D.3440

154 DAUMIER, 'Physiognomies of the spectators at the Porte St Martin during a
performance of Richard III.' *Current Events*, 1852. D.2274

164

down broad boulevards – they are part of the spectacle of Paris parading 'to see and be seen'. This was the period of the great World Fairs, the Expositions Universelles of 1855 and 1862. Daumier drew several series on the fairs, concentrating on the responses of the visitors.

In this same period, Daumier attended the theatre frequently.[21] The diversity and detail of his theatre audience, and the interactions between them, reflect his close attention to spectator as spectacle. They are distinguished by the posture and gesture of his figures which vivifies rather than typifies. In *Physionomies de spectateurs de la Porte Saint Martin pendant une représentation de Richard III* of 1852, he focused on four variations of standard bourgeois poses but with distinctive facial expressions.

The individuation of the spectator is expressed in the conflicts between spectators. In the series *Croquis pris au théâtre* (1864), Daumier conveyed a conflict of will between husband and wife through their gestures: the woman pointing to the stage with her husband determined to stalk out – but with his torso turned, responding to his wife's tug. In another theatre audience, one man weeps and the other laughs at him. A man challenges an interloper in his seat.

The bourgeois audience was Daumier's own, demanding in its passivity. It was in this period, the late 1850s and early 1860s, that Daumier's popularity was beginning to wane. Daumier captured the spectators' confusion and conservatism at the Salon, their boredom and bewilderment at the artifacts of progress at the Exposition Universelle. He depicted the Salon spectator with less sympathy than his bourgeois at their domestic pursuits: there is no one in these scenes at the Salon with whom Daumier identified.[22] He showed people critical and uncomprehending before the work of Courbet and Manet, women shocked by realist nudes, men strutting proudly before their own portraits. Daumier himself had submitted his paintings to the Salons, and experienced rejection and neglect.

In 1860, after thirty years of constant employment, Daumier was dropped from *Le Charivari*. Baudelaire wrote: 'Think of Daumier! free, kicked out of the doors of *Charivari* in the midst of the month and with only a half-month's pay . . . and with no other occupation than painting.'[23] Philippe Burty described Daumier in 1862 as in a 'cruel state of privation . . . having no longer either lithographs or woodcuts to do. The newspapers won't have anything from him any longer. *Charivari* did not renew his contract. *Le Monde illustré* won't accept his series; his wood engravings, I hear from Champfleury, make subscribers drop off.'[24]

The most likely reason for Daumier's dismissal was a shift in editorial staff at *Le Charivari*. Philipon had moved from there to *Le Journal amusant*. There is no further documentation on why Daumier's readers lost interest, if they had, or whether this was the real reason for *Le Charivari*'s decision.

Daumier's repetitiveness and lack of verve in some prints of the 1850s, and the competition of Cham's more light-hearted weekly report with its multiple images, may have contributed to Daumier's eclipse.

In 1861, Daumier published no new work. Since 1853, he had spent his summers in Valmondois, twenty-three miles from Paris. Friends of his own generation, Romantic landscape painters – Corot, Daubigny and Rousseau – lived and worked nearby at Barbizon; and during this period of unemployment he spent his time with oils and watercolours. In 1862, he was commissioned by the weekly illustrated paper *Le Boulevard* (edited by the caricaturist and photographer Etienne Carjat). Eleven of the twelve lithographs for *Le Boulevard* in 1862 and 1863 appeared under the title *Souvenirs d'artistes* (the last was a *portrait charge*). They are very diverse in theme and treatment (only one, *Paysagistes au travail*, 'Landscapists at Work', has painters as its theme) but among them are some of his finest scenes. They were executed under less immediate pressure than his daily work for *Le Charivari*; their composition is more careful, without any loss of directness or verve. *Nadar élevant la photographie à la hauteur de l'art* (Nadar Elevating Photography to the Level of Art), of 1862, is the best-known and most spectacular example. Several – one post-Haussmann street scene in particular – are tightly packed with figures and complex in composition. All show gradations of tone which may be associated with his concentration on painting in this period. There are also cross-overs of motif: the figure of the child in the painting *Femme et enfant sur un pont* (1845–8), *Départ pour l'école* (1852), and again in the repeated theme of *La Laveuse* (The Laundress) and *Le Fardeau* (The Burden) from 1852 to 1863, appears in the lithograph *Le Dimanche au jardin des plantes* (Sunday at the Zoo). A Don Quixote illustration in the *Le Boulevard* series is almost unchanged from two oil sketches around 1858. This lithograph also used, as its dramatic focus, a technique of scraping the greasy crayon off the stone, which introduced a new tonal element. This use of patches of varied tone to build up forms is a partial reversion to the style of his earlier *portraits charges* but now it is painterly as well as sculptural.[25]

Seven of his watercolours of the 1860s depicted lawyers and courtroom scenes, the third-class carriage and other train scenes, street performers, actors on the stage and print collectors. Daumier's emergence as a genre painter and watercolourist coincided with the first exhibited works of Manet, Monet and Degas.

In 1863 *Le Charivari* offered Daumier a new contract and its readers were informed:

> We announce with satisfaction to all our subscribers that our old colleague Daumier who for three years had given up lithography to dedicate himself exclusively to painting, has decided to take up the crayon again which he had wielded with such success. We present today a first plate of Daumier, and

Imp. Bertauts Paris.

155 DAUMIER, 'The New Paris: How pleasant it is for busy people now that they've broadened the routes of communication.' *Artists' Souvenirs*, 1862. D.3245

167

from this day on, we will publish, every morning, six or eight lithographs of this draftsman who has the talent of making even his caricatures true works of art.[26]

From 1863 to 1866 Daumier returned to familiar subjects, *Croquis parisiens, Types et physionomies, Croquis pris au Salon, Les Bons Bourgeois* and an occasional lawyer; and those subjects that the Impressionists were just beginning to adopt: café scenes, theatre audiences and spectators at large. Some of these lithographs were published in *Le Journal amusant* and the *Petit Journal pour rire*, both publications of the Maison Aubert.[27]

In 1866 censorship laws were lifted in an optimistic gesture on the part of Napoleon III, confident of his public support. International conflict had taken centre stage. And for all the complaints over the inconvenience and great expense of the reconstruction of Paris, internal politics were not under excessive attack. Napoleon had made France into a major military power, entering into wars with almost every major power in Europe except England. The military engagement of France with Italy, Russia, Austria, Prussia and Turkey unsettled the European balance of power.

Daumier depicted the growth of Italy and the threat of Prussia, and the attempt to ally with unreliable countries. But above all, his concern was with the threat to peace: he showed Europe personified balanced on the tip of a bayonet and, two variations, the globe balanced on the tips of bayonettes, and the figure of Europe trying to balance on a globe.

Issues of diplomacy and the threat of war now became Daumier's prevalent themes. With the shift from national to international politics, Daumier's caricature became more symbolic. He invented and used symbolic figures: Peace as an emaciated figure, Prussia as an obese woman with a military hat, Diplomacy as an old hag in eighteenth-century costume, France as Prometheus with a vulture picking at its liver. These figures, in topical references, were set against evocative but unspecific landscapes of devastation, reminiscent of Goya's *Caprichos* and black paintings, known in France through engravings. (His *The Disasters of War* were not published until 1863.) This new simplicity of background, together with the galvanizing symbolic figures, made Daumier's late political caricature enduring in its reference.

The defeat of Napoleon III in 1870 and the moral bankruptcy of France is conveyed in *La Toile* (The Curtain): the audience has called for the curtain to be pulled down – it is marked 'Theatre of politics'. On the face of it, this was the end of a long struggle that Daumier had championed all his life: Monarchy was dead; but what replaced it was not yet a republic such as Daumier had fought for. His caricatures at this time are admonitory: 'If the workers fight among themselves, how shall the house be built?' It was not until 1877 that the republic became a viable reality.

168

156–158 DAUMIER, *Right*,
'European Equilibrium',
Current Events, 1857.
D.3566
Below left, 'The Universal
Exhibition. The Exhibition:
"Forgive me if I don't offer
you a chair, but you
understand . . . "'; Peace:
"Don't bother, I am
used to not being seated".'
Current Events, 1867. D.3593
Below right, 'If the workers
fight among themselves,
how shall the house be
built?' *Current Events*, 1872.
D.3925

159, 160 *Left*, DAUMIER, 'She definitely has a stonger voice.' 1869. D.3717. *Right*, 'Le Charivari. Forced to draw a new view of the site where the Temple of Peace stood.' *Current Events*, 1867. D.3610

In 1867, twelve years before his death, Daumier introduced a last emblematic type (after his Macaire, Ratapoil and Monnier's Prudhomme). He turned from his society and to himself as caricaturist in his portrayal of the jester. As early as 1833 Daumier had identified the jester with *La Caricature* and *Le Charivari* caricaturists, but now the figure became less elfin and more human. Daumier had earlier presented types with whom he might have identified, but never with such explicit self-reference. *Don Quixote*, Daumier's favourite book, was a frequent subject in his painting, but did not appear in his caricature. Don Quixote who nobly misapplied moral categories was a recurrent tragic-ironic self-image for Romantics in a bourgeois society.

The jester, on the other hand, is explicitly the caricaturist: he seems to have Daumier's nose and Don Quixote's beard. With crayon-holder as his weapon he confronts, on Daumier's behalf, the politicians, clergy, disarmament, universal suffrage and reactionaries. From 1867 to 1872, Daumier drew the jester repeatedly.[28]

Daumier's jester is in the same profession as the street performer, the clowns and *saltimbanques* that he drew and painted repeatedly from the 1850s to the last years of his life.[29] But the jester of the lithographs keeps up his professional high spirits: he actively comments, records, and

170

opposes, while the *saltimbanques* of Daumier's paintings and watercolours are consistently dejected and passive. The street performers had been subject to the same censorship laws as the caricaturists – their skits were full of political reference. Daumier depicted the street clowns with the same three-cornered hat, the fool's cap, of the jester. In the most pathetic images they are seen moving from place to place in the city – perhaps an echo of Daumier's own childhood.

The clown or jester as the image of the artist outside society appears also in the writings of De Musset, Champfleury and De Banville.[30] The caricaturists who in 1830 had been influential in turning public opinion against the monarchists, had realized over the next thirty to forty years the limits of their political influence. The jester as a self-image is that of the critic at large who lives by his wits and can criticize only as long as he is entertaining.

We have assigned an emblematic self-image to three of our principal caricaturists – Gavarni's Vireloque, Monnier's Prudhomme and Daumier's jester. In polar contrast with Prudhomme, a plump *diseur de rien* and a quintessential bourgeois, the jester is outside society, lean, perceptive and a conscious contender. Prudhomme gradually swallowed up Monnier; Daumier's self-image emerged at the end of his career, and the jester is not his incubus but his comrade-in-arms.

In 1872 Daumier's eyesight began to fail. He retired from Paris to Valmondois and he drew little after that.

A major exhibition of Daumier's work was organized by his friends in 1878, sponsored by Hugo, the prominent novelist; Nadar, the photographer; Champfleury, the old champion of Realism; Daubigny, the Romantic Barbizon landscape painter; and many others. Altogether 94 oils, 139 watercolours and drawings, and some sculpture and lithographs were shown at the Galerie Durand-Ruel, the sponsor of the 'Impressionist' exhibitions. The critics enthusiastically praised Daumier's work, though little was sold. Only a few months later, in February 1879, Daumier died; and the local curate of Valmondois refused him church burial because of his politics.

The obituaries in the Paris newspapers reflected the public appreciation of his caricatures. *Le Monde illustré*, 22 February 1879, wrote:

> The collection of his works constitutes one of the most original and caustic satires of our contemporary society. He found the means to sum up in a few decisive traits the dominant character of a physiognomy; he brought out the ineffaceable signs of ridiculousness and vice. . . . A profound observer, he presented the men of his time with a particular manner, a firmness of expression. His bourgeois were living beings portrayed from life from top to bottom, with their personal manner of dressing, of holding themselves, of walking and of looking.

171

The intersection of pictorial codes, revealing each character's nature, nurture, ambition and immediate feeling constitutes the generative strength of Daumier's art; he developed the language of physiognomy, bearing and gesture, to a new level at which it could express a *comédie humaine* adequate to an evolving political and social state.

Daumier's one recorded adage was: 'One must be of one's time.' For the Impressionist/Realist painters of the next generation, Daumier's work was not only a brilliant journalistic record of modern Paris, it was a liberating example which they incorporated into their advanced programme: a style at one with its subject, and a rich source of naturalistic themes, improvisatory technique and audacious framing.

Duranty's description in *La Nouvelle Peinture* (1876) of the task of modern drawing could have been based on Daumier as much as on Degas: it is Degas' explicit programme but it describes Daumier's practice.[31] Duranty wrote:

What we need is the particular note of the modern individual, in his clothing, in the midst of his social habits, at home or in the street.

. . . By means of a back, we want a temperament, an age, a social condition to be revealed; through a pair of hands, we should be able to express a magistrate or a tradesman; by a gesture, a whole series of feelings. A physiognomy will tell us that this fellow is certainly an orderly, dry, meticulous man, whereas that one is carelessness and disorderliness itself. An attitude will tell us this person is going to a business meeting, whereas that one is returning from a love tryst. *A man opens a door; he enters; that is enough; we see that he has lost his daughter.* Hands that are kept in pockets can be eloquent. The pencil will be steeped in the marrow of life. We will no longer see mere outlines measured with a compass, but animated, expressive forms, logically deduced from one another . . .

The idea, the first idea, was to take away the partition separating the studio from everyday life . . .

It is the study of how morals reflect on physiognomies and on costume. The observation of a man's intimacy with his dwelling, of the special characteristics which his profession imposes on him, the gestures which it induces him to make, points of view from which he shows himself most clearly.[32]

Champfleury dedicated *Les Excentriques* to Daumier in 1852 with these words:

You must often have smiled at the difficulty felt by the novelist who tries to sketch a physiognomy in words – you who in a few strokes of the pencil give eternal life to those beings whom future historians will consult with delight in order to learn what the bourgeois exterior of our century looked like.[33]

161 DAUMIER, 'To think that with the stone from all these pedestals one could build a good dozen primary schools,' 1867. D.3600

Epilogue

The observer is a prince who rejoices in his incognito.

CHARLES BAUDELAIRE[1]

WE announced the theme of this study as an intersection in popular culture, with caricature at its crux. We have traced two aspects of a visual language: physiognomy as a guide to *decoding* character and physiognomy as a schema for *encoding* human interactions pictorially or in performance. This double tradition acquired new life in a context of vigorous popular journalism, with new techniques of reproduction, responding to the unhinging of traditional structures of class, power and métier, and to a new mass audience. We have seen how caricature was part of a broader enterprise of social mirroring and modelling: a consciously modern *comédie humaine*.

Daumier, who deployed and developed this language with heroic range and depth, has now brought us to the point where this enterprise of social description (record and comment) began to come apart into two cultures. Balzac as a matter of course assimilated his own vast endeavour to that of the great scientific observers and organizers. But we trace in our epilogue how Baudelaire (who has been throughout this study the most acute of our guides to the time) separated the sciences from the imagination. Objectivity belongs to the sciences; the value of art now lies in subjectivity. The Realist programme, with hindsight, was an often poignant last stand against this impoverishing split – to which Baudelaire gave the coup de grace.

The role of photography is a portent and an emblem. In practice, photography and photogravure, 'literal' purveyors of things seen, undermined the task of the illustrator and forced new polarization between illustration and painting, eroding the position of the caricaturist in whom the power to inform, to *indicate* character and moral action, is dependent on selectivity and emphasis. By mid-century, the daguerreotype was a current metaphor for the Realist spectator/artist.

In his *Ce qu'on voit dans les rues de Paris* (1858), Victor Fournel endowed the spectator with the dignity of an active collaborator in the artistic enterprise:

> This life of the spectator is, for one who can understand it and practise it, the most active and the most fruitful in useful results: an intelligent and conscientious spectator who fulfills his obligations scrupulously, that is to say, who

observes everything and registers everything, can play the leading roles in the republic of art. This man is a mobile and dedicated daguerreotype, who retains the slightest traces, and in whom are reproduced, with their changing reflections, the march of things, the movement of the city, the multiple physiognomy of public morale, of the beliefs, the antipathies and the admirations of the crowd.[2]

The metaphor of the daguerreotype marks a significant stage in the evolving motif of the urban observer. Balzac's bird's-eye view was authoritative (by virtue of its high viewpoint) but not impersonal: it presupposed the powerful personal grasp of the artist as natural historian who observes and decodes with special attention to the visual language of physiognomy, bearing and gesture, who organizes his observations into a unified map or chart. The 'mobile daguerreotype', like Stendhal's mirror which is walked along the street, stands for the literal registration of things seen, rather than personal organization or interpretation: it is the emblem of Realism which aspired to 'scientific' impersonality. In his 'Salon of 1859' Baudelaire put Daguerre's invention in its place with the same firm distinction with which he excluded the Realist programme from true Art:

> [Photography's] true duty . . . is that of handmaid of the arts and sciences. Let it, in short, be the secretary and record-keeper of whomsoever needs absolute material accuracy for professional reasons . . . But if once it be allowed to impinge . . . on anything that has value solely because man adds something to it from his soul, then woe betide us.[3]

The Realists, both writers and artists, adopted the man-in-the-street as their emblem; he is the recorder of city life, and specifically of the modern, the transitory, the circumstantial and fragmentary.[4] His virtues are fidelity and diligence; his attributes are the mirror and the daguerreotype. The Realist is still concerned with physiognomic clues, both those which contribute to the recognition of a person and those which typify the present time.

In mid-century Baudelaire brought about a further change: the conscious spectator, the *flâneur*, begins to shift his preoccupation from the city scene to his own relation to the scene; he becomes the emblem of the Modernist artist. Baudelaire welcomed 'the value and the privileges afforded by circumstance; for nearly all our originality comes from the stamp that the time impresses on our sensibility'.[5]

Baudelaire in his self-portrait as *flâneur* is as confident of his own illuminating consciousness as Balzac. But contrast Balzac's 'sublime bird of prey' with Baudelaire's private eye. Balzac's ideal product was a complete systematic map of social reality, a guide to its codes and its masks, which would allow his typical protagonist, and himself, to impose themselves successfully on the city and win its rewards. Baudelaire, like his 'hero of modern life', the *flâneur*, explored the city from within: 'To see

175

the world, to be at the very centre of the world, and yet to be unseen of the world, such are some of the minor pleasures of those incandescent, intense and impartial spirits'.[6]

Baudelaire's rewards lay in the imaginative skirmishes along the way, as he dwelt on visual contacts between strangers. His preoccupation was not with decoding visual evidence, still less with defining himself in the eyes of others, but with the electricity of the contact itself.[7]

Baudelaire also uses the metaphor of the mirror to describe the observer-artist (in this case Constantin Guys, his paradigmatic 'painter of modern life'), but he introduced an essential change: 'He, the lover of life, may also be compared to a mirror as vast as this crowd: a self athirst for the not-self, and reflecting it in energies more vivid than life itself, always inconstant and fleeting.'[8] Baudelaire's imaginative 'mirror' is more powerful than the would-be neutral mirror of the Realist programme; it yields images more vivid than those it receives.

In 'Salon of 1859', Baudelaire also stated his position vis-à-vis the Realists (or Positivists as he called them) with high panache and generality: 'The positivist says "I want to represent things as they are, or as they would be on the assumption that I did not exist. The universe without man." In the other camp there are the imaginative ones who say "I want to illuminate things with my mind and cast its reflection on other minds".'[9]

Baudelaire's *imaginatifs* clearly include himself. Here, the turn inward to self-reference has been made: external things are the reflectors of the imaginative artist's mind; the particular light it casts on these things is now the *subject* of the work of art. We saw in Chapter Four how Monnier responded to apathy and alienation, by succumbing to it and depicting it with chilling literalness. Baudelaire, by contrast, took an active grasp on his own separation from society, his 'feeling of an eternally solitary fate', and transformed it into a new and powerful beauty, of which his 'prince in incognito' is the agent. Baudelaire no longer classified or codified the urban crowd, but he still, like Manet, depicted his own Paris, vividly and with passion, in his verse and prose poems. The next steps towards Modernism come when the artist turns completely away from society and then from the external scene in general.

As the artist relinquishes the humane role of helping his public to make sense of its surroundings, social observation takes a complementary path of professionalization, subdivision and quantification, and begins to claim the autonomous dignity of scientific method. The task of human classification and codification falls to the developing social sciences: sociology, criminology, demography. And the artist's picture of his own activity takes an accelerating path to autonomy, to reflexive preoccupation with his own languages, rather than with the languages of nature and society.

Notes

Introduction

1 See above all, Walter Benjamin, *Charles Baudelaire: A Lyric Poet in the Era of High Capitalism*, translated from the German by Harry Zohn, London 1973; and Georg Simmel, *Soziologie*, 4th edn, Berlin 1958 (quoted by Benjamin).

2 For example, from Honoré de Balzac, *The Rise and Fall of César Birotteau*, English translation by Ellen Marriage, New York 1896, p. 47:

'At first sight his weasel face was not displeasing; but after more observation, you detected the strange expressions which are visible on the surface of those who are not at peace with themselves, or who hear at times the warning voice of conscience. His hard, high color glowed under the soft Norman skin. There was a furtive look in the wall-eyes, lined with silver leaf, which grew terrible when they were fixed full on his victim. His voice was husky, as if he had been speaking for long. The thin lips were not unpleasing, but the sharply-pointed nose and slightly-rounded forehead revealed a defect of race. Indeed, the coloring of his hair, which looked as if it had been dyed black, indicated the social half-breed, who had his cleverness from a dissolute great lord, his low ideas from the peasant girl, the victim of seduction; who owed his knowledge to an incomplete education; whose vices were those of the waif and stray.'

3 See Louis Chevalier, *La Formation de la population parisienne au XIXe siècle*, Paris 1950.

4 See George Boas, 'Il faut être de son temps', *Journal of Aesthetics*, Vol. I, 1941, pp. 52–65.

Chapter one

1 Georg Simmel, *Soziologie*, Berlin 1958; quoted by Walter Benjamin, *Charles Baudelaire: A Lyric Poet in the Era of High Capitalism*, London 1973, p. 38.

2 The first complete edition of Jean de la Bruyère, *Les Caractères de Théophraste, traduits du grec, avec les caractères ou moeurs de ce siècle*, was published in Paris in 1688. There were numerous eighteenth- and nineteenth-century editions. In 1836 it was published under the abbreviated title, *Des caractères ou les moeurs de ce siècle*, with subsequent editions in 1843, 1844–5, 1859, 1865, 1871, 1883 and 1891.

Georges Louis Leclerc de Buffon, *Histoire naturelle générale et particulière avec la description du cabinet du roi* appeared in forty-four volumes over the period 1749 to 1804. In the nineteenth century there were numerous editions of the *Oeuvres complètes de Buffon* issued in from twelve to forty volumes in the years 1817–18, 1819–22, 1828–9, 1826–36. Editions continued to be published throughout the century.

In La Bruyère's introduction to his translation of Theophrastus' *Characters*, often published together with his own *Moeurs de ce siècle*, he contrasts the simplicity of life in Theophrastus' Athens (when eminent men could be met going into shops to buy their own groceries) with the artificiality and stratification of his own time. Although vices are constants of human nature, the descriptions of their manifestations have to be updated – this is La Bruyère's rationale for his own work.

Theophrastus was a pupil of Aristotle and his successor as head of the Peripatetic School, where his lectures were attended by as many as 2,000 pupils, including the comic dramatist Menander. Theophrastus was a natural historian and, in society, a famous mimic: 'At a regular hour Theophrastus used to appear in the Garden spruce and gay, and taking his seat proceed to his discourse, indulging as he went along in every pose and gesture imaginable.' (*Ibid.*, p. 39.)

Theophrastus' dedicatory letter to the *Characters* opens with a reference to the assumption that climate and upbringing affect character:

'I have often marvelled . . . that, albeit the whole of Greece lies in the same clime and all Greeks have a like upbringing, we have not the same constitution of character. . . . Therefore, Polycles, having observed human nature a long time (for I have . . . had converse with all sorts of dispositions and compared them with great diligence) I have thought it incumbent upon me to write in a book the manners of each several kind of men both good and bad . . . for I am persuaded, Polycles, that our sons will prove the better men if there be left them such memorials as will, if they imitate them, make them choose the friendship and converse of the better sort, in the hope they may be as good as they.'

Theophrastus' chapter headings are usually abstract nouns, of which 'complaisance', 'self-seeking affability' and 'opsimathy' ('late learning') are perhaps the least condemning. After an opening definition in Aristotelian style of the quality, each vignette moves quickly to an evocation of 'the complaisant man', 'the snob' – often with snatches of exemplary behaviour. For example, the Flatterer:

'Of all the guests will be the first to praise the wine; and will say in his patron's ear "You are eating nothing"; or picking up some of the food upon the table exclaims "How good this is, isn't it?" and will ask him whether he is not cold?, and will he not have his coat on? . . . and saying this, bend forward to whisper in his ear; and will speak to another with his eye on his friend. He will take the cushions from the lackey at the theatre and place them for him himself.' (*Ibid.*, p. 47.)

3 Stendhal, *Le Rouge et le noir, Oeuvres complètes*, Paris 1831.

4 *Démarche* means walk and bearing, but also procedure or way of proceeding, although 'bearing' is usually closest. Honoré de Balzac, *Théorie de la démarche, La Comédie humaine: études analytiques*, Paris 1968, Vol. 19, pp. 210–51.

5 Balzac affects to despair of finding the opposing qualities combined in one mind:

'It is necessary to be at the same time as

patient as were Muschenbrock and Spallanzani [microscopists, discoverers of micro-organisms] . . . then one must also possess that *coup d'oeil* which makes phenomena converge to a center, that logic which arranges them in columns, that perspicacity which sees and deduces, that slowness which serves to never discover one of the points of the circle without observing the others, and that promptitude which goes in one leap from the feet to the head.' (*Ibid.* pp. 226–7)

6 Buffon, 'Premier discours de la manière d'étudier et de traiter l'histoire naturelle', *op. cit., Oeuvres complètes*, Vol. I, Paris 1749.

7 *Ibid.*, p. 39; quoted by Michel Foucault, *The Order of Things*, New York 1970, p. 147.

8 J. C. Lavater, *Physiognomische Fragmente zur Beförderung der Menschenkenntniss und Menschenliebe*, Leipzig and Winterthur 1775–8.

9 The English edition, translated by T. Holcroft, *Essay on Physiognomy, for the Promotion of the Knowledge and the Love of Mankind*, first appeared in London in three volumes in 1789. There were numerous other editions in all three languages, in full and abridged, and it was also widely imitated and parodied. By 1810 there were fifty-five editions, and, by the 1840s, 156 publications. See John Graham, 'Lavater's Physiognomy: A Checklist', *Bibliographic Society of America*, Vol. 55, 1961, p. 297.

10 See Graham, 'Lavater's Physiognomy in England', *Journal of the History of Ideas*, Vol. 22, 1961, pp. 561–72.

11 Holcroft, *op. cit.*, Vol. I, p. 10.

12 Charles Le Brun was founder, director and principal theorist of the French Academy from 1663 until his death in 1690. He developed a comprehensive system for the expression of the passions in painting. First presented as a lecture in 1668, it was published as a small treatise in 1698, *Méthode pour apprendre à dessiner les passions proposée dans une conférence sur l'expression générale et particulière*. Le Brun's *Conférence*

sur l'expression des différents caractères des passions was reprinted in the Lavater edition of 1820.

Le Brun's treatises draw on Descartes' *Les Passions de l'âme* (1649), in which the body is described as a machine. The passions are a set of reflexes in response to external stimulation (as opposed to the emotions, which are 'excited in the soul by the soul itself'). These external causes are received by the pineal gland and transmitted to the extremities of the body, as facial expression and gesture. The manifestation of passion is due to the inhibiting or enhancing effect an emotion has on the blood stream. Desire, for example, 'agitates the heart more violently than any of the other passions and furnishes more spirits to the brain, which passing from thence into the muscles, render all the senses more acute, and all the parts more mobile.' (*Ibid.*, article 101.) Responses to external stimuli are not uniform. They vary with one's constitution, which depends on the humours: 'The envious have a leaden complexion, yellowish, black, like battered blood. The yellow bile which proceeds from the lower portion of the liver, and the black from the spleen expand from the heart by the arteries into all the veins, and the latter causes the blood in the veins to have less heat, and to flow more slowly than usual, which suffices to render the colour livid.'

He observed that certain physical signs are more accurate indices to character than others, because they depend less on nerves and muscles, over which we have some control. Thus, blushing or blanching, or the colour of one's hair, are considered to be more direct indications. See E. Gilson, *Etudes sur le rôle de la pensée médiévale dans la formulation du système cartésien*, Paris 1930, pp. 51–100.

Le Brun's rules and precepts became the basis of academic practice. Historical narrative, making extensive use of his classification of expressions, became central to the programme of the Academy. Le Brun's main source of examples was his near-contemporary Nicolas Poussin (1593/4–1665), whose work combined classical rhetoric and Renaissance depiction (classical sculpture, Raphael, Giulio Romano).

Le Brun combined Descartes' explanatory system with the Italian treatises for painters. He was not so much concerned with physiognomics, the study of the permanent characteristics, as with pathognomics, the temporary affections of the soul, that are manifested in the external changes of the body. His reliance on schemata rather than *ad hoc* observations of nature had a slightly earlier proponent in Giovanni Pietro Bellori, who in 1675 had published *Vite dei pittori, scultori e architetti*, where he argued that nature was an inadequate model because of its constant changes. The artist, he said, required pre-established formulas into which the natural phenomena could be fitted. (See E. H. Gombrich, *Art and Illusion*, New York 1961.)

In his section on physiognomy, Le Brun set out rules for inferring moral quality, perhaps drawing from pseudo-Aristotle, The valour or 'animal instinct' of man or animal is given by the direction of eyes and the eyebrows: an upward slope denoting a spiritual quality; a downward one, a base character. Courage is discernible from the shape of the nose: the courageous have aquiline noses, but if the whole nose is aquiline, it denotes a talker like a parrot, and if the bump is too low, a mere croaker like a crow.

This was Le Brun's closest approach to animal-human comparisons in the manner of Giacomo della Porta whose *De humana physiognomica* was translated into French in 1655 and 1665 and must have been known to Le Brun. Della Porta phrased the same example as a syllogism: 'All parrots are talkers, all men with such noses are like parrots, therefore all such men are talkers.'

Le Brun accepted Descartes' explanation of the causal effect of the pineal gland on the flow of the animal spirits. Unlike his Italian predecessors, he was principally concerned with facial expression for, if the passions are controlled from the pineal gland, close to the brain, then the face is the most precise calibration of the passions: 'Expression is that which reflects the movements of the heart and which makes visible the effects of the passions. Ordinarily, anything which causes a passion in the soul produces some action in the body.' (Le Brun, *op. cit.*, reprinted in Henry Jouin, *Charles Le Brun et les arts sous Louis XIV*, Paris 1889, p. 372.)

He described and illustrated principal passions and their manifestations in facial expressions as required in the depiction of historical or religious scenes: admiration, esteem, veneration, rapture, scorn, horror, terror, simple love, desire, hope, fear, jealousy, hatred, sorrow, physical pain, joy, laughter, weeping, anger, despair, rage and compassion.

'*Admiration* or wonder is a surprise which causes the soul to consider attentively objects which seem to it rare and extraordinary and this surprise is sometimes so powerful that it pushes the spirits towards the place whence the impression of the object is received and they are so much occupied in considering this impression that there are none to pass thence into the muscles; the body therefore becomes motionless as a statue. This excess of wonder leads to Astonishment and this astonishment may happen before we know whether the object is good for us or not. Thus it seems that the movements of the blood and spirits are caused by the simple passions.

'One notes that Wonder causes no alteration in the heart, nor in the blood, such as one finds in the other passions, the reason for which is, that having neither good nor evil as its object, but only knowledge of the things about which we are wondering, this passion has no concern with the heart or the blood, on which the whole welfare of the body depends.

'*Esteem*. The body will be a little more bowed, the shoulders very slightly raised, the arms bent and close to the body, the hands open and near together, the knees bent.

'*Rapture or Ecstasy*. The whole body is bent backward, arms raised, hands open, whole action manifesting a transport of joy.

'*Scorn or Aversion*. The body can be drawn back, the arm in a gesture of repulsing the object for which one feels Aversion; they can also draw back, with the legs and feet doing the same.'

These and a great many other gestures from Le Brun's repertoire became current in caricature as well as painting in the nineteenth century. Le Brun's was the primary systematic collection of expressive heads; his illustrations served as a pattern book for painters for the next hundred and fifty years and were incorporated into the work of Lavater.

For a translation and complete discussion, see Jennifer Montagu, 'Charles Le Brun's "Conférence sur l'expression générale et particulière"', University of London, doctoral dissertation, 1959. Dr Montagu traces Le Brun's influence through the early twentieth century.

Le Brun's *Conférence* was the basis for subsequent theories of expression in the eighteenth century such as C. H. Watelet, *L'Art de peinture, poème, avec des réflexions sur les différentes parties de la peinture*, Paris 1760.

There were other eighteenth-century interests in the codification of gesture and expression. In 1795 the Count de Caylus set up a contest in the French Academy for a drawing of the most expressive head – the 'Concours de la tête d'expression' – as a means of vivifying the tradition of Le Brun. Ironically, these student drawings were then circulated among provincial academies as new schemata.

The many nineteenth-century publications for painters on the study of expression were essentially reworkings of Le Brun: they include Paillot de Montabert's nine-volume *Théorie du geste dans l'art de la peinture* (1813); Humbert de Superville's *Essai sur les signes inconditionnels dans l'art* (1827–31); J. B. Delestre's *Etude des passions appliquées aux Beaux-Arts* (1833); Charles Blanc's *Grammaire des arts du dessin* (1867).

By the end of the nineteenth century 'Le Brun's deducing expressions from a few assumptions as to the physiology of the human mechanism of the body was discredited and the way was open for more serious anatomical studies.' (Montagu, *op. cit.*, p. 215.)

13 'Each trait contains the whole character of man, as in the smallest works of God, the character of the deity is constant.' (Holcroft, *op. cit.*, Vol. II, p. 31.)

14 William Hogarth (1697–1763) took the painters' physiognomic schemata and precepts into the field of caricature and

urban comment. He did not contribute directly to the literature on physiognomy, but his *Analysis of Beauty* (1753) demonstrated his interest in the ways of capturing character, both naturalistic and exaggerated, as in his engraving *Characters and Caricatures*. He did not believe that copying from nature or from art led to a vivid grasp of character in painting. Rather, he proposed – unlike Le Brun's closed system of types – a language, a kind of generative grammar of character and expression which could yield an infinite variety of characters. His 'technical memory' provided an alternative to copying nature outright: mnemonic devices, formal means for recalling figures, emphasizing abstract shapes, such as the oval and serpentine line. He used line as shorthand: 'two or three lines at first is sufficient to show the intention of an attitude'. He described the force of habit and custom in action. . . . The peculiar movement of each person, as the gait in walking, [is] particularized in such lines as each part describes by the habits they have contracted.'

Hogarth was well informed of his predecessors' views. In his preface to *Analysis of Beauty* he quoted this passage from the neo-Platonist art theorist, Giovanni Paolo Lomazzo (1538–1600): 'for the greatest grace and life that a picture can have is that it expresses motion: which the painters call the spirit of a picture'. Hogarth was also familiar with and testified to the utility of Le Brun's work.

Commenting on the effect of pathognomy on physiognomy, Hogarth observed that common expressions, like frowning, 'in time bring those parts to a constant state of the appearance of ill-nature. . . . It is by the natural and unaffected movements of the muscles caused by the passions of the mind, that every man's character would in some measure be written in his face, by the time he arrives at 40 years of age, were it not for certain accidents which often, though not always, prevent it.' Hogarth, like Descartes, believed that 'the face is the index of the mind'.

Hogarth was interested in Dr James Parsons's (1705–70) studies of the changes in facial muscles and the play of features which determine expression. (See J.

Parsons, 'Human Physiognomy Explained', *Proceedings of the Royal Society*, presented in 1746, published in 1747.)

Another adumbration of Parsons's theories can be seen in the work of P. Camper (1722–89), a Dutch painter who developed Della Porta's analysis of facial angle into a quantitative theory. Camper's studies, *The Manner of Delineating the Different Passions* and *Dissertation sur les variétés naturelles qui caractérisent la physionomie des hommes des divers climats et des différents âges suivie de réflexion sur la beauté; particulièrement sur celle de la tête; avec une manière nouvelle de dessiner toute sorte des têtes avec la plus grande exactitude*, first conceived in 1768, were published in 1792; an English translation, *The Works of the Late Professor Camper*, was translated by T. Cogan, London 1794.

Though his work is barely cited in the nineteenth century, Camper's method prefigured Francis Galton's and Louis-Adolphe Bertillon's anthropometric measurements. Camper relates his statistical knowledge to reflections on beauty and offers 'a new manner for drawing all sorts of heads with the greatest exactitude'.

15 Holcroft, *op. cit.*, Vol. III, p. 207.

16 *Ibid.*, Vol. II, p. 60.

17 Lavater distinguished: *physiognomy* – the air of the face, the knowledge of the features and of their expression; *physiological physiognomy* – discovering in the proportions, etc. of the members, the expression of the predominant character; *constitutional physiognomy* – quality of blood, warmth and coldness of the constitution, the grossness or delicacy of the organs, the moisture, dryness, flexibility, irritability of man; *moral physiognomy* – disposition toward good or evil; *intellectual physiognomy* – faculties of human understanding as disclosed by confirmation of the visible parts, figure, complexion, movements, the whole exterior; *pathognomy* – interpretation of the passions.

Here are two examples of Lavater's descriptions and analysis:

'Signs of weakness: Disproportionate length of body; much flesh, little bone . . . hollow outlines of forehead . . . smallness of nose and chin; little nostrils; re-treating chin; long cylindrical neck; the walk very hasty or languid without firmness of step; the timid aspect, closing eyelids; open mouth; long teeth; jaw bone long, but bent toward the ear; whiteness of complexion; teeth inclined to be yellow or green; fair, long or tender hair; shrill voice.' (*Ibid.*, Vol. III, p. 78.)

'Certain individual parts of the human body: forehead shows the propensity, degree of power, thought, and sensibility of man. Weak eyebrows denote phlegm and debility.' (*Ibid.*, Vol. III, p. 182.)

The theory of humours and temperaments was one of the most ancient and fundamental methods of classifying human types. Beginning as an aspect of science and philosophy, it became part of the lore of practical knowledge.

The theory of humours had its origins in Galenic medicine and the idea of crasis which described and divided people according to elemental and climatic divisions: heat and cold, moistness and dryness. Melancholics are dry and cool; phlegmatics, warm and damp. The humours provided a framework of dispositions – at first physiognomic or physiological, when combined with the theory of temperaments, they became characterological: sanguines, sweet; cholerics, bitter.

Correspondences were also established between temperaments, seasons, and the ages of man. (See Klibansky, Saxl and Panofsky, *Saturn and Melancholy*, London 1964.) Children were viewed as sanguine; young men, choleric; middle-aged men, melancholic; and old men, phlegmatic.

The popularization of character traits according to humours and temperaments began in the fourteenth and fifteenth centuries in broadsheets, almanacs and popular pamphlets, and continued on through the nineteenth century. La Bruyère in the eighteenth century utilized the description of humoural types in his character portraits. In the nineteenth century reference to humours and temperaments was wide ranging. Kant gave an aesthetic and ethical interpretation to the tradition. At the other extreme, fashion magazines suggested diets according to one's temperament (*Ibid.*, p. 122). Lavater used the model of humours in descriptions of types, but during the course of the nineteenth century new theories and alternative groupings began to supplant that of the humours.

18 A Polish painter and director of the Berlin Academy, Daniel Chodowiecki, did most of the engravings for the Lavater editions.

19 There is some disagreement among scholars as to which edition Balzac owned. Théophile Gautier and Alfred de Vigny also referred to Lavater, as did Flaubert, particularly in *Bouvard et Pecuchet*, and in his *Dictionnaire des idées reçues*, testifying to the prevalence of these notions, rather than using them. Zola, in his theories of hereditary and psychological disposition in *Thérèse Raquin* and *Madeleine Pérat* used explicitly Lavaterian characterization. See M. F. Baldensperger, 'Les Théories de Lavater dans la littérature française', *Etudes d'histoire littéraire*, 2nd edn, Paris 1912, p. 77.

20 J. J. Engel in his *Les Idées sur le geste* (reprinted in Lavater, *L'Art de connaître . . .*, 1806 edn, Vol. 7, pp. 235–46) wrote:

'I call physiognomy an art resembling that of pantomime, because both are concerned with sensing the expression of the soul in the modification of the body, with this difference, the first directs its studies to fixed and permanent traits, from which one can study man in general and the other on the momentary movements of the body which indicates a particular situation of the soul.'

Also introduced by Moreau were discussions on the physiognomy of the sick and the insane, national physiognomic differences based on the research of Camper and Jean-Frédéric Blumenbach and remarks on the passions by Labranche.

21 L. J. Moreau de la Sarthe, 'Observations sur les signes physionomiques des professions', in Lavater, *op. cit.*, Vol. 6, pp. 222–47. (These quotations from pp. 222, 227, 242.)

22 *Ibid.*, p. 245.

23 Honoré de Balzac, *Physiologie du mariage*, Paris 1830 (written in 1825).

24 Balzac, *Une Ténébreuse Affaire*, cited in Baldensperger, *op. cit.*, p. 77.

25 Balzac frequently affixed animal equivalents or attributes to his characters as in *La Fille aux yeux d'or* (Girl with the Golden Eyes), p. 352:

'Never did an African physiognomy more graphically express grandeur in vengefulness, rapidity in suspicion, lightning speed in translating thought into action, the strength and child-like impetuosity of the Moor of Venice. His black eyes had the fixed stare of a bird of prey, and like those of a vulture, were framed in a bluish membrane devoid of lashes.'

26 See Louis Chevalier, *Labouring Classes and Dangerous Classes in Paris during the First Half of the Nineteenth Century*, London 1973. First published in Paris 1958.

27 *Ibid.*, p. 374.

28 *Loc. cit.*

29 *Ibid.*, p. 379. The depiction of street merchants hawking their wares has its source in the Cries of the City, a genre which began in the late fifteenth century in France and Italy and continued into the nineteenth century. Annibale Carracci developed the genre in the sixteenth century. The common Cries of London appear frequently in seventeenth- and eighteenth-century prints. Carle Vernet's *Cris de Paris* is perhaps the most distinguished nineteenth-century edition: a hundred coloured lithographs depict almanac and newspaper hawkers, the marionetteers and the bill-poster.

30 Balzac, *History of the Thirteen*, translated and introduced by Herbert J. Hunt, London 1978, pp. 317–18; first published as *Histoire des treize* (1831).

31 *Ibid.*, p. 32.

32 Balzac, *La Femme de trente ans*, cited in Baldensperger, *op. cit.*, p. 73.

33 Balzac, *Ferragus*, in Hunt, *op. cit.*, p. 112.

34 Balzac, *A Harlot High and Low*, translated by Rayner Heppenstall, London 1970, p. 19; first published as *Les Splendeurs et misères des courtisanes* (1839–47).

35 Balzac, *Ferragus*, in Hunt, *op. cit.*, p. 31.

36 *Ibid.*, p. 33.

37 Balzac, 'Girl with the Golden Eyes', *ibid.*, p. 310.

38 *Ibid.*, p. 317–18. Upward mobility from the working class was in fact exceptional. There were more failures than successes, as Chevalier, *op. cit.*, has pointed out.

39 Balzac, *op. cit.*, p. 319.

40 *Ibid.*, p. 320.

41 Quoted in Peter Brooks, 'The Text of the City', *Oppositions*, Vol. 8, 1977, pp. 7–11.

42 F. J. Gall, *Anatomie et physiologie du système nerveux*, Paris 1818. In *Physiologie du mariage*, Balzac referred to Gall's system as carrying out Lavater's notions more methodically, and Daumier caricatured phrenological interest in 'Le Cranioscope-Phrénologistocope', *Le Charivari*, 14 March 1836). The accompanying text describes phrenology as a kind of Parisian folly – seeking in external traits the non-existent internal ones. The writer comments that he does not mean to attack the whole system which is making incontestable progress in science, but cites that Lacenaire and Fieschi, notorious murderers, had the phrenological traits of honest men.

'Lacenaire et la phrénologie', published in *Gazette medicale* of 1836, gives a phrenological analysis of Lacenaire:

'We have had an opportunity of examining the heads of the two executed men, Lacenaire and Avril: Avril's face has no expression except stupid ferocity. It is a typical skull of a robber and murderer. The phrenologists will not fail to seize upon this circumstance; but the head of Lacenaire provides more evidence against them.

'In fact, Lacenaire, whose cold cruelty and impassivity among the most frightening circumstances has shocked the whole of France, is *phrenologically* a saintly man, with all the qualities of one who is good, gentle, religious, with a horror of injustice and robbery, and a thousand leagues from a murder. The organs of benevolence and especially of the knowledge of God are remarkably developed.'

Quoted (in the original French) in Charles Simond, *Paris, 1800–1900*, Paris 1900, Vol. 2, pp. 120–1.

In 1836 the art critic Théophile Thoré-Burger, later a leading proponent of Realism, edited the *Dictionnaire de phrénologie et de physionomonie à l'usage des artistes* (Paris 1836): 'These unusual forms (bumps) shocking to the eye are precisely the expression of moral and intellectual character.'

43 See Jacques le Thève, 'Balzac et la Phrénologie', *Aesculape*, 1951, pp. 55–62.

44 Quotations cited in Le Thève, *op. cit.*, from Balzac's *Ursule Mirouet* and *Grandissant*.

45 See Marthe Niess Moss, 'The Masks of Men and Women in Balzac's *La Comédie humaine*', *The French Review*, February 1977, Vol. 1, No. 3.

46 Balzac, *Théorie de la démarche, La Comédie humaine: études analytiques*, Paris 1968, Vol. 19, p. 228.

47 Balzac, *Grandeur et décadence de César Birotteau, L'Oeuvre complète*, Paris 1959, p. 36; first published Paris 1837.

48 Cited in P. Lacombe, *Bibliographie parisienne, tableaux de moeurs 1600–1880*, Paris 1887, p. 122.

49 Louis Huart, author of many physiologies and an editor at *Le Charivari*, also claimed to have originated the *Physiologies*. See Andrée Lhéritier, 'Les Physiologies', *Etudes de presse*, Vol. IX, No. 17, 1957, pp. 1–58.

50 Walter Benjamin, 'Paris, Capital of the Nineteenth Century', *op. cit.*

51 Claude Pichois, 'Le Succès des physiologies', *Etudes de presse*, Vol. 18, No. 17, 1957, pp. 13–56.

52 *Le Charivari*, 19 March 1837.

53 For a complete list, see Lacombe, *op. cit.*; and Lhéritier, *op. cit.*, Here are some titles of particular interest for our subject (the numbers refer to Lhéritier's listing, and all were published in Paris):

1826–40
1. Baron Jean-Louis Albert, *Physiologie des passions ou nouvelle doctrine des sentiments moraux*, 1826.
2. Anthelme Brillat-Savarin, *Physiologie du goût ou méditation de gastronomie transcendante*, 1826.
4. Balzac, *Physiologie du mariage*, 1830.
6. S. P. Peytel, *Physiologie de la poire*, 1832.
13. Hippolyte Auger, *Physiologie du théâtre*, 1839–40.

1841
25. Louis Huart, *Physiologie de l'étudiant*, ill. by Alophe, Trimolet and Maurisset, 1841.
30. Louis Huart, *Physiologie du flâneur*, ill. by Alophe, Daumier and Maurisset.
33. *Physiologie de l'homme de loi par un homme de plume*, ill. by Trimolet, Maurisset.
34. Maurice Alhoy, *Physiologie de la lorette*, ill. by Gavarni.
37. Louis Huart, *Physiologie du médecin*, ill. by Trimolet.
45. Balzac, *Physiologie de l'employé*, ill. by Trimolet.
48. Henry Emy, *Physiologie des quartiers de Paris*, ill. by Emy.
51. Léon d'Amboise, *Physiologie du parterre, types du spectateur*, ill. by Emy.
54. *Physiologie des physiologies*, ill. by Emy.
61. Emile de la Bedollière, *Les Industriels, métiers et professions de France*, ill. by Monnier.
74. Frédéric Soulie, *Physiologie du bas-bleu*, ill. by J. Vernier.
81. P. Bernard and L. Couailhac, *Physiologie du jardin des plantes et guide des promeneurs*, ill. by Emy.
83. *Physiologie de la presse, biographie des journalistes et des journaux de Paris et de la province*.
88. Henry Monnier, *Physiologie du bourgeois*, ill. by Monnier.

91. Louis Huart, *Physiologie de la grisette*, ill. by Gavarni.
95. Edouard Gouidon, *Physiologie de l'omnibus.*
96. Charles Marchal, *Physiologie du parisien en province*, ill. by Traviès, Daumier and Gavarni.
97. Taxile Delord, *Physiologie de la parisienne*, ill. by Menut-Alophe.

1842

107. Emmanuel Destouches, *Physiologie des barrières et des musiciens de Paris.*
129. Charles Philipon, *Physiologie du floueur*, ill. by Daumier, Lorentz, Vernier and Trimolet.
130. Paul Lacroix, *Physiologie des rues de Paris.*
136. James Rousseau, *Physiologie du Robert Macaire*, ill. by Daumier and Emy.

54 Among these omnibus volumes on popular types were the following (all published in Paris):

From P. Lacombe, *op. cit.* Other references, Jules Brivois, *Bibliographie des ouvrages illustrés du XIXe siècle*, Paris 1883.

Bibliothèque pour rire, Les Physiologies parisiennes, 1869.

J. K. Huysmans, *Croquis parisiens*, 1880.

Théodore de Banville, *Esquisses parisiennes. Scènes de la vie*, 1859.

Les Fous de Paris, types curieux de Paris, par un nain-sensé, 1842. Portraits and diverse types.

C. Paul de Kock, *La Grande Ville: nouveau tableau de Paris, comique, critique et philosophique*, ill. by Gavarni, Adam, Daumier, D'Aubigny and Emy. 2-volume in 8, 1842–3. 2nd volume texts by Balzac, Dumas, Soulié, Briffault, De Mirecourt, Ourliac, etc. Parisian types and institutions: Les Chemins de fer, Bains a domicile, Restaurants, Rotonde du Temple, Monographie de la presse parisienne, Boulevard du crime, Filles, Lorettes et Courtisanes.

Alfred Delvau, *Les Heures parisiennes*, 1866. Describes Paris hour by hour beginning at 3.00 a.m. and ending at 2.00 a.m.

Jules Janin, *L'Hiver et l'été à Paris*, ill. by Eugène Lami. 2 vols, 1846.

Louis Huart, *Muséum parisien.* Histoire physiologique, pittoresque, philosophique et grotesque de toutes les bêtes curieuses de Paris et de la banlieue, pour faire suite à toutes les éditions des oeuvres de M. de Buffon. 350 vignettes by Grandville, Gavarni, Daumier, Traviès, Lécurieur and Monnier, 1841.

Charles Monselet, *Le Musée secret de Paris*, 1859.

Nouveau tableau de Paris au XIXe siècle, 7 vols, 1834–5.

Frances Trollope, *Paris and the Parisians in 1935*, 2 vols, 1836.

Paris, ou le livre des cent-et-un, 1831–4, 15 volumes in 8, almost without illustrations. Chapters include: 'Le bourgeois de Paris', 'Le bibliomane', 'Les soirées d'artistes', 'La concierge', 'Les bibliothèques publiques', 'La morgue', 'Un voyage en omnibus', 'Charlatans jongleurs', 'Les musiciens', 'Les jeunes filles de Paris', 'Les petits métiers', 'Le juste milieu et la popularité', 'Les fêtes publiques de Paris', 'L'ouvreuse de loges', 'La manie des albums', 'Le flâneur de Paris par un flâneur', 'Le costume parisien', 'Le gamin de Paris', 'Les théâtres de société', 'Une scène de magnétisme', 'L'écrivain public', 'Les médecins de Paris', 'Les petits théâtres du boulevard'.

Léo Lespès, *Paris dans un fauteuil. Types, histoires et physionomies*, 1855.

A. Privat d'Anglemont, *Paris inconnu*, 1861.

Les Petits Paris par les auteurs de 'Mémoires de Bilboquet', 25 vols, 1854–5.

A. de Belloy, *Physionomies contemporaines*, 1859.

Physionomies parisiennes, 11 vols, 1867–8.

Le Prisme, encyclopédie morale du XIXe siècle, 1841. 24 brief vignettes on Parisian types with small engravings in the text.

Le Tableau de Paris, Histoire, description, physiologie, 1876.

Le Tiroir du diable, Paris et les Parisiens, Moeurs et costumes, caractères et portraits des habitants de Paris, tableau complet de leur vie privée, publique, politique, artistique, littéraire, industrielle, etc. by Balzac, Sue, Sand, Karr, Monnier, Stendhal, Janin, De Musset, Nodier and others. Ill. by Gavarni and Bertall. Reprint of 2nd volume of *Diable à Paris*, Paris, n.d.

Maxime Rude, *Tout Paris au café*, 1877.

55 L. Curmer, *Les Français peints par eux-mêmes*, 'Encyclopédie morale du dix-neuvième siècle', 1840–2, 8 vols; first 4 vols on Parisian types, the rest on the provinces.

56 Quoted from the English edition of the above, *Pictures of the French*, London 1840, p. xiv.

57 *Ibid.*, p. xvi.

58 *Le Diable à Paris, Paris et les parisiens*, ed. Jules Hetzel, 2 vols, Paris 1845–6, p. 82.

59 Texier drew attention to the distinction between public and private:

'As far as Paris shows itself, the painter has striven to reproduce the city's image – he has painted its everyday physiognomy and its physiognomy for special occasions . . . but the observer may stroll the streets as long as he will . . . Paris decorously maintains its privacy; it will not allow the intimate events of its life to be seen – at most, they can be guessed at . . . in order to get at the particular physiognomy of Paris in the flesh, the bone, and the intelligence, we need to describe private life.'

60 Conversely, in the mid-1860s and 1870s, in the work of Claude Monet (his *Boulevard des Capucines* was painted from Nadar's studio in 1873) and of Gustave Caillebotte, the local view of the city street from a window or balcony comes into prominence: the sensibility of the urban observer re-establishes itself in partial views.

Chapter two

1 Théophile Gautier, *Histoire de l'art dramatique en France depuis vingt-cinq ans*, Paris 1858–9, Vol. V, p. 23.

2 *Commedia dell'arte* troupes had visited Paris since 1570, and from 1600 on they were popular at the Italianate court of Henri IV and Maria de Medici. The Théâtre des Italiens became a permanent institution, and began to introduce French dialogue, although its virtuosity in panto-mime had made it popular even with those who could not follow the Italian. Expelled from France in 1679 because their play *La Fausse prude* was taken as a satire on Madame de Maintenon, Louis XIV's second wife, the actors returned in 1716 after the king's death. They grew steadily more established – competitive with the Comédie Française. Their reportory now included new French plays, most notably those of Pierre Marivaux, and a range of productions that went beyond the *commedia* tradition: ballet-pantomimes and vaudeville. In 1803 they became the Opéra Comique. Meantime, the stock characters and improvisational tradition of the *commedia* survived among the mime and acrobatic troupes of the fair grounds.

3 Charles Baudelaire, 'Some French Caricaturists', 1857, *Selected Writings on Art and Artists*, translated with an introduction by P. E. Charvet, London 1972, p. 230.

4 For further information on audiences see Albert Monnier, 'Excursions dans les petits théâtres, Les Funambules, étude de moeurs', *Le Journal pour rire*, 19 May 1855. The audience could take out a monthly subscription to the Funambules. In 1850, tickets ranged in price from 1.50 to 0.32 sous in the orchestra, loges and balcony; 0.40 sous in the second gallery, and 0.15 sous in the third gallery. The theatre was called the 'theatre of four sous' – the price for the *paradis* in the 1830s. A typical working salary in 1830 was 2 francs a day (20 sous = 1 franc). A loaf of bread cost 17 sous in 1829, and 13 sous in 1832. A newspaper cost 11–22 sous by 1839. Figures cited in Albert George, *The Development of French Romanticism*, Syracuse University Press 1950, pp. 50–62.

5 For a history of the Boulevard du Temple, see Georges d'Heylii, *Théâtre du Boulevard du Temple*, 2 vols, Paris 1881.

6 Legislation of 1806 regarding the theatres was reprinted in M. L. Veron, *Les Théâtres de Paris*, Paris 1860. Liberty of the theatre was established in 1791, and there were forty-five live theatres in Paris: by 1806 there were only eight speaking theatres. Liberty of genre and speech in theatre was restored only in 1864.

7 For the most complete history of the Funambules, see Louis Péricaud, *Le Théâtre des Funambules, ses mimes, ses acteurs, et ses pantomimes*, Paris 1897. Most of the performers at the Funambules came from artisan families and maintained trades and métiers for additional income. Deburau was an upholsterer, locksmith, wood-worker and clock-maker; Cassandre, a cardboard-maker, and Léandre, a wine-seller. In addition, Deburau was propman for the Funambules, building and repairing the props for the plays. He was paid like an artisan and treated worse. His contracts of 1826, 1828 and 1831 stipulated 35 francs a week (about four times what the musicians earned and less than one-third what Daumier made as a beginner), plus 10 francs for the care of the props. He performed six times daily; and nine times on Sundays. He was not allowed to travel, perform in other theatres or miss a performance. There was no sick pay, and there was a penalty for mistakes in performance. In the mid 1830s, his salary was raised to 200 francs a month and, in 1835, to 240–50 francs a month on a ten-year contract.

8 Jules Janin, *Deburau: histoire du théâtre à quatre-sous*, 2 vols, Paris 1832, p. 75.

9 Gautier, *op. cit.*, Vol. V, p. 23.

10 See Champfleury, *Souvenirs et portraits de jeunesse*, Paris 1872, pp. 64–5.

11 George Sand, *Questions d'art et de littérature*, Paris 1878, Ch. XV, p. 217.

12 For further discussion on Bouquet, see Champfleury, *Auguste Bouquet, le peintre ordinaire de Gaspard Deburau*, Paris 1889. No date is given for Vautier's print, nor for the start of Deburau's use of naturalistic costume.

13 Edmond Texier, *Tableau de Paris*, Paris 1852–3:

'Without grand gestures, without contortions, without apparent effects, but by the sole play of his pale physiognomy, so fine and animate; he knows how to render all the impressions, sentiments, nuances, and to have a perfect communication with his audience . . . With what enthusiasm and penetration of the least intention on his whitened face, so intelligently mobile. . . . In this mass of nameless pieces, he brings the life of art, he assimilated various types and imposes on the fantasy of his librettists, being always himself, loyal to his exceptional form, to the unity of his nature. . . . He brings to all his characters a rare verity.

'This Pierrot who gives and receives kicks in his Funambulesque life, who delivers punches, trips and somersaults is nearly incalculable. But in his long battle which forms all his repertory, with what inimitable grace he receives these blows, what marvellous agility, what aplomb in the gaucherie, and with what exquisite tact he tempers, by the half-tones of the game and the finesse of the smile, a gross piquancy and obscenity suited to the place. . . . What superb mobility of the mask, what variety of expression in his apparent monotony. This man has seen all, felt all, understood all his sphere. He knows his populace by heart, he possesses all the métiers, he plays by turns, a coal man, ragman, grocer, clothes merchant, water carrier, cobbler, as if he had only done each thing all his life.'

14 George Sand, *op. cit.*, p. 219.

15 Paul de Saint-Victor, 'Mort d'un artiste et son art', July 1846, in Funambules file, Bibliothèque de l'Arsenal, Paris, Rondell Collection.

16 See Champfleury, *Souvenirs . . .*, Ch. XII.

17 Emile Bouvier, *La Bataille réaliste*, Paris 1913. Bouvier's account, based mainly on Champfleury's *Souvenirs des Funambules* (Paris 1859) and Péricaud, *op. cit.*, helps to relate Pierrot-Deburau and his Romantic and Realist admirers.
The scenarios for the Funambules are

published in Péricaud, *op. cit.*; Emile Goby, *Pantomime de Gaspard et Charles Deburau* (preface by Champfleury), Paris 1889; Champfleury, *op. cit.*; D'Heylli, *op. cit.*; Albert Monnier, *Biographie de Deburau*, Paris 1859.

18 Péricaud, *op. cit.*, pp. 11–12.

19 From Champfleury, *op. cit.*, p. 85:

'Ah! if I had ten actors as intelligent as Paul, Deburau, de Rudder, Laplace and the Colombine Ismène, I would read them a piece in the form of a story, and turn them loose on the stage.... But with lesser talents, every character, every entry, every exit, every trick has to be described as if with a pair of compasses ...

'Another system uses *words* in pantomime. A bad expedient which makes me tremble when I have to use it. Mimes should be made to speak as little as possible. You should see the effect on the spectators of the spoken word following after a mimed scene.... The spoken word is chilling, it breaks up the agreeable harmony of mime language.'

20 George Sand, *op. cit.*, p. 220, described the audience demanding complete silence in the theatre for fear they would lose a word of Pierrot.

21 Péricaud, *op. cit.*, p. 309.

22 Péricaud, *op. cit.*, pp. 69–73, summarized the plot of *Le Boeuf enragé*:

1. Boissec has a marriage contract with Columbine. Love and the three sorcerers vow to get it from him. Arlequin too seeks Colombine's hand. Love transforms the miserable Boissec, with the help of a splendid costume.

2. Boissec challenges Arlequin to a duel and hires Pierrot to fight for him. Arlequin plays dead, and Boissec and Pierrot run off. Arlequin runs off with Colombine.

3. The lovers hide in a porcelain factory. Pierrot thinks that he has found Arlequin and attacks, but instead the 'object' is a box of porcelain.

4. In order to hide his love in a crowd, Arlequin goes to the Funambules, but Pierrot, who is a frequent attendant there, wants to denounce Arlequin to Cassandre. Arlequin threatens Pierrot, and after a fight, Pierrot is barred entrance and is arrested.

5. 'A Striking Sign.' Arlequin and Colombine stop at an inn, The Golden Mallet, where they dine on some fish, Pierrot steals food and wine. When he enters the inn, Pierrot is hit on the head by the sign as is Cassandre and Boissec.

6. Pierrot enters a laundry and all the laundry disappears. Pierrot is accused of theft. Arlequin has the power to bring the laundry back.

7. Pierrot is exonerated and, aided by his friends, he encircles Arlequin whose legs are so elastic that he jumps out to his escape.

8. The pursuers are thirsty. They enter a wine shop which becomes a pharmacy. The wine they drink gives them a stomach ache and they swallow some pills which cause an explosion of diarrhoea.

9. 'Le boeuf enragé.' A fat bull resisting slaughter runs loose, breaking up Cassandre's porcelain shop and ensnaring Pierrot on its horns.

10. 'Will Pierrot die?' Arlequin perceives that the contract can now be seized and burnt, the wedding up in smoke.

11. Boissec doesn't believe that his contract is null and void and goes to get his wedding clothes. Pierrot takes advantage of his absence and dresses up like a dandy of the Boulevard de Gand.

12. Love and the three sorcerers feel that enough confusion has occurred and decide to be helpful. They order Cassandre to unite Arlequin and Colombine and throw Boissec out. Arlequin is satisfied. Escorted by Pierrot, Cassandre conducts Arlequin and Colombine to the temple of Marriage.

23 Théodore de Banville, 'Les Anciens Funambules au Boulevard du Temple', *Le Journal pour tous*, January 1892; *Gil Blas*, 12 March 1892; see also *Mes souvenirs*, Paris 1882.

24 *Pierrot en Afrique* is summarized by Péricaud, *op. cit.*, pp. 247–51:

Plot: 1. Two Arabs enter with a wounded colleague and announce to Zelmire that her father has been captured. Pierrot is caught. The Arabs want to decapitate him but Zelmire stops them. A comic scene ensues between Pierrot and the Arabs. The Arabs announce that the French are coming and hide underground. Ali guards Pierrot, Zelmire stays with them. The French enter and recognize Pierrot. An exchange is set up between Zelmire's father and Pierrot. The French officer falls in love with Zelmire. Pierrot captures Ali and during a melee, Ali escapes and Pierrot pursues him.

2. The Bey is seen with his odalisques. Mohammed, Zelmire's suitor asks her where her bracelet is. Scene of jealousy. The French are announced, a fight ensues. Comic scene with Pierrot and a bedouin. The Arabs are disarmed. Everyone disbands.

3. Mohammed asks Hassan for his daughter Zelmire's hand in marriage. She says she's in love with the French officer, Léon. Mohammed vows revenge. Pierrot, disguised as a sultan, enters on a giraffe. A feast is held in his honour. Then comes a love scene between Zelmire and Léon. Mohammed tries to kill Léon but is vanquished. At Mohammed's call, the Arabs join to help him. Léon is almost dead, when Pierrot comes to the rescue. There is another fight and the Arabs flee.

4. Bedouins are lying around. Upon hearing of the Bey's arrival, they get up. The French are announced. Mohammed hides his troops. Léon enters, is attacked, tied up, about to be shot. Pierrot arrives with the French. There is a big fight and the bedouins flee. Léon and Zelmire are united.

25 Cham's illustrated parody of the pantomime represents:

1. The orchestra of the Funambules.

2. The French army march toward the Palace of the Bey.

3. Arabs coming to help the sultan. Pierrot takes out his knife but it is broken. He grabs the broomstick of the janitor of the palace with which he attacks the Arabs and rejoins the French army.

4. Pierrot is installed as a new sultan with his African servants chosen from the Faubourg St Antoine. Pierrot is seen with pipe and pillows.

5. Wanting to keep his subjects in good humour, Pierrot learns the can-can which is known in French Africa. The French and the Arabs join and the can-can is performed by Deburau with all the chic of the famous Alex Chicard of Paris.

26 Champfleury, *op. cit.*, p. 87.

27 *Ibid.*, p. 86.

28 *La Pandore*, 19 July 1828.

29 Janin, *op. cit.*, p. 75.

30 See Richard Holmes, 'Poor Pierrot', *The Times*, Saturday Review, 10 January 1976.

31 Baudelaire, 'Of the Essence of Laughter', *op. cit.*, p. 156.

32 Champfleury, *op. cit.*, p. 63.

33 For summary and analysis of *Pierrot marquis*, see Edouard Thierry and Gautier's articles reprinted in Champfleury, *op. cit.*, pp. 87–103.

34 In all, the Deburau brothers played some 79 roles. See Monnier, *op. cit.*:

Les 3 Planètes, Madame Polichinelle, Pierrot ministre, Arlequin Phoebus, Pierrot savatier, La Reine des carottes, Pierrot le possédé, Amour et contrariété, Les Filles à Cassandre, La Chasse au succès, Les Naufrageurs de la Bretagne, La Vie militaire de Pierrot, Les 3 Nigardinos, Les 2 Pierrots, Pierrot et Les noirs, Les 2 blancs, Sebastiano le bandit, Polichinelle vampire, Les 3 Pierrots, Pierrot maçon, Les 2 Cuisiniers, Les Pêcheurs napolitains, Les Amours de Pierrot, Les Prétendus, Les Mille et une tribulations, Pierrot et les bandits, Espagnols, Les Circassiens, Bamboches et taloches, Les Joujoux de bric-à-brac, Pierrot sorcier, Pierrot chez les maures, Les 2 Arlequins, Le Mousquetaire et le bandit, Pierrot et Polichinelle, L'Etoile de Pierrot, La Queue de lapin, Pierrot à 2 Faces.

Among Baptiste's roles that Charles recreated: *Le Tonnelier et le somnambule, Pierrot marquis, Pierrot pendu, Une Vie de*

189

Polichinelle, Pierrot pacha, Pierrot récompensé, Pierrot marié, Les Bohémiens, Pierrot en Espagne, Pierrot réactionnaire, La Cruche cassée, La Bataille d'Isly, Les Noces de Pierrot, Le Corsaire algérian, Pierrot valet de la mort, L'Oeuf rouge et l'oeuf blanc, Amour et désespoir, La Chaumière des Cévennes, Colette ou la fête au village, Pas de plaisir sans peine, Les 26 infortunes de Pierrot, Noir et blanc, Les Dupes, Les Epreuves, Pierrot partout, Satan ermite, Pierrot et l'aveugle, Pierrot en Afrique, Le Boeuf enragé, Les Jolis Soldats, Pierre le rouge, Le Songe d'or, Le Billet de 1,000 francs, La Veuve du soldat, L'Enfant révélateur, Richard coeur-de-lion, Fra-Diavolo.

35 The series of photographs is not extant. A few of the photographs can be found in the folders on Deburau at the Bibliothèque de l'Arsenal and the Musée Carnavalet, and in the Adrien Tournachon file at the Bibliothèque Nationale, Paris, Cabinet des Estampes. See André Jammes, 'Duchenne de Boulogne, la grimace provoqué et Nadar', *Gazette des Beaux-Arts*, December 1978, pp. 215–20.

36 Baudelaire, 'Of the Essence of Laughter', *op. cit.*, p. 155.

37 Gautier, *op. cit.*, Vol. V, p. 23. Pierre le Grand, Charles Deburau's contemporary and competitor, merely broadened the type further. He was a stock figure who wore a comical hat that detracted from the face. Le Grand was successful in England where broad clowning was still associated with pantomime.

38 See Francis Haskell, 'The Sad Clown: Some Notes on a 19th-Century Myth', in *French 19th Century Painting and Literature*, ed. Ulrich Finke, Manchester University Press 1972, pp. 2–17. And Paula Hays Harper, 'Daumier's Clowns: Les Saltimbanques et les Parades. New Biographical and Political Functions for a Nineteenth Century Myth'. Stanford University doctoral dissertation, 1976.

39 *Vieux Saltimbanque* La misère absolue, la misère affublée, pour comble d'horreur, de haillons comiques, où la nécessité bien plus que l'art avait introduit le contraste', *Oeuvres complètes*, ed. Pléiade, Paris 1966, p. 295.

40 K. E. Maison, *Honoré Daumier, Catalogue Raisonné of Paintings, Watercolors and Drawings*, New York and London 1967: I, p. 144.

41 Maison, *op. cit.*, and Haskell, *op. cit.*, both maintain that the drawing is of Charles Deburau.

42 Since the seventeenth century writers and the upper class had been interested in the puppet theatre. In 1713 the Duchesse du Maine had set up a puppet theatre in her house; the Duchesse de Berry brought a puppet theatre to Versailles to entertain the aging Louis XIV. Voltaire was an enthusiast, admiring the puppets' dramatic simplification and anti-authoritarian manners.

43 J. W. von Goethe, *Wilhelm Meister*, Berlin 1957. First published 1795–6.

44 Heinrich von Kleist, 'Über das Marionettentheater', in *Kleine Schriften*, 1810. Reprinted in Herbert Pluegge, *Grazie und Anmut; ein biologischer Exkurs uber das Marionettentheater von Heinrich von Kleist*, Hamburg 1947.

45 Among the best known were the Guignolet, founded in 1818 at the Champs-Elysées; the Bobino, initiated in 1836 at the Place des Vosges; the Théâtre Babylas at the Luxembourg; the Théâtre Guignol at the Rue de Sèvres; the Polichinelle at Ranelagh; and the Guignol des Batignolles at the Place de l'Eglise. See John Grand-Carteret, *L'Histoire – la vie – les moeurs et la curiosité par l'image, le pamphlet et le document*, Vol. 5 (1830–1900), Paris 1928, pp. 305–41.

46 Maurice Sand, *Masques et bouffons*, Paris 1860.

47 Other puppets included Guignol, Pupurin, Combrillon, Isabelle della Spada, Capitaine Arbait, a policeman and a green monster.

48 They used real hair for the head and beard. In place of the glass eyes of dolls, they used nails, 'round and bulging like plums, that caught the light with each movement of the head and gave the

illusion of a glance'. In his marionnettes
Sand developed both chest and shoulders
that added to the range of poses, postures
and movements. Ernest Maindron, *Marionnettes et guignols*, Paris 1900, p. 274.

49 Quoted in Maindron, *op. cit.*, pp. 277–80.

50 The *vis motrix* (motor force) was Leonardo
da Vinci's concept of the animating force
of the source of movement.

51 In his essay 'Sur la physionomie', *La
Revue liberale*, II, 1867, pp. 499–523, and
in a series of articles on gesture in paintings at the Louvre, 'Promenades au
Louvre', *Gazette des beaux-arts*, 1878
Edmond Duranty, expressing his interest
in gesture and physiognomy, suggested an
updating of Lavater.

52 Cited in Marcel Crouzet, *Un Méconnu de
réalisme: Duranty*, Paris 1964, p. 152.
Champfleury epithet cited in J. Troubat,
*Un Coin de littérature sous le second empire;
Sainte-Beuve et Champfleury*, Paris 1908, p.
204, and F. de Moimandre, 'Un Molière
en miniature; Le Théâtre de marionnettes de Duranty', *La Revue*, July 1917,
pp. 71–82.

53 See M. Parturier, 'Les Marionnettes de
Duranty', *Bulletin du bibliophile*, No. 3,
1950, pp. 111–25.

54 Duranty did find support and encouragement from Nodier who had written about
puppet drama in his *Fantaisies d'un
dériseur sensé*, Paris 1853.

55 Parturier, *op. cit.*, pp. 119–22.

56 Duranty, *Théâtre des marionnettes*, Paris
1880. In the preface to his collected plays,
Duranty observed that society is like a
pyramid, with types like Pierrot and
Arlequin at the bottom, and lawyers and
commissionaires at the top, while the
devil, represented by Polichinelle, has the
final word. We see the confrontation of
innocent citizenry and corrupt institutions in *Les Plaideurs malgré eux*. The plot
is as follows:

'Two lawyers are complaining to each
other about their lack of business. They
devise a plot to hoodwink Pierrot and a

Mme Begriche into a legal case. Pierrot
and Mme Begriche are brought to trial.
Pierrot is accused of killing her bird.
Mme Begriche responds, "He has done
me a great service. The parakeet was only
a drunk." Nevertheless, the commissionaire condemns them both to hang. The
lawyer first demands his fee of Pierrot.
Pierrot assaults him and the lawyer com-
plains to the commissionaire, demanding damages as well as his fees. The
lawyer's line reads like a caption under a
Daumier caricature of lawyers:
'If you give me 20,000 francs we'll
appeal your case and I'll save you.'
Pierrot again attacks the lawyer. Pierrot
and Mme Begriche meet at the gallows
and claim their innocence to each other
and seek revenge. They attack the lawyers
with batons. The lawyers begin to accuse
each other; they come to blows and they
kill each other.

57 There was also Lemercier de Neuville, a
contemporary journalist turned puppeteer, who set up his Théâtre Erotikon in
1862–3 in the garden of the caricaturist
and photographer, Carjat, and went on
to perform in Salons. In these protected
settings, with their pre-selected audiences,
he found an enthusiastic following for his
puppets of Dumas, Rossini, Zola, Hugo
and Sarah Bernhardt. Among their productions were Monnier's *L'Etudiant et la
grisette*, Hugo's *Les Misérables*, Lemercier's
Les Fourberies de Monsieur Prudhomme and a
verse play by Champfleury. Berlioz played
the accompaniment, and Carjat drew the
faces of many of his puppets.
    He began with eight puppets, sculpted
by an actor, Demareu, with 12 costumes
and 36 décors. According to his prospectus, he inaugurated a 'spoken and acted
journal . . . a Parisian chronicle with its
heroes of the day, its celebrations of tomorrow, its reputations of the old'.
    There were direct political allusions in
Lemercier's productions, such as to Gam-
betta and Emile Olivier. Other contemporary artistic characters figured among
his marionettes. There was a Joseph
Prudhomme puppet, and one of Victor
Hugo, who said:

*'Bon appétit, good sirs! Have you a taste for
    poison?
Mantraps and daggers, thieves behind the arras,*

Bandits, or castellans, or courtesans?
Victor Hugo himself is at your service –
I who sang lately of the Emir's battles
And the veiled throats of sultans' ladies. . . .
Ah, mock me if you will! Your insults may
Spatter my shoes, but cannot touch my brow,
My brow so vast it constitutes a world!
I am the leader of my school, no schoolboy
following his teacher down that muddy road
Foul Classicism squats on. . . .'

Lemercier wrote and produced 106 plays between 1862 and 1891, but his theatre never extended beyond a small coterie and the impact of his contemporary characterizations of individuals never had the currency of the pantomime theatre or the caricaturists. See Lemercier de Neuville, *Histoire anecdotique des marionnettes modernes*, Paris 1892.

Chapter three

1 Charles Baudelaire, 'Some French Caricaturists', *Selected Writings on Art and Artists*, translated by P. E. Charvet, London 1972, p. 216.

2 This was one of four ordinances of repression. The other three were: the dissolution of the Chamber recently elected; restriction of the franchise to the wealthiest 25 per cent of the existing electorate; convocation of the electoral colleges to choose a new chamber. See Alfred Cobban, *A History of Modern France*, Vol. 2, 1799–1871, London 1961; Penguin edn 1973, p. 90.

3 In December 1831, the right of hereditary peers to sit in the assembly was suspended: the upper chamber was to consist instead of the nominees of the 'bourgeois king'. The propertied class, which still held the majority of seats, had successfully ousted the legitimist and clericalist regime and, on the other hand, prevented Republicans from acceding to power. The government of France was now 'a bureaucracy and plutocracy'. Louis-Philippe 'stood between France and a Republic'. (Cobban, *op. cit.*, pp. 97–8.)

4 After *Le Charivari* was well established, Charles Philipon founded and edited other publications in which caricature and illustration played a major role:

Musée Philipon; Journal pour rire which became *Journal amusant; Petit journal pour rire; Modes parisiennes: Toilettes de Paris; Musée français, revue des peintres*, which illustrated painting exhibited at the Salon; and *Revue pittoresque*, which illustrated popular contemporary novels. (He also published *Paris au daguerréotype* in 1840.

Other newspapers with caricatures and illustrations were the short-lived *Le Boulevard*, 1848–50, edited by the caricaturist and photographer Carjat, *Le Monde illustré, L'Illustration, L'Univers illustré* and *Le Journal illustré*.

Caricature newspapers and publications continued to proliferate between 1860 and 1890 but they are beyond the purview of our study. (See Philippe Robert-Jones, 'La Caricature française entre 1860–1890', Univ. Libre de Brussels, December 1958.)

5 Charles Baudelaire, 'The Painter of Modern Life', *op. cit.*, p. 394.

6 Henry James, *Daumier, the Caricaturist*, London 1954, p. 14.

7 Philibert Audebrand, *Petits Mémoires du XIXe siècle*, Paris 1892, p. 248.

8 Nadar, *Le Journal amusant* and *Le Charivari*, 2 February 1862.

9 'Le Dedans jugé par le dehors', excerpted in Audebrand, *op. cit.*, pp. 239–46. There appears to be no official publication of this essay and it is not clear whether Philipon actually distributed it among his staff and friends. I have found no other mention of the essay.

10 *Ibid.*, p. 242.

11 *Ibid.*, pp. 244–6. (See note on Theophrastus and La Bruyère, Chapter One, note 1.)

12 Champfleury, *Histoire de la caricature moderne*, Paris 1865, p. 272.

13 Baudelaire, 'Some French Caricaturists', *op. cit.*, p. 216.

14 *La Caricature*, 14 November 1831.

15 Sébastien-Benoît Peytel, *Physiologie de la poire*, Paris 1832, Ch. IV.

16 *Le Charivari*, 16 September 1835.

17 *Le Charivari*, 8 November 1835.

18 For a study of the Association Lithographique Mensuelle see Edwin de T. Bechtel, *Freedom of the Press – L'Association Mensuelle – Philipon Vs. Louis-Philippe*, New York 1952.

19 Lithography, invented by Aloys Senefelder, a Bavarian playwright, in 1798, was as widely used as engraving in Paris by 1819. This more immediate graphic process – the artist could draw directly on the lithography stone rather than giving his drawing to a professional engraver – allowed for greater speed of execution and publication.

Significant to the popularization of caricature was the increasing mechanization of the printing press, imported from England at the end of the 1820s, doubling the number of exemplars that could be produced hourly, and halving the cost. The newspaper industry expanded while reducing its costs. In 1833 there were twelve presses for producing newspapers on a large scale. The papers of Emile de Girardin, the nineteenth-century newspaper magnate, lowered their subscription rate in 1835 from 80 to 40 francs and circulation rose rapidly. (See Albert George, *The Development of French Romanticism*, Syracuse University Press 1955, pp. 19–20). Thus, the technology for mass literature and illustration existed by 1830.

Before 1830, newspapers had been essentially limited to a wealthy upperclass readership. In 1824 papers had been available by subscription at 80 francs a year, the equivalent of one-tenth of a worker's annual wages. A total of between 50,000 and 61,000 copies of French newspapers were sold daily in 1830. In the first three months of 1831 the readership rose to 77,500, and by the next month to 81,490. By 1832, the number of newspapers sold in France jumped by 50 per cent. And the figures continued to increase. Between the July Revolution and 1833, six million copies of newspapers, broadsheets and circulars were distributed by 1,500 hawkers (see Irene Collins, *The Government and the Newspaper Press in France, 1814–1881*, Oxford 1959, p. 80). The principal political dailies in Paris doubled circulation from 73,000 to 148,000 between 1836 and 1845. By 1858, 235,000 newspapers were sold daily in Paris (Bechtel, *op. cit.*).

But still newspapers reached a limited audience. In 1858 the Paris population measured approximately one and a half million. And only a small minority of the overall Parisian readership subscribed to the caricature newspapers. In 1846, while *Le Siècle*, a major liberal paper, sold 32,885 copies in daily sales and 21,500 outside the city, *Le Charivari* sold 2,740 copies daily in the city, and 1,705 subscriptions outside the city. (See *Histoire générale de la presse française*, II, Paris 1969, p. 146, published under the direction of C. Bellanger, J. Godechot, P. Ourial and F. Terrou.) Commercial literary success was measured on a lower scale then than now. In the first half of the nineteenth century, the sale of 2,500 copies of a popular novel of Hugo or Paul de Kock, was considered exceptionally high. (Theodore Zeldin, *France 1848–1945*, II, Oxford 1973, p. 368.)

The audience for caricature was also expanding. There was a constant growth of the number of caricatural publications, newspapers, journals, albums and series of prints. There was no systematic accounting of the papers' readership. Nor is there any 'scientific' way to measure their impact and influence. Still, we can glean from contemporary comments and illustrations at least a partial view of their constituency (Zeldin, *op. cit.*, II, p. 1126). *La Caricature* announced that it was edited 'by young people, addressed to young people'. Baudelaire described Daumier's readership as 'honest bourgeois, business man, youngster and fine lady'. Daumier depicted bourgeois men reading *Le Charivari*. People often read papers in cafés or public reading rooms. Founded during the Restoration, these *cabinets de lecture* reached their peak around 1844, when there were 215 of them. They subsequently dwindled as a result of the availability of pirated cheap editions published in Belgium. Most of the clientele in these public reading rooms were bourgeois and young people – the reading rooms were primarily located in bourgeois neighbourhoods. (See Claude Pichois, 'Les Cabinets de lecture à Paris, durant la première moitié du XIXe siècle', *Annales*, 1959, pp. 521–34.)

There is some evidence that the caricatures in *Le Charivari* reached a wider audience. An article on *Le Charivari* published in London in 1838 observed that in contrast to London, in Paris 'even very poor families have prints of all kinds . . . gay caricatures of Granville [sic], of Monnier – military pieces of Raffet, Charlet Vernet'. Presumably these were clipped from the newspapers. Crowds are described gathered outside the window of the Maison Aubert where the day's caricatures were posted. Daumier and others depicted such scenes as well.

Contributing to the audience for Republican caricatures was the growing number of people with some literacy and education. Between 1840 and 1870 the number of secondary school graduates doubled and this at a time when there was little suitable employment (Zeldin, *op. cit.*, II, p.126). These newly educated, unemployed and dissatisfied people flocked to the Republican party and were undoubtedly sympathetic to the views of the Republican newspapers and caricaturists, particularly Daumier.

However, illiteracy rates were still high. Despite the new education laws that had been passed in 1833, in 1866 35 per cent of the population of France could not read (Zeldin, *op. cit.*, II, pp. 542–3). Caricature, as seen in the papers in the café, may have been a means of getting a visual report and editorial on the day's political and social activities (as photojournalism and television provide in the twentieth century).

20 For a general illustrated history of prints and their public see Ralph Shikes, *The Indignant Eye; the artist as social critic* Boston 1969, and Hyatt Mayor, *Prints and People*, New York 1971.

21 L. L. Boilly, *Grimaces*, 92 lithographs 1823–8, reissued by the Maison Aubert in 1837 as *Groupes physionomiques connus sous le nom de grimaces par Boilly*. 200–300 exemplars of first edition, up to 1,000 on

a few. Also issued in more limited editions in London.

Some titles: *La Félicité parfaite, L'Enfance, Le Baume D'Acier, Les Cinq Sens, L'Adroit Barbier, Consultation de médecins, Les Petits Ramoneurs, Les Savoyards, Les Figurantes, Les Moustaches, Le Printemps, L'Eté, L'Automne, L'Hiver, La Punition, La Récompense, Les Sept Péchés Capitaux, La Gourmandise, L'Orgueil, La Paresse, La Luxure, L'Avarice, La Colère, L'Envie, Les Fumeurs et les Priseurs, La Bonne Aventure, Les Papillotes, Les Oreilles percées, Les Faux Toupets, Le Pouvoir de l'éloquence, Les Epoux assortis, Les Mangeurs d'huitres, Les Mangeurs de glaces, Les Mangeurs de raisins, Les Mangeurs de noix, La Dégustation, Les Aveugles, La Frayeur, Le Jour de barbe, Les Cornes, Les Journaux, Le Tireur des cartes, Le Petit Mendiant, Réjouissances publiques départ pour le distributions, Réjouissances publiques retour des distributions, Les Canons, Le Petit Jaloux, La Marchande de beignets, Le Portrait, Les Chantres, Le Magnétisme, La Vaccine, La Marchande d'eau-de-vie, Les Sangsues, Les Bossus, Nez ronds, Les Nez camards, Les Nez longs, Les Amateurs de café, La Malade, La Fête de la grand-mère, Osage, Peuplade sauvage de l'Amérique Septentrionale dans l'Etat du Missouri, Les Oranges, La Lecture du Roman, Les Ivrognes, La Lecture du testament, Le Concert, Les Antiquaires, Le Second Mois, Le Neuvième Mois, Les Amateurs de tableaux, La Famille Africaine, Les Gueux, La Mariée, La Rosière.*

22 Jean Wasserman, *Daumier Sculpture*, Cambridge 1969, pp. 69–72.

23 The censorship laws were published in *La Caricature*, 27 August 1835. See also Bechtel, *op. cit.*, pp. 39–40.

24 The assassination attempt was made by a Corsican, Fieschi, assisted by two members of the Leftist Society for the Rights of Man.

25 Quoted in Oliver Larkin, *Daumier, Man of his Time*, Boston 1966, p. 29.

26 See Irene Collins, *The Government and the Newspaper Press in France 1814–1881*, Oxford 1959, p. 85.

27 Georges Doutrepont, *Les Types populaires*

de la littérature française. Académie Royale de Belgique. Mémoires, Vol. 22, 1926, p. 5.

28 The dates indicate their primary period. See the entry on Mayeux, *Le Grand Dictionnaire du XIXe siècle*, Larousse, Paris 1874; and Félix Meurie, *Les Mayeux Essai iconographique et bibliographique, 1830–1850*, Paris n.d.

29 Champfleury, *Histoire de la caricature moderne*, Paris 1865, p. 205, citing A. Bazin, *L'Epoque sans nom, esquisses de Paris, 1830–1833*, Paris 1833.

30 Jules Janin, *Histoire de la littérature dramatique*, I, p. 95, observed: 'The prints, the songs on the passions, loves and angers of Mayeux one can't count. He gave his name to clothes, handkerchiefs, hats, stores, vaudevilles. One sports hats à la Mayeux.'

31 Champfleury, *op. cit.*, pp. 206–10, reports that a number of journals were published using Mayeux; for example, *Du nouveau . . . Attention, nom de d . . .! Mayeux*, 1830–2, a monthly journal. Aware of his popularity Mayeux published his collective work as a monument to himself. *Oeuvres de feu M. Mayeux, de son vivant chasseur de la garde nationale parisienne. Membre de sept académies, aspirant à l'ordre royal de la légion d'honneur, et l'un des braves des trois journées. Episode de l'histoire de France*, Paris 1832.

When he did not achieve the power he sought, he joined the cause of democracy, publishing *Mayeux à la société des droits de l'homme* (1833), where he uttered his famous adage: 'A chaque crime, élevons un poteau, nom de D.' (For every crime we shall raise a scaffold . . .'). Cited in Champfleury, *op. cit.*, p. 205, he memorialized the cholera epidemic in verse and prose: *La France, M. Mayeux et le choléra* (1833). Mayeux returned briefly with the 1848 Revolution; he published six issues, *Mayeux, journal politique*, and a reactionary brochure, *Voyage de M. Mayeux en Icarie, ses aventures curieuses dans le pays de M. Cabet*. In 1851 he made a final appearance: *Mayeux l'indépendant, homme politique, etc. appelant les hommes du jour par leur nom. Suivi d'une revue critique sur diverses positions de sa vie et quelques pages sur l'évènement du 2 décembre*, Paris 1851.

32 Champfleury, *op. cit.*, p. 205.

33 *Ibid.*, p. 205.

34 See Stanislav Osiakovski, 'The History of Robert Macaire and Daumier's Place in It', *The Burlington Magazine*, Vol. 100, no. 668, Nov. 1958, pp. 388–92.

35 *Ibid.*, p. 390.

36 Baudelaire, 'Some French Caricaturists', *op. cit.*, p. 222.

37 Cited in Osiakovski, *op. cit.*, pp. 389–90.

38 *Westminster Review*, Vol. 33, 1838.

39 Osiakovski, *op. cit.*, p. 389.

40 *Ibid.*, p. 389.

41 Théophile Gautier, *Histoire de l'art dramatique*, Vol. V, p. 260.

42 Gerard de Lairesse, *The Art of Painting in All Its Branches*, London 1838, pp. 18–19.

43 Lavater, *op. cit.*, Holcroft edn, Vol. 3, p. 212.

44 Politics had simmered down between 1836 and 1848; but in that year attacks on government corruption increased in the liberal papers which called on the people of Paris to take up the struggle. In February 1848 Paris revolted and, with the aid of the National Guard, toppled the monarchy. A split had occurred between the supporters of Louis-Philippe, the Bourbon monarchists, and the Republicans. Louis-Philippe abdicated; the new Republican government, which emerged from the meeting of the National Assembly, proclaimed universal male suffrage. The voting population increased from a quarter of a million to nine million, and laid the foundation for the subsequent Bonapartist dictatorship. Cobban, *op. cit.*, p. 319.

45 Workers were dismissed from factories and craftsmen were unemployed. There was little government assistance, credit or charity.

46 Ledru-Rollin, Minister of the Interior, who was responsible for the election of the Constituent Assembly, realized that if the vote was held, with universal suffrage, the

illiterate peasants were likely to follow the lead of the clergy and the landowners.

47 Louis-Napoleon had the Orleans family banished from France and encouraged a plebiscite in support of the revival of the empire.

48 Philippe Robert-Jones observed that Ratapoil's physiognomy is grafted onto the God Mars in Daumier lithographs of 1867 and 1869. See 'Etude de quelque types physionomiques dans l'oeuvre lithographique de Daumier', doctoral dissertation, Brussels 1949–50.

49 Gustave Geffroy, quoted in Jean Wasserman, *Daumier Sculpture*, Cambridge 1969, p. 161.

50 Jules Michelet (1798–1874), letter to Daumier, 30 March 1851. Published in *Daumier, raconté par lui-même et par ses amis*, Paris 1945, p. 87.

51 *Le Charivari*, 23 September 1835.

52 *Le Charivari*, 4 October 1835.

53 *Le Charivari*, 16 October 1835.

54 Holcroft edition of Lavater, *Essay on Physiognomy, for the Promotion of the Knowledge and the Love of Mankind*, 1789, Vol. 4, p. 380.

55 Traviès was born in Switzerland of working-class origins and came to Paris before the end of the 1820s. Little has been written about him apart from the brief sections in Baudelaire, *op. cit.*, in Grand-Carteret, *Les Moeurs et la caricature en France*, Paris 1888, and in Champfleury, *Histoire de la caricature moderne*, Paris 1865. Still less has been reproduced. Albums of his work are available at the Bibliothèque Nationale, Paris, Cabinet des Estampes.

56 Champfleury, *op. cit.*, p. 231.

57 Grandville was his grandparents' stage name. Grandville came to Paris in 1825 to study miniature painting after apprenticing to his father. For a major reproduction of his work see: *Grandville, Das gesamte Werk*, 2 vols, Munich 1969.

58 Quoted from English edition, *Public and Private Lives of Animals*, introduction by Edward Lucie-Smith, London 1977, p. 85.

59 Baudelaire, *op. cit.*, pp. 226–7.

60 *Public and Private Lives of Animals, op. cit.*, p. vii.

61 Edmond and Jules de Goncourt, *Gavarni, L'homme et l'oeuvre*, Paris 1879, p. 263.

62 For example, the following series: *L'Artiste*, 1838, *Les Actrices*, 1839, *L'Etudiants de Paris*, 1839–40, *Les Grisettes*, 1839, *La Vie de jeune homme*, 1840, *Les Débardeurs*, 1840–1, *Les Lorettes*, 1841–3.

63 The Goncourts report that the Republicans of 1848 thought Gavarni's work aristocratic and conservative, maintaining that he had a pernicious effect on the masses. He was dubbed 'a corrupter of the people'. Goncourt, *op. cit.*, p. 217.

64 *Ibid.*, p. 314.

65 *Ibid.*, p. 315.

66 *Ibid.*, p. 354.

67 See also Anne Coffin Hanson, 'Popular Imagery and the Work of Edouard Manet', in *French 19th Century Painting and Literature* (ed. Ulrich Finkel), Manchester 1972, pp. 133–63, and *Manet and the Modern Tradition*, New Haven 1980.

68 On the fascination with the rag-picker in the period, see Walter Benjamin, 'The Paris of the Second Empire in Baudelaire', *Charles Baudelaire: A Lyric Poet in the Era of High Capitalism*, London 1973, pp. 19–20.

Frédérick Lemaître, who played Macaire in *L'Auberge des adrets*, also acted in a social drama, *Le Chiffonnier* (The Ragpicker), in 1847 and was regarded as influencing the Revolution of 1848.

Cited in James H. Billington, *Fire in the Minds of Men*, New York, 1980, p. 237, where he quotes A. Zévaès 'Le mouvement social sous la restauration et sous la monarchie de juillet', *La Révolution de 1848*, 1936–7, p. 235.

69 Goncourt, *op. cit.*, p. 358.

Chapter Four

1 Baudelaire, 'The Painter of Modern Life', *Selected Writings on Art and Artists*, London 1972, p. 403.

2 Champfleury, *Histoire de la caricature moderne*, Paris 1863.

3 Monnier's successful début was attended by the literary and artistic élite – Delacroix, Gerard and Vernet among painters; Chateaubriand, Lamartine and Hugo among the writers. Dumas gave an account of the occasion, comparing Monnier's virtuoso realism with that of Lemaître in his portrayal of social types. See Alexandre Dumas, *Mes mémoires*, Vol. VIII, Paris 1869, pp. 173–4.

4 Champfleury, 'Henry Monnier', *Gazette des beaux-arts*, Vol. 15, April 1877, p. 368.

5 Alphonse Daudet, 'Henry Monnier', *Trente Ans de Paris*, Paris 1880, pp. 57–60.

6 For a comparison of Monnier and Flaubert see Edith Melcher, 'Flaubert and Henry Monnier: A Study of the *Bourgeois*', *Modern Language Notes*, Vol. 48, March 1933, pp. 156–62, and Melcher, *Life and Times of Henry Monnier*, ch. XII, Cambridge 1950.

7 Henry Monnier, *Les Mémoires de Monsieur Joseph Prudhomme*, Vol. II, Paris 1857, p. 215.

8 Théophile Gautier, 'Henry Monnier', *La Presse*, 20 February 1855, reprinted in his *Portraits contemporains*, Paris 1874, p. 35.

9 Gautier, article in *La Presse*, 8 July 1849; English translation cited in Melcher, *op. cit.*, p. 18.

10 This reflexiveness can be compared with that of Dostoevsky in *Notes from Underground*, an almost contemporary prototype of the anti-hero.

11 Gautier, *op. cit.*, p. 35.

12 *Ibid.*, pp. 35–6.

13 Emile de la Bedollière, *Les Industriels, métiers et professions en France*, Paris 1842.

This statement recalls Moreau de la Sarthe's gloss on Lavater (see p. 25).

14 Among the scenes, *La Femme du condamné* (The Wife of the Condemned) tells the story of a woman who visits her husband before his hanging. She shows little concern for his plight and fear, as she schemes to secure his watch and clothes before the end. Other scenes: *Un Agonisant* (At Death's Door), *L'Exécution*, *Les Misères cachées* (Hidden Miseries), *Une Nuit dans un bouge* (A Night in a Slum).

On the frontispiece by Félicien Rops, Prudhomme is shown shocked as he looks through a man-sized camera. The lens is uncapped by a skeleton with a jester's cap and a cloak bearing the inscription 'Gaité Parisien' – a modern variant of the *vanitas* motif. The camera bears the title: 'Basfonds de la Société par Joseph Prudhomme, Photographe à Paris.' Below is the figure of naked truth – a reprobate woman, with sagging breast and old shoes perched on a plinth marked 'vérité'. Above, the sun covers its eyes and around the central figures are eight vignettes illustrative of the text.

Rops (1838–98), an illustrator and caricaturist born in Brussels, lived several months a year in Paris during the 1860s and settled there in 1870. He depicted the diabolic aspect of the Second Empire in erotic drawings of the Parisians:

'I have the desire to depict the scenes and characters of the 19th century that I find so fascinating and curious. . . . Above all the love of brutal enjoyments, the preoccupation with money, the mean interests, have glued to the faces of our contemporaries a sinister mask where the instinct of perversity, as Poe says, can be read in capital letters. All this seems to me to be sufficiently amusing and should be stressed by the devoted artists who desire to establish the physiognomy of their times.'

Quoted in *The Graphic Work of Félicien Rops*, notes on the life of Rops by Lee Revens, New York 1975.

15 Gautier, *op. cit.*, p. 34.

16 Reported in Melcher, *op. cit.*, p. 112.

17 Quoted in Marcel Crouzet, *Un Méconnu du réalisme: Duranty*, Paris 1964, p. 439.

18 Such as *Six Quartiers de Paris*, 1828, *Scènes du jour*, 1829, *Boutiques de Paris*, 1829; *Galerie théâtrale*, 1829; *Récréations*, 1839–40; *Nos Contemporains*, 1845.

19 Jules Janin, 'Grandeur et décadence de Joseph Prudhomme', *Journal des débats*, 29 November 1852.

20 Quoted in Aristide Marie, *L'Art et la vie romantique: Henry Monnier*, Paris 1931, p. 66.

21 Baudelaire, 'Some French Caricaturists', *op. cit.*, p. 225.

22 *Loc. cit.*

23 Gautier, *op. cit.*, p. 36.

24 Marie, *op. cit.*, p. 78; reported in an obituary by Bertall of Monnier in *L'Illustration*, 6 January 1877.

Chapter five

1 Charles Baudelaire, 'Some French Caricaturists', *Selected Writings on Art and Artists*, London 1972, p. 219.

2 Cited in *Daumier. Raconté par lui-même et par ses amis*, Paris 1945, p. 16. Paul Valéry wrote:

'It has been said of his work that it reminds us of Michelangelo and Rembrandt; and nothing could be more apt.... A resemblance also to the most powerful writers, creators of types, is to be seen in a draftsman so swift and prolific ... who can endow capital sins, vices, madness, with their true anatomy, their essential attitudes and expressions. That is why the names of Dante, Cervantes and Balzac in turn come to mind.... I mean that what compels us to group these genuine "creators" together is a common urge, instinct, passion for employing the human image to serve a profound purpose, instilling it with a charge of life, quite other than any real living being can convey.'

P. Valéry, *Degas, Manet, Morisot*, translated by David Paul, New York 1960, pp. 155–6.)

3 See Jean Adhémar, *Honoré Daumier*, Paris 1954.

4 The loss of a significant role for artisans in mid-nineteenth century Paris, concomitant with the rise of the bourgeoisie, led to high levels of mental derangement among this class. See T. J. Clark, *The Absolute Bourgeois: Artists and Politics in France, 1848–1851*. London 1973.

5 Baudelaire, *op. cit.*, p. 215.

6 Dante's *La Divina commedia* was so called because he intended it to be popularly accessible and with a cheerful outcome. See *Oxford English Dictionary*; also Philippe Bertault, *Balzac and the Human Comedy*, New York 1963, for possible sources of the title.

7 Baudelaire, *op. cit.*, p. 222.

8 There was a Musée Dantan in the Passage des Panoramas, and Philipon sold lithographs based on the Dantan figurines.

9 See Maurice Gobin, *Daumier sculpteur*, Geneva 1952; and Jean Wasserman, *Daumier Sculpture*, Cambridge 1969.

10 Gobin, *op. cit.*, also refers to examples of the sculptor David d'Angers and his phrenologically informed heads. Both Daumier and Grandville satirized phrenology in a few lithographs.

11 Daumier depicted D'Argout frequently: D. 49, 50, 62, 91, 92, 101, 179, 194, 210, 218 – but most notably in *Les Masques de 1831*, D. 42, and *Le Ventre législatif*, D. 131.

12 Also see Clark, *op. cit.*, p. 105.

13 Theodore Zeldin, *France 1845–1945*, Oxford 1973, Vol. I, p. 23.

14 In *Les Français peints par eux-mêmes*, 1845–6, L. Roux observed:

'Since religious faith has become enfeebled in France, the physician and the lawyer have acquired a stronger influence over society. What false shame prevents us from revealing to the priest, we are forced by pain to avow to the physician or by interest to unveil to the lawyer. The physician is the necessary confidant of all mysteries, and of the most sacred affections; and the honour of families is protected by his professional discretion. The physician supersedes the confessor.... The semi-science of a doctor renders him a materialist. He believes only what he sees. This love of the real results in an idolatry of gold.'

15 See F. D. Klingender, 'Daumier and the Reconstruction of Paris', *Architectural Review*, July–December 1941, pp. 55–60.

16 It should be acknowledged that there were widely differing levels of commitment; throughout his working life he continues to fall back, now and again, on simple and undemanding caricatural schemes and techniques, for instance, the large-headed manikins, which are stereotypes almost without physiognomic interest or special social insight, but which seem to have remained popularly acceptable.

17 Baudelaire, *op. cit.*, p. 223.

18 Le Brun's schemata are discussed in Chapter One, footnote 12.

19 See also Otto Baur, *Bestiarium humanum*, München 1974.

20 Edmond Duranty, 'Daumier', *Gazette des Beaux-Arts*, Vol. 17, May 1878, pp. 433–4.

21 Daumier's attendance at the theatre is discussed by Jean Cherpin, *Daumier et le théâtre*, Aix-en-Provence 1978; his assertion that Daumier only began to attend the theatre regularly after 1851 is challenged by Paula H. Harper who introduces evidence for earlier attendance, *op. cit.*

22 Daumier participated in the Salons of 1849, 1850/1 and 1861, exhibiting a total of six works which did not receive much attention.

23 Quoted in Loys Delteil, *Le Peintre-Graveur illustré*, Paris, 10 Vols. 1925–30, Vol. 28, notes under D. 3255; English translation quoted from Oliver Larkin,

Daumier: Man of his Time, Boston 1966, p. 157.

24 Larkin, *op. cit.*, p. 157.

25 It is thought that most of Daumier's finished watercolours are from this period (1860–4). Daumier's friend Geoffroy-Dechaume saw a dozen watercolours when he visited him in 1862. See Larkin, *op. cit.*, p. 146.

26 *Le Charivari*, 18 December 1863. This announcement is puzzling, as Daumier produced only two caricatures weekly; and nothing was said about the paper's responsibility for his previous absence. In 1865 a new editor was appointed to *Le Charivari*, Pierre Veron, a loyal Republican and admirer of Daumier.

27 The stronger contours and simpler background in these caricatures were in part Daumier's accommodation to the 'Gillotype', a new technique of reproduction, used by *Le Journal amusant* and adopted by *Le Charivari* in 1870. From the original drawing, which could have been on lithographic stone or paper, an impression was transferred to a zinc plate which was then etched. This method allowed more prints to be pulled from one original (*Le Charivari*'s circulation had increased) and was cheaper; A. Hyatt Major, in *Prints and People*, New York 1971, pl. 665, characterized the result: 'The gillotype granulates the grays in a grit that disintegrates any drawing short of heroic.'

28 3582, 3595, 3610, 3631, 3649, 3660, 3684, 3717, 3760, 3768, 3772, 3887, 3893, 3927.

29 The jester appears in a few of Daumier's earliest lithographs, less explicitly as a caricaturist, but clearly in opposition to the Republic. See D. 142, 187, 188.

30 Flaubert, in his *Dictionnaire des idées reçues*, defines 'Artistes. Tous Farceurs'. And Diderot, in *Le Neveu de Rameau*, depicts the artist as a clown who keeps his patron amused. For further discussion of clowns and saltimbanques see Paula Harper, *op. cit.*; Francis Haskell, 'The Sad Clowns: Some Notes on a 19th Century Myth', *French Painting and Literature*, ed. Ulrich

Finke, Manchester, 1972; Jean Staro-binski, *Portrait de l'artiste en Saltimbanque*, Geneva, 1970; T. J. Clark, *The Absolute Bourgeois*, London, 1973.

31 Degas owned 1,800 of Daumier's prints, half his lithographic oeuvre, and learned many specific devices from him. See Theodore Reff, *Degas: The Artist's Mind*, New York 1976, p. 39, and his discussion on Daumier's influence on Degas, pp. 70–87.

32 Duranty, *La Nouvelle Peinture*, Paris 1876; English translation (up to the last paragraph) quoted from Linda Nochlin, *Impressionism and Post-Impressionism, 1874–1904, Sources and Documents*, Princeton, 1966, p. 5.

Daumier's insistence on direct observation is explicitly contrasted with all the received formularies of physiognomic expression – from Le Brun to Lavater. Duranty is clearly advocating direct observation as an alternative to these. In 'Sur la physionomie' (*Revue liberale*, t. II, 25 July 1867, pp. 499–523) Duranty examined critically and sceptically the theories of Gall and Lavater; he concedes that facial expression is more informative than utterance which is often dissimulating. He discusses the difficulties of observing people and reproaches Balzac for never having known how to make a physically specific portrait.

Duranty makes the distinction between transient and permanent characteristics, as Le Brun and Lavater had done: he speaks of 'feelings which pass' and 'those feelings which lodge in a person'. He further distinguishes between the 'clear impression' of our first sight of a person and the successive and contradictory judgments through which, if we are acquainted with someone over time, we arrive at a settled opinion. Duranty parallels this to the difference, in writing, between the immediate record of an impression and a detailed analysis.

He reaches a sceptical conclusion: 'The best advice to someone who wants to recognize a man, or men, is to have plenty of wits and sagacity for sorting out confusion, for words are untruthful, action is hypocritical, and physiognomy is deceptive.'

33 Champfleury, *Les Excentriques*, p. 10.

Epilogue

1 Charles Baudelaire, 'The Painter of Modern Life', *Selected Writings on Art and Artists*, London 1972, p. 400.

2 Victor Fournel, *Ce qu'on voit dans les rues de Paris*, Paris 1858, p. 263.

3 Baudelaire, 'Salon of 1859', *op. cit.*, p. 297.

4 'Modernity is the transient, the fleeting the contingent'; from Baudelaire, 'The Painter of Modern Life', *op. cit.*, p. 403.

5 *Ibid.*, p. 405.

6 *Ibid.*, p. 400.

7 See Baudelaire's poem 'A une passante', from *Fleurs du mal*. Perhaps the comparable moment in painting is the confrontational gaze of Manet's Olympia which forces the viewer to recognize his and the painter's position as voyeur. The balcony motif in Degas and Caillebotte also forces back the viewer's attention to the painter's viewpoint: the viewpoint becomes the subject of the painting.

8 Baudelaire, *op. cit.*, p. 400.

9 Baudelaire, 'Salon of 1859', *op. cit.*, p. 307. The chapter headed 'The Intellectual Physiognomy in Characterization' in Georg Lukács, *Writer and Critic and Other Essays*, New York 1970, draws the consequences of these two procedures in his contrast between 'description' and 'narrative', as exemplified by Zola and Tolstoy. Zola enumerates observed details, Tolstoy *uses* and *heightens* events so that they emerge from character and advance our understanding of it.

Selected bibliography

ADAM, Victor, *Cris de Paris et moeurs populaires*, Paris 1832.

ADHÉMAR, Jean 'Grandville le maudit', *Bizarre*, Paris 1953; *Honoré Daumier*, Paris 1954; 'Daumier et Boilly', *Arts et livres de Provence*, Marseilles 1955.

ALEXANDRE, Arsène, *Honoré Daumier*, Paris 1888; *L'Art du rire et de la caricature*, Paris 1892.

ANTAL, Frederick, *Hogarth and His Place in European Art*, London 1962.

ARAGO, Jacques, *Physiologie des foyers de tous les théâtres de Paris*, Paris 1841.

ARMINGEAT, Jacqueline, catalogue and notice, *Daumier: les gens du spectacle*, preface by Francois Périer, Paris 1973.

AUDEBRAND, Philibert, *Petits Mémoires du XIXème Siècle*, Paris 1892.

AUERBACH, Erich, *Mimesis*, Princeton, N.J. 1953.

BALDENSPERGER, Fernand, 'Les Théories de Lavater dans la littérature Française'; *Etudes d'histoire littéraire*, Paris 1910.

BALTRUSAITIS, Jurgis, *Aberrations. Légendes de formes*, Paris 1957.

BALZAC, Honoré de, *Petit Dictionnaire critique et anecdotique des enseignes de Paris*, Paris 1826; *Physiologie du rentier de Paris et de province*, ed. P. Martinon, Paris 1841; 'Théorie de la démarche', *Etudes analytiques*, Paris 1853.

BANVILLE, Théodore de, *Esquisses Parisiennes*, Paris 1859; *Mes Souvenirs*, Paris 1882; 'Les Anciens Funambules au boulevard du Temple', *Le Journal pour tous*, January 1892.

BARASCH, Moshe, 'Character and Physiognomy: Bocchi on Donatello's St George, A Renaissance Text on Expression in Art', *Journal of the History of Ideas*, 36: 413–30, July 1975; *Gestures of Despair*, New York 1978.

BATY, G. and Chavance, R., *Histoire des marionnettes*, Paris 1972.

BAUDELAIRE, Charles, *L'Oeuvre complète*, ed. Claude Pichois, Paris 1961; *L'Art romantique*, Paris 1968 edn; *Selected Writings on Art and Artists*, translated with an introduction by P. E. Charvet, London 1972.

BEAULIEU, Henri, *Les Théâtres du boulevards du crime (1752–1862)*, Paris 1905.

BECHTEL, Edwin de T., *Freedom of the Press – L'Association Mensuelle – Philipon vs. Louis-Philippe*, New York 1952.

BENJAMIN, W., *Charles Baudelaire: A Lyric Poet in the Era of High Capitalism*, translated from the German by Harry Zohn, London 1973.

BENOIST, Louis, *Physiologie de la poire*, Paris 1832.

BLANC, Charles, *Grandville*, Paris 1855; 'Grammaire des arts du dessin', *Gazette des beaux-arts*, Vol. 6, 1860, pp. 5–8, 321.

BOAS, George, 'Il faut être de son temps', *Journal of Aesthetics and Art Criticism*, Vol. I, 1941, pp. 52–65.

BOLL, Jules, *Histoire Pittoresque des passions, chez l'homme et chez la femme*, Paris 1846.

Le Boulevard, journal littéraire illustré, ed. Etienne Carjat, Paris 1862–3.

BOUVIER, Emile, *La Bataille réaliste*, Paris 1914.

BOUVY, Eugène, *Daumier, l'oeuvre gravé du maître*, 2 Vols, Paris 1933.

BRAZIER, Nicholas, *Chronique des petits théâtres de Paris*, Paris 1883.

BROOK, Peter, 'The Text of the City', *Oppositions*, Vol. 8, 1977, pp. 7–11; *The Melodramatic Imagination*, New Haven, Conn. 1977.

BURTY, Philippe, 'Traviès', *Gazette des beaux-arts*, September 1859, pp. 315–16.

CALVET, Jean, *Les Types universels dans la littérature française*, Paris 1928.

La Caricature, ed. Charles Philipon, 1830–5.

CHADE-FEUX, 'Le Salon caricatural de 1846 et les autres salons caricaturaux', *Gazette des beaux-arts*, March 1968.

CHAM (pseudonym of Amédée Noé), *Paris comique . . . revue amusante des caractères, moeurs, modes, folies, ridicules, bêtises, sottises*, Paris 1840.

CHAMPFLEURY (Jules-François-Félix-

Husson, called Fleury), *Les Excentriques*, Paris 1852; *Souvenirs des Funambules*, Paris 1859; *Histoire de la caricature moderne*, Paris 1865; *Souvenirs et portraits de jeunesse*, Paris 1872; 'Henry Monnier', *Gazette des beaux-arts*, Vol. 15, April 1877, pp. 363–81; *Catalogue de l'oeuvre lithographique et gravures de Daumier*, Paris 1878; *Henry Monnier – sa vie, son oeuvre*, Paris 1889; *Auguste Bouquet: le peintre ordinaire de Gaspard Deburau*, Paris 1889.

Le Charivari, ed. Charles Philipon *et al.*, 1832–72.

CHERPIN, Jean, *Daumier et le théâtre*, Aix-en-Provence 1978.

CHESNAIS, Jacques, *Histoire générale des marionnettes*, Paris 1947.

CHEVALIER, Louis, *La Formation de la population Parisienne au XIXème siècle*, Paris 1950; *Classes laborieuses et classes dangereuses à Paris pendant la première moitié du XIXème siècle*, Paris 1958.

CHRISTOUT, Marie-Franèoise, *Le Merveilleux et le théâtre du Silence*, The Hague 1965.

CLAPTON, G. T. 'Lavater, Gall and Baudelaire', *Revue de littérature comparée*, 13:59–298; 429–56; April, July 1933.

CLARÉTIE, Léo, *Histoire des théâtres de société*, Paris 1905.

CLARK, T.J., *The Absolute Bourgeois: Artists and Politics in France 1848–1851*, London and New York 1973; *The Image of the People: Gustave Courbet and the 1848 Revolution*, London and New York 1973.

COINDRE, Victor, *Théâtre des marionnettes*, Paris 1880.

COLLINS, Irene, *The Government and the Newspaper Press in France, 1814–81*, Oxford 1959.

COURSAGET, René, and Anne d'Evgny, *Au Temps de Baudelaire, Guys et Nadar*, Paris 1954.

CROUZET, Marcel, *Un Méconnu du réalisme: Duranty (1833–80)*, Paris 1964.

DARWIN, Charles, *The Expression of the Emotions in Man and Animals*, London 1872.

DAUDET, Alphonse, *Trente ans de Paris, à travers ma vie et mes livres*, Paris 1888.

Daumier, Arts et livres de Provence, No. 27.

1948 (*Bulletin Daumier*, No. 2).

DELTEIL, Loys, *Le Peintre-Graveur Illustré . . .*, Vols xx–xxix (Daumier), Paris 1925–30.

DELVAU, Alfred, *Histoire anecdotique des cafés et cabarets*, Paris 1862; *Les Lions du jour: physionomies parisiennes*, Paris 1867.

DESCARTES, René, *Les Passions de l'âme*, Paris 1649.

DESNOYERS, Fernand, *Le Théâtre de Polichinelle*, Paris 1861.
Le Diable à Paris, Paris 1845–6.

DIDEROT, Denis, 'De la pantomime', *Oeuvres de Diderot*, Vol. 7, Paris 1875, pp. 378–87.

DISDERI, Adolphe-Eugène, *L'Art de la Photographie*, Paris 1890.

DOUTREPONT, G., 'Les Types populaires de la littérature française', *Académie Scientifique Belgique*, No. 2, pp. 1–660, 1928.

Drouot. Catalogue des Tableaux, Aquarelles, Dessins, Bronzes, etc. à Henry Monnier, Paris 1875.

DUBECH, Lucien, *Histoire générale illustrée du théâtre*, Paris 1931; *Histoire de Paris*, Paris 1931.

DUCHARTE, P.L., *La Commedia dell'arte et ses enfants*, Paris 1955.

DUCHENNE DE BOULOGNE, G.B., *De l'électrisation localisée et de son application à la physiologie, à la pathologie, et à la thérapeutique*, Paris 1855; *Mécanisme de la physionomie humaine, ou analyse électro-physiologique de l'expression des passions, applicable à la pratique des arts plastiques*, Paris 1862; *Physiologie des mouvements, démontrée à l'aide de l'expérimentation électrique et de l'observation clinique, et applicable à l'étude des paralysies et des déformations*, Paris 1867.

DUMAS, Alexandre, *Oeuvres: mes mémoires*, Paris 1869, pp. 173–9.

DURANTY, Edouard, *Théâtre des Marionnettes au Jardin des Tuileries*, Paris 1863; 'Sur la physionomie', *La Revue Libérale*, II, 1867, pp. 499–523; *La Nouvelle Peinture*, Paris 1876; 'Promenades au Louvre: remarques sur le geste dans quelques tableaux', *Gazette des beaux-arts*, Series 2, Vol. 15, January 1877, pp. 15–37; February 1877, pp. 172–80; March 1877, pp. 281–9. 'Daumier', *Gazette des*

beaux-arts, May 1878, pp. 429–43;
June 1878, pp. 528–44.

EKMAN, Paul, ed., *Darwin and Facial
Expression, a Century of Research in
Review*, London 1973.

ENGEL, J.J., *Idées sur le geste et l'action
théâtrale*, Paris 1788.

ESCHOLIER, Raymond, *Daumier et son
monde*, Paris 1965.
Etudes de presse, Vol. IX, No. 17,
1957. Issue on the physiologies.
(Articles also listed alphabetically by
author.)

EUDEL, Paul, *Champfleury et la pantomime*,
Paris 1892.

FARWELL, Beatrice, ed., *The Cult of
Images. Baudelaire and the 19th Century
Media Explosion*, Santa Barbara 1977.

FESS, Gilbert M., *The Correspondence of
Physical and Material Factors with
Character in Balzac*, Philadelphia 1924.

FINKE, Ulrich, ed., *French 19th Century
Painting and Literature*, Manchester
1972.

FOCILLON, Henri, 'Honoré Daumier',
Gazette des beaux-arts, Vol. II, 1929,
pp. 74–106.

FOURNEL, Victor L., *Les Cris de Paris,
types et physionomies d'autrefois*, Paris
1887; *Ce qu'on voit dans les rues de Paris*,
Paris 1858.

Les Français peints par eux-mêmes, ed.
E. Curmer, 8 Vols, Paris 1840–2.

FREUND, Gisèle, *La Photographie en France
au XIXème siècle*, Paris 1936.

FRIED, Michael, 'Toward a Supreme
Fiction: Genre and Beholder in the
Art Criticism of Diderot and his
Contemporaries', *New Literary History*,
Vol. 6, Spring 1975, No. 3, pp.
543–85.

GARNIER, Charles, *Le Théâtre*, Paris 1871.

GAUTIER, Paul, *Le Rire et la caricature*,
Paris 1906.

GAUTIER, Théophile, 'Shakespeare aux
Funambules', *L'Art moderne*, Paris
1856; *Histoire de l'art dramatique en
France depuis vingt-cinq ans*, Bruxelles
1858–9; *Portraits contemporains*, Paris
1874.

GAVARNI, *Masques et visages*, Paris 1857.

GEORGE, Albert J., *The Development of
French Romanticism*, Syracuse, N.Y.
1955.

GOBIN, M., *Daumier, sculpteur*, Geneva
1952.

GOBY, M. Emile, ed., *Pantomimes de
Gaspard et Charles Deburau*, Paris 1889.

GOETHE, J.W., *Wilhelm Meister*, Berlin
1795–6; reissued Berlin 1957–60.

GOMBRICH, E.H., *Art and Illusion*, London
1959; 'On Physiognomic Perception',
Daedalus, Cambridge, Mass. 1960, pp.
228–41; 'Moment and Movement in
Art', *Journal of the Warburg and
Courtauld Institutes*, Vol. 27, 1964, pp.
293–306; 'Ritualized Gesture and
Expression in Art', *Philosophical
Transactions of the Royal Society of
London*, Series B, Biological Science,
No. 772, Vol. 251, London 1966, pp.
393–401; 'The Cartoonist's
Armoury', *South Atlantic Quarterly*,
1963, pp. 189–223; 'The Evidence of
Images', *Interpretation, Theory and
Practice*, Baltimore 1969, pp. 35–104;
'Action and Expression in Western
Art', *Non-Verbal Communication*,
R.A. Hinde, ed., Cambridge 1972;
'The Mask and the Face: The
Perception of Physiognomic Likeness
in Life and in Art', *Art, Perception and
Reality*, Baltimore 1972.

GOMBRICH, Ernst and Kris, E., 'The
Principles of Caricature', *British
Journal of Medical Psychology*, Vol. 17,
1938, pp. 319–42; *Caricature*,
Harmondsworth 1940.

GONCOURT, Edmond and Jules, *Gavarni,
l'homme et l'oeuvre (1822–96)*, Paris
1879.

GOUPIL, F., *Panorama des passions et leurs
manifestations, étude applicable aux
beaux-arts et à la littérature, à la peinture,
à la sculpture, à l'art dramatique, etcetera*,
Paris 1879.

GRAHAM, John, 'Lavater's Physiognomy:
A Checklist', *Bibliographic Society of
America*, Vol. 55, 1961.

GRAND-CARTERET, John, *Les Moeurs et la
caricature en France*, Paris 1888.
XIXème siècle (en France); *classes,
moeurs, usages, costumes, inventions*,
Paris 1893; *L'Histoire – la vie – les
moeurs et la curiosité par l'image, le
pamphlet et le document*, Vol. 5,
(1830–1900), Paris 1928.

GRATIOLET, Pierre, *De la physionomie et
des mouvements d'expression*, Paris 1865.

GROSE, François, *Rules for Drawing
Caricatures* (pamphlet), 1788; *Principes
de caricature*, Paris 1802.

libres, Paris 1918 and New York 1921.

HARPER, Paula Hays, 'Daumier's Clowns: Les Saltimbanques et Les Parades', Stanford University Doctoral Dissertation 1976.

HARRISSE, Henry, *L.L. Boilly, peintre, dessinateur, et lithographie; sa vie et son oeuvre, 1761–1845*, Paris 1898.

HASKELL, Francis, 'The Sad Clown: Some Notes on a 19th Century Myth', *French 19th Century Painting and Literature*, ed. U. Finke, Manchester 1972.

HAUSSMANN, Georges-Eugène, *Mémoires du Baron Haussmann*, Paris 1890–3.

HEYLLI, Georges d', *Théâtres des boulevards*, Paris 1881.

HILLAIRE, J., *Dictionnaire historique des rues de Paris*, Paris 1963.

HOGARTH, William, *The Analysis of Beauty*, Oxford 1955.

HONOUR, Hugh, *Romanticism*, New York 1979.

HOUSSAYE, Arsène, *Les Confessions, souvenirs d'un demi-siècle*, Paris 1885–9.

HUART, Louis, *Physiologie du flâneur*, Paris 1842.

HUART, Louis and Maurice Alhoy, *Les Cent et un Robert Macaire*, Paris 1839.

HUGOUNET, Paul, *Mimes et Pierrots*, Paris 1889.

HUON, Antoinette, 'Charles Philipon et la Maison Aubert (1829–1862)', *Etudes de presse*, 1957, pp. 67–76.

JAMES, Henry, *Daumier, the Caricaturist*, London 1954, p. 14.

JAMMES, André, 'Duchenne de Boulogne, le grimace provoqué et Nadar', *Gazette des beaux-arts*, Dec. 1978, pp. 215–20.

JANIN, Jules, *Deburau – histoire du théâtre à quatre-sous*, Paris 1832.

JANIN, Jules with Gérard de Nerval, Eugène Briffaut, Théophile Gautier, Albert Monnier *et al*, *Deburau*, Paris 1856.

JOUIN, N., *Charles Le Brun et les arts sous Louis XIV*, Paris 1889.

KLEIST, Heinrich von, 'Über das Marionettentheater', published in Pluegge, H., *Grazie und Anmut; ein biologischer Exkurs über das Marionettentheater von Heinrich von Kleist*, Hamburg 1947.

KLIBANSKY, R., Saxl, F. and Panofsky, E., *Saturn and Melancholy*, London 1964.

KLINGENDER, F.D., 'Daumier and the Reconstruction of Paris', *Architectural Review*, July–December 1941, pp. 55–60; *Hogarth and English Caricature*, London 1964.

KOCK, Paul de, *La Grande Ville*, Paris 1842.

LA BRUYÈRE, Jean de, *Les Caractères ou les moeurs de ce siècle*, Paris 1844–5.

LACOMBE, Paul, *Bibliographie parisienne*, Paris 1887.

LAIRESSE, Gerard de, *The Art of Painting in all its Branches*, London 1738.

LAMBERT, Abbé, *Le Langage de la physionomie et du geste*, Paris 1865.

LARKIN, Oliver, *Daumier, Man of His Time*, Boston 1966.

LAROUSSE, *Grand Dictionnaire du XIXème siècle*, Paris 1866–76.

LAVATER, Johann Caspar, *Essay on Physiognomy for the Promotion of the Knowledge and the Love of Mankind*, London 1789; *L'Art de connaître les hommes par la physionomie*, Paris 1806–9, ed. Dr Moreau de la Sarthe

LE BLANC, H., *Catalogue de l'oeuvre complet de Gustave Doré*, Paris 1931.

LE BRUN, Charles, *Conférence de M. Le Brun sur l'expression générale et particulière des passions*, Amsterdam 1698; *Méthode pour apprendre à deviner les passions*, Amsterdam 1702; *La Physionomie humaine comparée à la physionomie des animaux, d'après les dessins de Le Brun*. Introduction by Lucien Métivet, Paris 1927.

LE COMTE, Louis Henri, *Un Comédien au XIXème siècle*, Paris 1892; *Histoire des théâtres de Paris*, Paris 1912.

LEE, Rensselaer, 'Ut Pictura Poesis: The Humanistic Theory of Painting', *Art Bulletin XXI*, 1940, pp. 197–260. Reprinted New York 1967.

LEMAÎTRE, Frédérick, *Souvenirs*, Paris 1880.

LEMERCIER DE NEUVILLE, Louis, *Histoire anecdotique des marionnettes modernes*. Paris 1892; *Souvenirs d'un montreur de marionnettes*, Paris 1911.

LETHÈVE, J., 'Balzac et la phrénologie', *Aesculape*, March 1951, pp. 52–62.

LHÉRITIER, Andrée, 'Les Physiologies', *Etudes de presse*, Vol. IX, No. 17, 1957, pp. 1–58.

LOMBROSO, Cesare, *Criminal Man*, New York 1911.

LUKÁCS, Georg, *Writer and Critic*, New York 1970.

MAINDRON, Ernest, *Marionnettes et guignols*, Paris 1900.

MAISON, K.E., *Honoré Daumier. Catalogue Raisonné of the Paintings, Watercolours, and Drawings*, London and New York 1967.

MARASH, Jessie G., *Henry Monnier, Chronicler of the Bourgeoisie*, London 1951.

MARIE, Aristide, *L'Art et la vie romantique: Henry Monnier (1799–1877)*, Paris 1931.

'Marionnettes et Guignols', *Revue artistique*, Nice 1918–24.

MARRAST, Robert, 'Le Théâtre de Henry Monnier', *Réalisme et poésie au théâtre*, Paris 1960.

MATORÉ, Georges, *Le Vocabulaire et la société sous Louis-Philippe*, Paris 1951.

MELCHER, Edith, *Stage Realism in France between Diderot and Antoine*, Bryn Mawr, Pennsylvania 1928; *The Life and Times of Henry Monnier (1799–1877)*, Cambridge, Mass. 1950.

MERCIER, Louis Sébastien, *Le Nouveau Paris*, Brunswick 1862.

MONDOR, Henri, *Doctors and Medicine in the Works of Daumier*, Boston 1970.

MONNIER, Henry, *Physiologie du bourgeois*, Paris 1841; *Les Industriels. Métiers et professions en France*, Paris 1842; *Les Bourgeois de Paris*, Paris 1854; *Mémoires de M. Joseph Prudhomme*, Paris 1857; *Oeuvres diverses*, Paris 1857; *Les Bas-fonds de la société*, Paris 1862; *Paris et la province*, Paris 1866.

MONTAGU, Jennifer, 'Charles Le Brun's Conférence sur l'expression générale et particulière', University of London Doctoral Dissertation 1959.

MUSSET, Alfred de, *Un Spectacle dans un fauteuil*, Paris 1834.

NADAR, 'Charles Philipon', *Le Journal amusant*, 2 February 1862; *Quand j'étais photographe*, Paris 1900; reprinted 1979.

NADAR-TOURNACHON, *Pierrot Boursier*, Paris 1856.

NOCHLIN, Linda, *Realism*, New York 1971.

OSIAKOVSKI, Stanislav, 'History of Robert Macaire and Daumier's Place in It', *Burlington Magazine*, Vol. 100, No. 668, November 1958, pp. 388–92.

PAILLOT DE MONTABERT, *Traité complet de la peinture*, Vol. IV, pp. 489–93; Vol. VII, pp. 487–96, Paris 1829; *Théorie du geste dans l'art de la peinture, renfermant plusiers préceptes applicables à l'art du théâtre, suivie des principes du beau optique, pour servir à l'analyse de la beauté dans le geste pittoresque*, Paris 1913.

Paris, ou le livre des cent-et-un, 15 Vols, No. 8, Paris 1831–4.

Paris Comique, ed. Charles Philipon, Paris 1844.

'Parisian Caricature', *Westminster Review*, 32:282–305, 1874.

PARTURIER, M., 'Les Marionnettes de Duranty', *Bulletin du bibliophile*, No. 3, 1950, pp. 111–25.

PAULSON, Ronald, *Hogarth, His Life, Art and Times*, New Haven 1971.

PÉRICAUD, Louis, *Le Théâtre des Funambules, ses mimes, ses acteurs et ses pantomimes*, Paris 1897; *Histoire des grands et petits théâtres de Paris*, Paris 1908–9.

PICHOIS, Claude, 'Les Cabinets de lectures durant la première moitié du XIXème siècle', *Annales*, 1959, pp. 521–34.

PIDERIT, T., *Mimik und physiognomik*, Detmold 1925.

PINKNEY, David H., 'Paris in the 19th Century: A Study in Urban Growth', Harvard University doctoral dissertation 1941; *Napoleon III and the Rebuilding of Paris*, Princeton, New Jersey 1958.

POËTE, Marcel, *Une Vie de cité de sa naissance à nos jours*, Paris 1929–31.

Le Prisme, tricyclopédie morale du XIXème siècle, Paris 1841.

REFF, Theodore, 'Harlequins, Saltimbanques, Clowns, and Fools', *Artforum*, October, 1971; *Degas: The Artist's Mind*, London and New York 1976.

REMY, Tristan, *J.G. Deburau*, Paris 1954.

REY, Robert, *Daumier*, New York 1966.

RIBEYRE, Félix, *Cham, sa vie et son oeuvre*, Paris 1884.

ROBERT-JONES, Philippe, 'Etudes de quelque types physionomiques dans

l'oeuvre lithographique de Daumier',
doctoral dissertation, Brussels
1949–50; 'Les Passants familiers chez
Daumier', *Arts et livres de Provence*,
No. 27, May 1955, pp. 28–34; 'La
Caricature française entre 1860–
1890', Univ. Libre de Brussels, 1958.
—'La Presse Satirique Illustrée entre
1860–1890', *Etudes de presse*, Vol. 8,
No. 14, 1956, pp. 5–113.
ROGER-MARX, Claude, 'Actualité de
Daumier', *Mercure de France*, Vol. 281,
January 1938, pp. 322–40.
ROGERSON, Brewster, 'The Art of
Painting the Passions', *Journal of the
History of Ideas*, XIV, 1953, pp.
68–94.
RUBIN, James H., 'Painting as Theater:
An Approach to Painting in France
from 1791 to 1810', Harvard
University dissertation 1972.
RUDÉ, George, *The Crowd in History,
1730–1848*, New York 1964.
SAALMAN, Howard, *Haussmann: Paris
Transformed*, New York 1971.
SAND, GEORGE, *Théâtre de Nohant*, Paris
1865; *Questions d'art et de littérature*,
Paris 1878.
SAND, Maurice, *Masques et bouffons*, Paris
1860; *Le Théâtre des marionnettes*,
Paris 1876.
SCHWARTZ, 'Heinrich, Daumier, Gill and
Nadar', *Gazette des beaux-arts*, Vol. 19,
February 1957, pp. 39–106.
SELLO, G. (intro.), *Grandville, Das
gesamte Werk (1803–47)*, 2 Vols.
Munich 1969.
SENNETT, Richard, *The Fall of Public
Man*, New York 1977.
SIDDONS, Henry, *Practical Illustrations of
Rhetorical Gesture and Action adopted to
the English Drama from a Work on the
Subject by J. Engel*, London 1822.
*La Silhouette. Journal des caricatures,
beaux-arts, dessins, moeurs, théâtres, etc.*
Paris 1830.
SIMMEL, Georg, *Soziologie*, 4th edn,
Berlin 1958.
SIMOND, Charles, *La Vie parisienne à
travers le XIX siècle*, 2 Vols, Paris
1900–1.
SMART, Alistair, 'Dramatic Gesture and
Expression in the Age of Hogarth

and Reynolds', *Apollo*, August 1965.
STAROBINSKI, Jean, *Portrait de l'artiste en
saltimbanque*, Geneva 1970.
STOREY, Robert, *Pierrot, A Critical History
of a Mask*, Princeton, New Jersey
1978.
'Street Trades in Paris', *Bentley's
Miscellany*, Vol. 56, 1864, pp. 56–68.
'The Street Trades of Paris', *Leisure
Hour*, Vol. 4, September, 1855,
pp. 586–90.
'The Streets of Paris', *New Monthly
Magazine*, Vol. 113, August, 1858,
pp. 490–500.
SUË, J.J., *Essai sur la physionomie des corps
vivans, considerée depuis l'homme jusqu' à
la plante*, Paris 1797.
SVELHA, Jaroslav, 'Jean Gaspard
Deburau. The Immortal Pierrot',
Mime Journal, No. 5, 1977.
TABARY, Louis, *Edouard Duranty. Etude
bibliographique et critique*, Paris 1954.
TEXIER, Edmond, *Tableau de Paris*,
2 Vols, Paris 1852–3.
THIERRY, Edouard, *De l'influence du
théâtre du silence*, Paris 1862.
THORÉ, Théophile, *Dictionnaire de
phrénologie et de physionomie à l'usage des
artistes*, Paris 1836.
TROLLOPE, Frances, *Paris and Parisians in
1835*, London 1836.
UDINE, Jean d' (pseudonym of Albert
Cozaret), *L'Art et le geste*, Paris 1910.
VÉRON, M.L., *Les Théâtres de Paris*, Paris
1860.
VICAIRE, Georges, *Le Manuel de l'amateur
de livres du XIXème siècle*, Paris 1907.
WASSERMAN, Jean, *Daumier Sculpture*,
Cambridge, Mass. 1969.
WEINBERG, Bernard, *French Realism: The
Critical Reaction, 1830–1870*, Chicago
1936 and New York 1937.
WINTER, Marian, *Le Théâtre du
merveilleux*, Paris 1862.
WOLFF, Kurt M., ed., *The Sociology of
Georg Simmel*, Glencoe, Illinois 1950.
WRIGHT, Thomas, *A History of Caricature
and Grotesque in Art and Literature*,
London 1865; reprinted New York
1968.
ZELDIN, Theodore, *France 1848–1945*,
2 Vols, Oxford 1973 and 1977.

Index

208